Praise for **The Impeccable Warrior of Light**

A Precious Gift to Humanity

I recommend this book to anyone I Love, as well as to those whom I find it difficult to love, for this book is not just about self-healing, but healing on a global level as well. It is a rare jewel that blesses my life on a daily basis. It teaches me to look through the spiritual eye regarding all situations. If you have ever experienced spiritual suffering or the effects of chaos that negative forces direct towards your life, then you will Appreciate this work.

Lola, USA

New Thought Patterns

The Impeccable Warrior Of Light is an amazing book of Truth, Wisdom and Universal Truths. The author, Peace Mother, has within her a way of explaining why and how we, as human beings, do not have to get caught in old programming and negative thinking from society or our parents and choose to be Happy, Joy-full and successful in our lives. Her book is truly profound and I recommend this to anyone who is a seeker of the truth and who wants real answers to problems. It reminded me to be open to new ways in dealing with old problems.

Her book touched me and it has changed my life and the way I will live my life in the future.

Lee, USA

Praise for **The Impeccable Warrior of Light**

The Key To Creator's Divine Protection

This is an excellent addition to the library of anyone who is interested in Spiritual Protection and who wishes to be an ally of the forces of Light on Planet Earth. Peace Mother Geeta Sacred Song writes as an individual who understands the nature of unseen realities and how dark forces can possess and corrupt individuals.

I have read other books on similar topics and in one book, a board-certified psychiatrist was amazed to discover that when she placed patients under hypnosis, a great number of her patients were possessed. Christians will recall that it is written in Ephesians 6:12, "For we wrestle not against flesh and blood, but against principalities, against powers, against the rulers of the darkness of this world, against spiritual wickedness in high places."

Peace Mother offers various techniques and suggestions that individuals can use to deal with malignant forces that cause depression, illness and create obstacles or other circumstances that impoverish or degrade Life on Planet Earth. Stating that Earth is the most beautiful planet in the Universe, Peace Mother explains the ambitions of the dark forces.

A devotee of Divine Mother, Peace Mother emphasizes that whatever tradition one follows—whether one is a Christian, Muslim, Jewish, Hindu, Buddhist or of any other religion—there is Spiritual Protection available to all, and that the key to accessing the Creator's Divine protection is Devotion and Love. Her mission is to uplift humanity; one way she accomplishes this is through sharing her knowledge of how we can all become Impeccable Warriors of Light.

Leatha, USA

Praise for **The Impeccable Warrior of Light**

Practical, Simple and Down-To-Earth Techniques

This book was a precious key to my release. I have always known that other worlds exist alongside our own and yet I had "forgotten" to pay full attention to their impact upon this very Life that we give most of our attention to.

The very practical, simple and down-to-earth techniques that Peace Mother shares had an immediate impact upon my Life. My spiritual practices became my highest priority once again and I felt the waves of Peace and Joy begin to affect every area of my Life.

My six-year old son took to the simple techniques like a fish to water. One day I heard him clap loudly three times as he rode in the back of our van. I asked what he was doing and he said, "I had a bad thought and I was driving it away!" (He had heard me do the same thing earlier and soon he was repeating my good example!) Since the first step to Freedom is awareness, it gave me great comfort to know that I had shared something that would help him "re-member" his own powerful "Warrior of Light" Self!

Cheryl, USA

I Am Amazed, So Much I Want To Quote From This Book

I am amazed to find that there is so much I want to quote from it and pass on to people, more than any other book I have read lately. Yes, please keep me informed with other articles and Teachings.

Annie, United Kingdom

Praise for **The Impeccable Warrior of Light**

Peace Mother Is Serving Humanity 24/7

Peace Mother is the clearest channel of Spirit that I've ever encountered. Her Wisdom and Compassion are truly inspiring. She walks the talk, serving humanity 24/7, and this book is just one example of this. In it she offers us all tools we can use every day to protect and expand the precious Light of Spirit within. The writing is straightforward and accessible, as Peace Mother challenges us to live as "Impeccable Warriors lof Light".

Suzy, USA

I Feel Vibrant and Energized

While recovering from surgery recently, it afforded me the opportunity to catch up on my reading. 'The Impeccable Warrior of Light' is clear and simple, yet detailed. It gives you the tools and procedures that will enable you to protect yourself from negative thoughts and forces. In these days of fears from war, terrorism, the ravages of Mother Nature and yes, health issues and surgical procedures, the book's enlightening message is both timely and powerful.

With Peace Mother Geeta Sacred Song's exuberant techniques, you can lighten your load and break the chain of anguish and discomfort and feel vibrant and energized.

Ira, USA

Praise for **The Impeccable Warrior of Light**

Thank You For The Positive Changes In My Son

I can't thank you enough for the positive changes that you have brought to my son and his friend. You have given them both the chance to live, as you say, the BIG Life. For that I am eternally grateful.

Dr. Robert, USA

Practical, Caring Advice For The Modern World

It is a very sensible book, every page was encouraging and I felt empowered to do some of the practices to change my circumstances. My favourite quote was, "We did not come here to lie in bed and eat bon-bons all day. No one ever earned a black belt by sitting around eating bon -bons".

That Teaching was just what I needed. It really was! One of the second most important things I remembered from Peace Mother's book was when things are not going well, that is the time to intensify your practice. That is the time to pray like you have never prayed before. SO, I prayed and I prayed!

Matthew, New Zealand

Praise for **The Impeccable Warrior of Light**

I Encourage Everyone To Keep This Book Handy As A Guide!

I have researched through books and through the Internet these last 6 years. I have had many dramas and many traumas in my life. I believe for me, this is what I needed to go through. I say this because I know that some of you will read this and can relate to most if not some of the experiences I have shared. All of you have the power within to enfold this Love and the Light to become the "Impeccable Warrior" that Holy Mother speaks of in her book.

My reading of Holy Mother's book, "The Impeccable Warrior Of Light" has been another eye opener to what is and what has always been. She offers many tools that help us on our journey in this Lifetime and she does so with All the Love, Light and Wisdom that only Peace Mother can offer.

I suggest this book to anyone who is truly responsible for their own Life, and who really wants to become more in-tune with their reality. This book helps protect you from negativity and dark energies in your life. Do not just read it once and put it on the shelf, for if you do, I promise you this much; you will not remember the Sacred Tools of Power and you will slip back into the throes of the Negativity that can surround you. Keep it handy as a guide…keep it in view, so that your Higher Self can lead you to it when the time is needed. Trust in Yourself and Love yourself, for only then can you truly Trust and Love others!

Piper, AZ

Praise for **The Impeccable Warrior of Light**

I Can Now See Spirit Is Trying To Awaken Me

Whether I am eating, sleeping or working, your Teachings are beginning to thrive in my every thought. I am able to see more visibly than ever how the forces can especially manipulate frames of mind, having repercussions on peoples' perceptions, awareness, choices, etc.

I see people around me feeling down because they believe the judgements that pop into their heads. I have witnessed that people act upon these thoughts without really inquiring into the SOURCE and nature of these negative thoughts. I now understand many of the Teachings that Divine Spirit has presented me with regarding the challenges of the path ahead. Recently, Divine Mother's words, channelled through Peace Mother's heart, have undoubtedly brought me ecstatic Joy and equipped me with the resources to sustain this Gusto. I have come to believe that an abundance and variety of practices must exist for one to be fully protected from the devious, myriad ways dark forces feed on our mind, body, spirit and environment.

J., Australia

THE IMPECCABLE WARRIOR OF LIGHT ™
Mantras and Rituals for Spiritual Protection
How To Protect Yourself From Negative or Evil Forces

Library of Congress Control Number: 2003109059 (1st Edition)

Second Edition
Published in 2009 by A Center for Peace & Healing, dba Sacred Peace Center
Printed in China

Sacred Peace Center, a 501 (c) 3 non-profit organization
1800 N. Bristol St., Suite #C224,
Santa Ana, CA 92706, USA
Phone: 1-866-987-3223
Websites: www.sacredpeace.org
Email: info@sacredpeace.org

ISBN 0-9741959-2-8
First edition printed under ISBN 0-9751959-0-1

Sacred Peace Center

To serve the Light, we practice Spiritual Protection...
With impeccable protection practices, we invoke Grace...
Enveloped by Grace we are armed with a Shield of Light...

Spiritual Protection is the core element of Peace...
By protecting ourselves diligently, we protect the Light...
In this way Devotion, Wisdom & Harmony flourish...

A Peace-full Heart embraces that all Paths...
Lead to The Sacred Temple Of The Heart...
In this way Balance, Mutual Respect...
And Harmonious Cooperation flourish...

The Golden Virtues birth unwavering Peace...
Through impeccable allegiance to the Golden Laws...
And Sacred Sounds of Peace...
A Valiant, Radiant, Peace-full Heart upholds...
The Goodness of the Universe...

The Universe around us is a reflection...
Of our inner state of being...
In order to transform turmoil and discomfort in our lives...
We must master the Divine Laws of Spiritual Protection...

Solidified in Impeccable Awareness...
We are ABLE to consciously choose Love and Peace...
Over discord at every opportunity...
Through loyalty to the Light...
We can transcend suffering and pain...

Sacred Peace Center Teaches...
How to Triumph over adversity…
Walk the Spiritual Path with Dignity…
And be an instrument for Love...

Working together…
We live The Sacred Way….
In Peace...

Pash In Lak'ech..We are ONE…

ASSIST IN UPLIFTING HUMANITY

People around the world often ask how they can assist others in receiving the profound Teachings from this book, as it holds the key to creating a peace-full society that is able to live in inner and outer Peace.

Many of you have the same desire and YOU CAN DEFINITELY MANIFEST A HEALING WAVE OF LIGHT ON THIS PLANET by creating greater exposure for the Wisdom Teachings in this book.

Here are easy direct ways you can uplift humanity immediately:
♦ Buy copies for family and friends as gifts
♦ Place a 5 star review on Amazon.com
♦ Ask local bookstores to carry it
♦ Donate a copy to libraries
♦ Buy the books from bookstores, rather than our website or Amazon.com to encourage media interest
♦ Send e-mails to friends and family about this book. Excerpts from the book are available on our website www.sacredpeace.org for people to read.

If there is some other way that you would like to help, then please feel free to e-mail the Peace Team at info@sacredpeace.org.

CONTENTS

DEDICATION

Eternal blessings upon my excellent parents, Yogini Julie and O.C., for gifting me this radiant human birth...your impeccable qualities inspired me to awaken fully and realize Enlightenment ... An Ocean of Grace unto you!

Boundless appreciation to my sister, The Oracle of the Light, Shree Dayananda...for her Great Wisdom and vast support for Divine Mother's Work...You are truly the Bliss of Compassion... May you live a long, healthy Life, All Ways exalted in your Impeccable service to the Light!

Eternal Liberation and an everlasting stream of sweet offerings unto all my Ancestors for paving the way for me...You are my Strength and I pray to honour each of you perfectly and complete your Work radiantly...

Infinite illumination unto my Spirit Guides, who patiently encourage me to write their words... Joy-full am I for the opportunity to be Your humble instrument... Pash In Lak'ech!

Endless salutations and praise unto my Perfect Teachers: Bhagawan Nityananda, Swami Muktananda Paramahamsa, Swami Gurumayi Chidvilasananda and Don Jacinto Tzab, for bestowing upon me Garments of Love, a Golden Mind and therefore Golden Life... Precious, Supremely Compassionate Gurus, my heart is forever at Your glory-us Lotus Feet...

Radiant Gurus, Masters of the Light, Parents, Venerable Oracle, Ancestors and Spirit Guides...You are the Loving winds beneath my wings...Every victory is Yours...I donate any merit attained, towards Your everlasting Enlightenment. May Your spirit forever be triumphant... continually rejoicing in the Light!

I surrender every-thing at the Lotus Feet of the Eternal Source, my Beloved Divine Mother...It is You who illumines my Path...Through Your Grace, may this Divine Work uplift all souls, dissolve suffering and infuse All Creation with Peace... May Thy Will All Ways be done, Maa ...

JAI JAI MAAAAAAAAAAAAAAAAAAAAAAAAAAAAAA!

ACKNOWLEDGEMENTS

Infinite praise to my Divine Protectors for gifting us a Sacred Peace Team to support the global expansion of Divine Mother's wondrous mission.

Special Recognition goes to Swami Durgadas, for wholeheartedly Devotion to Divine Mother's Will. Your commitment to serve as the Perfect Student, by mastering the Impeccable Warrior of Light Teachings, is a rare quest.

Eternal Appreciation to The Oracle of the Light, Shree Dayananda, for co-directing SPC's Highest Destiny through Mighty Prayer, Ceremony, and superb Divine Guidance. Heaven and Earth celebrate you and Swami Durgadas for walking the Heroic Path! May you both succeed every step of the Way and continue to illuminate the path for humanity.

A Fountain of Grace unto Yogini Julie, Yogini Sevadai, Premlayo, Suzanne 'Sunrose', Joyce Dreamweaver, J. Gordon Windwalker, Linda Karuna, Lawrence Dayadas, Julie "Golden Jewel", Roman Venkatesh, Amy B., Jessica Dhagavati, Harish and Rini, for offering their homes to me as a haven for Maa's Work. With Loving care, all of you nourished me and therefore sustained the completion of Divine Mother's mission.

Merit unto Roman Roth of Roth Photo Studio, for creating hundreds of radiant images for SPC. Your vast talent and Radiant Love is evident in this book cover and many CD covers you photograph for us....Great-fullness unto: Janara "Golden Heart", Lisa T., Maria M., Jazmin, Piper and Scott Jayendra for compassionately assisting this Divine Work. A special medal of honour goes to Scott Jayendra for years of exemplary Selfless, loyal service and my brother, Jose Maheshwara, for funding the first edition of IWOL and Faith-fully tithing to Maa's Work.

Everyone mentioned and many more have sacrificed to be of service...You are Angels of Mercy! Your Loving actions, donations and support help us carry on...and fortify the Goodness of the Universe. May the Grace you cultivated, return to you multiplied...to carry you, your Ancestors, and all future generations to Enlightenment! All my LOVE to you!

Peace Mother Geeta Sacred Song

ABOUT THE AUTHOR

Peace Mother Geeta Sacred Song is recognized as an Enlightened Master and manifestation of Divine Mother. Trained in Mayan Soul Retrieval by Don Jacinto Tzab, one of Mexico's most Power-full and Beloved Mayan Shamans, She is a Peace Shaman. The Holy Mother has been Divinely donated to humanity, in order to bring healing balance to humanity through Her thunderous Prayer Songs, Sacred Ceremonies and Teachings.

Before apprenticing to Don Jacinto, Her Holiness immersed herself in the Sacred Mantras of India and the Spiritual practices outlined by Her Guru, Siddha Master Gurumayi Chidvilasananda, the spiritual head of Siddha Yoga.

With the Grace of Gurumayi, Peace Mother mastered the healing power of sound to the highest degree and credits Her Beloved Guru, the Siddha Lineage of Masters and Mayan Shamans Lineage for the miraculous power that flows through Her.

To increase global Harmony and awaken Wisdom within all beings, Her Holiness has founded the non-profit organizations A Center For Peace And Healing, Sacred Peace Center, and Shamanic Training and Healing Institute.

To accelerate us all towards Enlightenment, the Holy Mother has recorded multiple CDs of Devotional, Protection and Peace Mantras, blending Mayan, Tibetan, Native American and India's sacred songs.

Her second book, The Shamanic Healing Art Journal, music CDs/DVDs and Impeccable Warrior Of Light Training tools are infused with a frequency that mystically uplifts us to a stronger, truer connection with our Angels, Spirit Guides and Protectors.

With Joy-full Zest, compassionate gaze and light-charged touch, Her Holiness activates the Light within us all, quickening our Divine Essence, opening doors to our highest destiny and clearing us of negative karmic patterns.

Performing Peace Rituals and Prayers with spiritual leaders from global traditions, Peace Mother upholds the Teaching that all paths lead to the Sacred Temple of the Heart. She lovingly calls on all of us to work together in mutual Respect, inviting us to transform all suffering by singing and dancing our prayers!

INTRODUCTION

In the first chapter of my Life, I experienced the sensations of psychic attack, without awareness of what was happening around me, to me, and others. In the next phase of my spiritual development, I embraced spiritual practices, which gave me tools and understanding I could apply toward a Happy and Balanced Life. During this part of my training, I studied the Teachings of my Gurus from India and proceeded to purify my intellect and heart through daily mediation, contemplation and devotional practices such as chanting of Sanskrit mantras. At this point, I was growing and getting stronger year by year, yet I still did not fully comprehend the rules of Life on planet Earth. My focus was on the rewards available to an initiate but I could not fathom the dangers. Although I had often read and heard the Teaching "The Spiritual Path is sharper than the razor's edge", I could not fully comprehend how the Spiritual Path could be more dangerous than walking on a razor's edge.

Every Teacher and each path have a particular assignment in addressing the myriad aspects of Life on planet Earth. My Gurus were addressing the risks and rewards in the traditional way as taught by the scriptures of India. They were giving Teachings on the nature of the limited mind and its vast trickery when it comes to robbing us of Peace. However, due to the veils clouding my Wisdom Mind, I was not able to accept the depth of the danger that surrounds every seeker. Blind to the invisible world, I was not able to be an Impeccable Warrior Of Light. I was still allowing negative energies to seep in to my mind, emotions, body and home which created ongoing drama in my Life. I did not have the knowledge to understand the nature of being a psychic instrument, but with my Guru's Grace, I was able to apply constant effort and Devotion to the Light. Grace led me to the third phase of my spiritual development.

During this part of my path, my Shamanic Training blossomed at the same time as my past Life Devotion to the Divine Mother of the Universe. Through my Shamanic Training, all the psychic sensitivities I had experienced during my entire Life were suddenly clarified and solutions were provided for transforming them. I feel that through my own discomfort and suffering at the hands of the negative forces, I was given thorough and first-hand knowledge of the unseen worlds and how they affect our lives. Having been given that insight, I have likewise been gifted Compassion for others who are being challenged by negative spirits. Knowledge is Freedom and as I have been freed from a world of ignorance, I am Happy to be able to share these Wisdom Teachings on the role of Grace and Spiritual Protection in the Impeccable Warrior of Light path.

For years, my Spirit Guides had been urging me to write down the techniques I was revealing in workshops and Soul Retrieval consultations. Finally, thanks to my patient Spirit Guides and Divine Mother Grace, these techniques and tools are now available to you in this book. It is an honour to know that the obstacles in my path have led to solutions that can ease the suffering of others.

The emphasis on Spiritual Protection is not just about recognizing the dark forces. Of equal importance is the recognition of Divine Grace, your Angels, Spirit Guides, Spiritual Protectors and the way both worlds are interrelating with you at all times. Being awake means acknowledging both the assistance and the hazards present on the Spiritual Path. There is endless Grace and Compassion available to us in the Universe...however it takes self-effort to draw it to us and then to maintain it within us and in our lives.

We make this self-effort through spiritual practices, which constantly align us with the Divine Forces of Light. Through the Faith-full calling of the Light, Grace is invoked and accumulated.

As the Light within us is Strengthened...the mystical secrets which have been utilized for psychic protection throughout the ages arise...they become known to us. This allows us to succeed in manifesting our most radiant health, wealth and Wisdom. Only when we master protection of our mind, body and spirit can we reach and sustain an Enlightened state of being.

This book has been donated to humanity by Divine Mother to help all beings increase their awareness of the invisible worlds around them. It will help you develop spiritual sight, hearing and sensitivity, as well as arm you with practical and power-full tools so you can deal with psychic phenomenon successfully. In order to reach our highest potential, we must be able to recognize what is REALLY going on around us and within us at all times. In this book, I impart guidelines that will help you de-code messages the Compassionate Universe is sending you. You will learn how to identify what the many signs mean and what the invisible world is trying to tell you.

The biggest mistake we can make on the Spiritual Path is to believe that only the "seen" world exists. The seen and unseen worlds are forever blending and blurring into each other. In order to be consistently Happy, balanced and vibrant on ALL levels, you will find it necessary to master the language of the unseen worlds, for they are constantly reaching out to YOU.

I grew up seeing e-v-e-r-y-t-h-i-n-g moving around during the night. We lived in a haunted house, which sat on land previously settled by Native Americans, and the area was layered with the heaviness of unresolved issues embedded into it. From early childhood to our teenage years, my brothers, sisters and I had the luxury of having wide open spaces to play in, but at the same time our psyches were being bombarded by the multitude of energetic forces roaming the land. These forces hypnotized us into an unconscious state, whereby we remained oblivious to the fact that there were numerous bodies buried in the large orchards around our house. Due to the angry entities assaulting us, my family's Balance of prosperity and Harmony was continually affected. Since we did not realize we were under psychic attack, we did not increase our Spiritual Protection and therefore continued to struggle and suffer.

Up until I was fourteen years old, my family spent part of every year in Mexico, where it is common conversation to speak of those in the village who are currently being attacked by witchcraft, vampires, ghosts, and other malevolent forms. Whether I was in America or Mexico, I feared each coming night, knowing fully well I would not be able to sleep. If I did somehow fall asleep I was tortured by horrible nightmares. It was pure miserable agony to lie there; witnessing fierce ugly forms come and go. The many voices I heard in my head and the horrible images flashing before me one after another, made sleep unattainable. I was easily able to sleep during the day, but each night seemed like an eternity and I was always relieved and supremely "Great-full" to see the sun coming up.

Before receiving the Impeccable Warrior Of Light Teachings, I mistakenly believed I could not sleep due to insomnia, and thought I was doomed to miserable, restless nights for the rest of my Life. It was only after meeting my Teacher, Mayan Shaman Don Jacinto Tzab, that everything I had felt, seen and wondered about, was confirmed as not only real, but quite universal. For none of this is new on this Earth plane. The only aspect that is new is the degree to which everyone is being attacked. Once I learned how to protect myself, I realized the nightmares were a message to alert me to the presence of negative energies in my space. Thanks to Grace, I was given ways to cleanse my space, which I do at least once per day. With these tools you too will be able to sleep better and arise more focused on the Grace that is forever illuminating your path.

IMPORTANT: READ THIS FIRST

The content of this book will open your eyes to the Light Forces that walk with you and the dark energies that exist on Planet Earth as well. The Good and malevolent forces that live in the invisible world have always been around you...they have been influencing your state of being all along, but once you become aware of them you automatically become more sensitized to them and will therefore feel their presence more graphically.

It may feel a bit uncomfortable at first, as you learn of the energies that are living side by side with you, yet KNOWLEDGE IS FREEDOM so do not allow dis-comfort to dis-tract you from your mission to take back your power through increased awareness of the invisible world. Contact with these Golden Teachings will increase awareness of every aspect of your Life. By being willing to see all that is around you, you will have a greater advantage in controlling the flow of events in your Life.

Impeccable Warrior of Light Wisdom will give you the necessary tools to TAKE CHARGE and TRANSFORM any challenges that may pose obstacles or dangers on your path...as well as READY AND STEADY YOU to accept and capitalize on any rewards available to you.

If you feel overwhelmed at any point by all you are learning, remember that this is the case with any new material you are exposed to. Driving a vehicle is a great example of this: When a person first learns to drive an automobile it can feel intimidating to be aware of all the people, objects and activity around them. However through daily practice it becomes second nature and then the accomplished driver amazingly manoeuvres safely through an ocean of traffic and objects, while drinking a beverage, answering a mobile phone and sometimes putting on makeup! I know of people who read while driving!

You can see how confident they have become with juggling so many details :) Likewise, in time, with regular practice, you too will be able to confidently manoeuvre through interactions with the invisible world, feeling fully supported by the Grace you have firmly connected with.

Another appropriate example is the arena of hygiene. If you do not delve into the dangers bacteria and parasites pose to you, you are not able to recognize the threat that is all around you, until you or someone you know becomes ill. If you were to research the world of germs you would suddenly become aware of the billions of invisible, deadly elements that are actively posing a threat to you in your environment. Discovering that harm-full germs are everywhere, your first reaction might be to lock yourself up in a bubble and never come out, but then you realize you can never totally escape these Life forms, for they are part of our existence on Planet Earth.

At all points of expanding your awareness in any area of Life, you are presented with a choice: To remain frozen with fear and become neurotic…or to take steps to limit the danger these invisible invaders pose. Eventually, you come to understand that you have many tools available to you for dealing with the invisible parasites and you take steps to minimize the dangers and increase your defence system.

The point of this comparison is that a wise person does not allow information to stifle the enjoyment of Life. Instead of becoming consumed with anxiety, the wise being will incorporate the data and research ways to prepare and counter hazardous conditions, so as to live in a healthier way. As we expand our awareness of our experiences, we grow in knowledge and gain greater Wisdom. When practiced, all that you learn from the Impeccable Warrior of Light Teachings will empower you and enable you to live your Life more vibrantly.

Do not let those malevolent forces that promote fear discourage you from becoming an Impeccable Warrior of Light! They do not want you or any seeker to commit to Spiritual Protection because it means your Freedom from smallness. Never let dark forces frighten you or obstruct your path to the Divine Knowledge that will bring you the growth that every soul must embark upon.

NO SOUL CAN EVER REACH MASTERSHIP WITHOUT MASTERING THE LAWS OF SPIRITUAL PROTECTION.

Mastering the art and science of Spiritual Protection is not something you can put off indefinitely. This area of your spiritual life is the core and any lessons tied to this Mastery will forever loom before you until you face this training responsibly and courageously.

Remember, it is not just information that is being imparted to you in this book…it is soul support for the very essence of your being. For we come to earth to walk the HEROIC PATH…yet we cannot do that success-fully without embracing our duty to protect our self…our inner·light.

If at any time you sense harmful or negative energies around you, a simple tool to use throughout the reading of this book is to snap your fingers or clap three times and order all negative forces to leave you in Peace. You must meet resistance with action and not ever allow sinister energies to over-run your Kingdom! For more information on the full technique, see Chapter 5.

Once you have become more aware of the images and thoughts wicked forces project onto your mind, you will be able to expertly spot them as they attempt to frighten or weaken you. Some of the ways they will attempt to block your empowerment is by:
a)   Discouraging you

b) Attempting to persuade you that these techniques won't work

c) Making you self-conscious of how others will perceive you once you begin implementing these techniques regularly.

d) Convincing you to put this book aside. They will attempt to stall your growth by implanting thoughts that this book is too much of an eye opener.

e) Hypnotizing you into a sleepy state every time you attempt to read this material. Whenever you constantly fall asleep while trying to read something important, it is the work of the evil forces that wish for you to remain unconscious. In this case, you must get creative and read at a time when your energy is more dynamic. If you can remain determined, you will all ways emerge triumphant in creating a solution, so the key is to PRESS ON! My Grace, Divine Mother Grace is with you as you strive to break free, so put forth a mighty effort, and let nothing dissuade you from liberation, for "God helps those who help themselves!"

Throughout your Life an onslaught of negative thoughts have already been appearing on your mind screen... however you may have chosen to not pay much attention to them...until now. Upon recognition of any limiting thought or feeling, if you immediately use the finger snapping technique you can instantly dissolve negative energies encroaching upon you. By doing this, instead of being weakened by the negative forces, you will instantly strengthen yourself.

Remember by picking up this book, your soul is calling out for Enlightenment. Therefore do not allow the trickery of the malicious forces to dissuade you in anyway. As you persist in completing these Teachings you will find that layers of unconsciousness fall away and that these techniques absolutely work, which will fill you with spiritual empowerment. You shall see that the more you persist, the easier it becomes, as you and these Wisdom Teachings become one magnificent flame of Light! VICTORY TO THE LIGHT! GLORY TO THE GRACE!

SPELLING NOTE

Throughout this book, you will find that many words are spelled in what appears to be an unusual manner, eg: 'All Ways', re-member or 'Beauty-full'. These are not 'typos', but have been purposefully used by Peace Mother to give power and emphasis to the meaning of the word. Words have a life of their own, each emitting their own energetic vibration and when combined with the intent of the user, can bring a new level of meaning to the reader, even if on a sub-conscious level. Words carry within their letters the secrets of their fuller meaning and can, to those who are open to receiving this information, reveal the sacred truths contained within them. Being an independent spirit, Peace Mother believes in spelling words according to the greater meaning She is imparting. She feels it is an excellent way to loosen the chains that enslave the mind to the hypnotic trance of pre-conditioning by society. If you read this book with fresh eyes and an open heart, you will receive all the blessings contained within.

Chapter 1

WE ARE ALL IN THE SAME BOAT

Regardless of our path, we all have a mind, we all possess an ego and we all hear voices urging us towards either the high road or the low road in Life's decisions. Every one of us will hear both the voice of evil and the voice of the Goodness within.

Regardless of the spiritual tradition we each follow, the terrain is the same. Although the names given to trials and tribulations may differ, they will still challenge us and the rewards may be referred to by different names, but they will still inspire us. Regardless of whether our spiritual mentors are Buddha, Jesus, or any of the other Saints, Prophets, Enlightened Beings and Ascended Masters from various traditions, Their lives have all revealed identical keys to master-ship. They have all demonstrated and taught that the way to Enlightenment consists of self-examination of the petty ego and all its attributes.

Their many writings have illustrated that embarking upon the Spiritual Path is the equivalent to walking on the 'razor's edge'. Therefore it doesn't matter which tradition or religion we follow… the goal of human existence is the same: to purify the mind and dissolve the petty ego, in order to birth within us the purest qualities of Compassion, Love, Respect, Strength and Faith. All of which leads us to existing in a Balanced way. The Masters would not be writing about the all-important purification process, if they had not also experienced the eternal battle with the dark side. Know that No matter who our Teachers, Gurus or Masters are, regardless of which Holy Books we consider sacred, no being is immune to psychic attack.

The writings of those Beings who have reached a state of Enlightenment have shared that confronting one's own 'demons' is a part of the purification process. The reason the word demon is used to describe one's inner torments is because whatever suffering torments us is attached to an actual demon. If you were to see their dark forms in your aura, or attached to you and others, you would describe them as demonic apparitions. As long as you have issues and are not totally pure, you will be controlled by these demons. Enlightened Beings are also attacked by demons, however, they do not fall prey to the demons trickery. They live by the following two steps and if you choose to live in the same aware manner, you will find that you no longer grant dark forces the opportunity to cause havoc in your Life. An Impeccable Warrior of Light is an expert at:

1. Recognizing dark forces.
2. Casting them out of mind, body, spirit and surroundings immediately.

If you choose to come to Earth and incarnate in human form, you automatically inherit some kind of weakness, whether it be in the mind or body. All Saints have been confronted by daunting challenges. Every Spiritual Heroine and Hero has confronted the forces of evil, which did everything in their power to hinder the Great Beings and convince them to 'throw in the towel'.

The Great Beings reached Their heightened state by learning many rituals, prayers and techniques through the course of Their Life experience, which equipped Them with the power to dissolve and drive away those evil forces that endeavoured to encroach upon the Master's equilibrium.

Each time the negative forces inflicted assault upon Them and ventured to seduce Them from Their vow of Purity, the Great Beings had to affirm Their Faith in the Light Forces. They had to Strengthen Their connection with Their Spiritual Protectors and the Spiritual Principles that formed the support for Their quest for Goodness.

It is necessary to understand the universality of this. When it comes to the tests and rewards of climbing the spiritual ladder, there is no difference between you and those Beings who have already become Impeccable Warriors of Light. Regardless of the individual's chosen tradition and path, everyone is subject to assault and these attacks will be especially apparent in the weak areas of your Life. Likewise, we all have tremendous assistance through our Angels, Guides and many types of Spiritual Protectors assigned to help us in our Life mission.

Everyone relates to the Forces of Light and Good by different names. Whether you call your source of higher inspiration Spirit/God/Higher-Self/Mother Earth/Angels or any other name, do not let it dissuade you from mastering the UNIVERSAL PRINCIPLES regarding Spiritual Protection. Regardless of our path, we all have a mind, we all possess an ego and we all hear voices urging us towards either the high road or the low road in Life's decisions. Every one of us will hear both the voice of evil and the voice of the Goodness within.

As an example, there is the presence of the constant choice between forgiveness and harbouring hurt feelings. All of us will have the choice whether to act in the name of Love or cruelty. Hence the temptation to fall from Grace is present for everyone. This is a universal peril. To avoid this hazard we must learn more about the nature of the ocean of delusion and all its agents, as well as the many available tools for successfully navigating around both the seen and unseen obstacles that our karma has set up for us.

WHY DO WE NEED TO PROTECT OURSELVES ?

We are all psychic beings...perfect psychic instruments that receive vibrations every moment of the day and night. We receive impressions from the seen world...such as our Loved ones who are thinking about us, the people we work with, people we cross in the street, in the grocery store, people who like us and those who don't. These people are each carrying psychic baggage, and when they cross your path they can project onto you their judgments, criticisms, envy or jealousy. There are many ways they can transfer negative vibrations unto you, for negative energies can easily jump from one host to another.

We are also receiving impressions from the unseen world of ghosts, spirits, demons, ancestors, and so on. If you were not brought up with the awareness of the myriad forms of energy that live alongside us, it's very easy to slip into denial or amnesia about these things. However, to succeed in Life…we must walk on the Beauty-full Mother Earth with FULL awareness…with IMPECCABLE focus and attention to our surroundings and the constant stream of activity that is affecting us.

If we do not accept this challenge of heightening our objective observance, we are choosing to be easy targets. While it is true that negative forces have the cosmic assignment to attempt to disrupt our Life and destroy our mind, body and spirit, it is WE who willingly and unwittingly open the door to them through lack of awareness, attention and focus.

If we choose to be half-hearted in our approach to them, know this: they are NOT half-hearted in THEIR focus toward us. They are totally devoted to our downfall. They are ALL-WAYS looking for ways to infiltrate our Life by filling it with pain. They create suffering on our path to ensure we NOT enjoy our time on the Beauty-full Flowering Earth.

If we look at the palm of our hand or a kitchen counter, we don't see the millions of bacterial germs, yet we accept that they do exist, can harm us, make us sick and possibly even kill us. It is the same way with the invisible beings from the invisible worlds. We may not always be able to see them, but nonetheless they are there. Some 'invisible' forces are help-full, some won't harm us, others can make us ill and some are strong enough to kill us.

Just as it is the day's nature to be full of Light and the night's duty to be dark, it is the job of negative forces to try to destroy us. Looking at it from a detached point of view, where it is recognized that no experience is 'bad' since it does make us stronger and wiser to some degree, we shall call 'negative' forces by that name for the sake of identification.

4

They are therefore not necessarily 'bad'; it is simply their nature and assignment to inflict suffering upon us. Just as it is a poisonous snake's nature to bite you, it is the nature of any malevolent energy to attach itself to you and infiltrate your Life. They will attack your mind, health, relationships, job and Prosperity. It is vital you clearly understand this: they have one focus and one only--to destroy you!

We have all seen the cartoons of the wicked being on one shoulder and the good Angel on the other, both trying to get our attention. That is what it is truly like. The negative voice will try to talk us into self-destructive thoughts and actions, while the positive voice will strive to steer us towards a beautiful, Peace-full existence. It is our Sacred Duty to learn to protect ourselves. With the assistance of the positive Earth and Celestial Forces, we can train ourselves to quickly identify negative influences and immediately take action to dissolve any danger.

You will come to realize that in these modern times, most people don't know much about protecting themselves...Hence, they don't have a sufficient protective shield in place to guard them. The negative forces on the other hand are FULLY PREPARED...they do know everything about US. We may chose to be casual towards them, perhaps feeling unsure we actually believe in their presence... but guess what? While we are standing with one foot in one boat and another foot in a second boat, leaving ourselves un-balanced and easy prey, THEY are not casual in their approach to us! They are one-pointed in finding our weak spots and beginning their assault strategy. So our doubts and laziness in doing research in the most basic of spiritual principles, which is protection of our spirit, plays right into their hands.

For example, Saint Bernard of Clairvaux, describes the Spiritual Path, as a battle that he felt absolutely had to be waged against the dark forces;

"If you desert your ranks, do you think you can escape the enemy? An armed multitude surrounds your house and yet you sleep. They are scaling the walls; they demolish the palisade; they will soon burst through the postern.... where are your arms of battle? Where

are the shields of Faith? The helmet of salvation? The breastplate of patience?"
(Source: The Life and Times of St. Bernard, by James C. Morrison in Darshan Magazine 1997, P. 59.)

BEING SENSITIVE MEANS BEING PRONE TO PSYCHIC ATTACK

Being sensitive is the same as being psychic. To the degree that you are sensitive, to that degree you are a psychically open instrument. In days past, for example, psychics/mediums/channellers/intuitives were called 'sensitives'. Therefore, whether you realize it or not, the more sensitive you are, the more psychic you will be. Your sensitivity will naturally open doors to other worlds and give you access to other realities, whether you welcome it or not.

To be psychic is to be open and this is why sensitive beings feel everything so intensely, including psychic attack. Sensitive beings are more likely to experience symptoms of being 'possessed' by negative energies. This means they will tend to have more phobias, fears, vulnerability and overall out-of-balance behaviour. This is because the malicious energies can easily access the sensitive being and then influence them towards negativity, which then causes suffering in the sensitive one's Life.

Anywhere you find someone steeped in a pain-full, ugly Life-path, whether that be from any destructive behaviour abuse such as: cruelty, overt weakness, obsessions, compulsions, violence, fears and so on, it reflects that the person is a good person at heart, but due to their nature being too sensitive/too open, they have been possessed by negative entities that now control the person and their Life Force.

These Teachings provide us with that long desired clarity as to why people such as our Loved ones, who do Love us, can at times be so intolerant, cruel and generally unconscious of the pain they inflict on us and themselves. Comprehension such as this can bring us great Peace of mind in understanding humanity's behaviour... particularly our own...and alert us to our duty to master our Spiritual Work in transforming and uplifting all situations.

Most sensitive souls are not aware that their spiritual homework is to balance out their sensitivity, their kind hearts, with Strength, Valour and Clarity. They don't know they have to become great warriors who are focused, intelligent and ready for action! They incarnate on the Earth plane already accomplished in the softer tones such as Compassion, Generosity and Selfless-ness...so they don't have homework to do in that area. Their studies, research and application in this Life-time must be in psychic self-defence. Once they have mastered that, they will be the strong, wise, kind Warriors we need on Mother Earth for Harmony to exist and last.

There Is Nothing New Under The Sun

Everything you have read about in myths and legends, plus more that you may not even be able to imagine, does exist. In my younger years, I often wondered if the numerous forms of dark energy that I saw portrayed in television programs, books and around me, really existed. I chose to believe that they didn't and proceeded to take refuge in my Gurus, spiritual practices, meditation, chanting of mantras and calling forth the Light. In this way, I called forth protection day and night, yet I still experienced being attacked by an onslaught of ugly persistent entities.

Divine Mother has blessed me with the finest Teachers one could pray for. In this Life-time, before meeting my Mayan Teacher, Shaman Don Jacinto in Yucatán, Mexico, I was blessed to fall in Love with these Golden Beings: Bhagwan Nityananda, one of India's Great Saints, who trained and initiated Swami Muktananda; Swami Muktananda, founder of Siddha Yoga, who trained and initiated Gurumayi Chidvilasananda and Gurumayi Chidvilasananda, an Enlightened Master who continues the work of the Siddhas as the Siddha Yoga Guru, is still living and blessing us all with Her Grace-bestowing Presence.

My three Gurus are all Siddhas, part of the Siddha Lineage of Perfect Miraculous Beings. Great Liberators of humanity, who illuminate the path for all, they are unwavering towers of Love, Devotion and Grace.

I was born with a special bright Light within me, but by being in Their presence, through keeping company with Their Golden vibration and Their Golden Teachings the inner Light grew and grew. Fanned by Devotion, it consumed me until all that was left was another Free Being and Tower of Light. The Masters birthed another Master and I can never repay them!

My Gurus taught me about the 'mind' and the negative tendencies produced by the inner demons of the mind. Through Their Beauty-full, golden example, they imparted unto me Confidence in the path of Purity. Although they did refer to the impurities of the mind and gave us an ocean full of Wisdom Teachings on how to break free of the inner tormenters, due to the huge amount of veils which still covered my Intuitive Vision at that time, I was not able to truly understand everything they were revealing to us. During this period of my path, I often asked Spirit if darkness really existed and if so, to reveal to me how the dark side was able to create so much distress in humanity and how the Light Forces functioned in protecting us. I yearned for clarity!

Until the day arrived when clarity was granted, even as I was engaged in intense daily spiritual practices, I would still find myself having fright-full experiences as I sensed and saw dark shadows around me. I also saw and continue to witness the same thing happening with endless spiritual aspirants from various paths. There are several reasons for this. The first cause is the veils that cover our Golden, All-Knowing Mind. It is difficult to purify the mind if we are not fully aware of the many unseen worlds that are trying to possess our mind. The path of meditation often teaches us about the tendencies of the mind, but meditation Teachings do not always graphically disclose how the outside forces trigger the mind and its tendencies, as the negative energies attach themselves to our mind, body and spirit. And until we comprehend the exact science behind their attacks, we will not value the science of protection.

The second cause is that not every Teacher will divulge every-thing they know about this science because it is not their assignment to do so. What a Teacher knows…what they will actually teach…and how they will teach it, will be directed by Their Spiritual Guides. None of the Masters do what They want to do…Each Master carries out what they are INSTRUCTED to do for humanity. Spiritual Protection IS my assignment and therefore Sacred Peace Center's Teachings focus on Peace through Spiritual Protection.

Meditation is supremely valuable on the Spiritual Path, as it does purify the mind and heart, expanding our understanding of ourselves, and the Cosmos. It assists us by creating a space within us for Grace to flow into, which then opens up the doors for further remedies and knowledge. While meditation in itself may not protect us from daily negative attack, it aligns us with our Protectors, who then help us establish the steady Strength, Determination, Intuition and Trust needed to recognize our true spiritual needs and call forth solutions to our challenges.

The more you meditate, the brighter Light you radiate! This seems like a good thing, doesn't it? Be aware that the brighter your Light is, the more the negative forces will be drawn to you. The negative forces feed on energy and the more Positive Energy you have, the more substantial a meal you can provide them. At the same time you become a power-full Light force, you also become a sought after prize for the dark force. Once you have great power, it is considered a greater triumph for the force of evil when they are able to turn you towards the dark side, by engaging you in negative behaviour, even for a moment.

Do not let this frighten you from progressing on the Spiritual Path. Whether you are a race-car driver, aeroplane pilot, brain surgeon or Light worker, the key to confidence is practice and knowledge. This book will arm you with many techniques and mantras for disintegrating any harm-full energies that try to attack you. With the help of the Impeccable Warrior of Light Teachings, you can quickly Strengthen your Courage and Victory Power. The continual infusion of Grace will make you a wiser, stronger Warrior, who is able to fearlessly reverse negativity.

As you take greater refuge in the Spiritual Laws you will become able to truly believe in the presence of your Protectors. Your Faith will allow you to perceive the Legions of Light that surround you and you will receive all the spiritual tools you need to stand your ground and be triumphant in every case.

I feel my first Teachers, my three Gurus, intensified within me my Love for God, saturating me with Devotion towards the daily spiritual practices of chanting and meditation. My Guru's Grace and the Light-producing spiritual practices they bestowed upon us, established a solid relationship between me and my Spirit Team. My Divine Gurus paved the way for the in-depth comprehension to arise of how the seen and unseen world intermingle and connect. However, it was my fourth Teacher, Mayan Shaman Don Jacinto Tzab, who confirmed the existence of these apparitions more than I ever imagined! As His apprentice I observed first-hand, case after case of Soul Retrieval consultations where I heard and saw other's experiences of psychic attack from beings, energies and dark practices that I would not have believed when I was younger.

Having served the Mayan people as a Yucatecan Shaman since he was fifteen years old, Don Jacinto was supremely knowledgeable of the endless types of sinister forces that pounced upon the many people who came to see him. Being an Impeccable Warrior of Light, armed with the Shaman's practices he inherited from his Teacher Don Feliciano, he was usually able to dispel the ill that had been cast upon the patient.

There were times when the case was too far-gone, but such cases were rare. In studying with him, I was shown that the many evils that have been written and spoken of throughout the ages do indeed exist. My questions were answered as it was revealed to me that these negative forces have appeared in different cultures in similar forms. Throughout history the Impeccable Warriors of Light have walked their path as Wise Beings by taking all of this into account, and in doing so, safe-guarded themselves against the perils of the spiritual journey.

My Life's path has further shown me that everything that expresses itself in an outer form has come from the universal Source of Creation and this birthing process has been going on from the beginning of beginningless Time.

Everything that might emerge as new in your Life has already repeatedly appeared and continues to materialize in other people's lives throughout all ages. For example, ghosts, goblins, trolls, evil witches, vampires, werewolves or demonic practices of any variation are not new, and have plagued humanity in countless variations. If you chose to do a thorough investigation into any of these subjects you would find a wide variety of people from all levels of existence, from every country and civilization, who have experienced these types of negative forces and more.

Just as there is a long history of Grace-bestowing Beings that watch over humanity, such as Angels, Archangels, Saints, Master Teachers and Spirit Guides, there is also a long history of the creative energy manifesting in dark forms.

Therefore, 'There is nothing new under the sun.' If you read something, see it in a movie, or somehow come across it, believe me, it has happened or been done before. Once you admit to yourself that other worlds exist right alongside of us, you are less likely to be caught off-guard. As long as you choose to be in denial, the malevolent forces will continually 'possess' you, meaning they will easily take over your Radiant nature and Divine intelligence, influencing you to leave behind the Golden Rules of being a Radiant Being. They will chip away at your Happiness to keep you un-balanced and in this way keep you from reaching your highest Joy-fullness and Destiny here on Earth.

Once you adopt some of the simple techniques in this book, you will have tools with which to defend yourself and by reacting with positive action instead of denial, you will start taking back the power you have unwittingly been feeding the negative forces around you.

WHY ARE WE IN DENIAL OF THE UNSEEN WORLDS?

The Universe is filled with diversity. After all, how many types of bugs are there? How many types of birds, flowers, others plants, etc. exist? Scientists are forever finding new species of Life forms that they previously thought non-existent. Human beings are constantly re-minded that what they see represents only a tiny fraction of what exists and that there are countless worlds, Universes and Galaxies which are alive, yet, unknown to us.

We must therefore learn from this that whether we know about destructive energies or not, whether we believe they exist or not, they still live and move amongst us.

For example, once someone asked my teacher Don Jacinto if extraterrestrials existed. He replied, "Which ones do you want to know about?" So whether we are discussing extraterrestrials, ghosts, entities, etc., it is not a matter of whether they exist. It is a matter of how many variations exist. It is important to always remember that just because we don't understand a caterpillar's world, or the Universe the hummingbird lives in, does not mean 'their world' does not exist.

Sometimes when people have experiences of psychic attack, as well as experiences with the benevolent Legions of Light, they wonder if they are 'going mad'. Although they may question whether they are losing their mind, what is actually occurring is simply an interaction with the other worlds. The uncertainty comes from not understanding the messages, signals and signs, which are being delivered to them in an unfamiliar language of the Universe. Rather than deny the existence of this language, the Impeccable Warrior of Light is willing to be open to receive the infinite Wisdom of the mysterious Universe.

The reason the Mystics all refer to Creation/The Universe/Life as 'the Great Mystery' is because it is unfathomable. No matter how much we learn of it, we will never ever be able to totally comprehend its enormous cosmic secrets.

We should not waste our Life Force by re-inforcing ignorance. Instead of getting caught up in confusion over whether other species, planets, planes and Life-forms exist, we can put that same energy towards our spiritual practices, so we can reach Enlightenment. We should not invest a huge amount of our Golden Energy in denying the existence of that which we have not seen in solid form. Some things in Creation were not intended to be perceived in dense form... however they may be sensed or recognized through Intuition and research. Even if we are not fully convinced that the unseen or undiscovered worlds are real, by honouring the possibility, we go forward with more awareness.

By being receptive we then expand our minds to many other possibilities within the mystical realms. The more we loosen our grip on the idea that only that which our mind can prove exists, the more we become available to communication from the other worlds. If, through expanding the perception of your beliefs, you inherit a stronger conviction to maintain Spiritual Protection, balance, good thoughts and good actions, then this can only fortify the connection between you and your Higher-Self.

The battle between Good and Evil has been going on from the beginning of beginningless Time. In certain ages, the negative forces succeeded in clouding the Sacred Memory of a huge majority of the people, causing the Earth Beings to live their lives in denial of the existence of the dark side and the extent of it's power to control and manipulate. Making Humanity oblivious to the movements of evil is the first way dark forces gain control over us. For how can we defend ourselves against something we choose not to see? How can we prepare for that which we deny exists?

Having hypnotized us into blindness, it is easy for sinister forces to create an illusion within us of separation from our God Self. They not only blind us to their ugly existence, but also blind us to the existence of God and our Oneness with the God Light. By erasing our remembrance of the Light, they have robbed us in the past of our Divine inheritance. To this day, they continue to assault us in the same way, in order to separate us from our Eternal Power, which enables us to create Beauty and Balance.

By the negative forces moving us away from our soul and further into the confines of the mental maze of Faith-less worries, doubts and denial, they have succeeded in converting most people into the 'walking dead'. They have successfully manoeuvred most living forms into a state of amnesia of the Impeccable Warrior Wisdom. We are physically alive, our lives are filled with many activities, many thoughts and many goals, but are we spiritually alive? Do we live Life as the sacred, fantastic, amazing, Glory-us and ecstatic gift it truly is?

13

WHY WOULD ANYONE WANT TO SUFFER?

On the one hand we say we don't want to suffer, yet on another level, we are not awake and by not living fully aware, we are casually accepting a Life-style that hypnotizes us into believing what society tells us about the world around us. This state of delusion is very much present in today's age, which has given more credence and power to that of materiality instead of spirituality. Too many people give much more attention to their favourite television programs, Internet activities, newspapers and magazines than their Spiritual Path. The media, science and technology have become deities to some.

Everyone registers unseen energies as "gut feelings" in their solar plexus or through some other reaction of the Wisdom Body. Yet, in spite of experiencing chills or the hair on the arm standing up and other signs of an invisible presence around them...they re-main in denial of what their energetic body is registering, rather than trusting their Intuition and listening to their Higher Wisdom. In the meantime, they continue to bow to those who keep them locked into the ever-chattering, fear-riddle, never-satisfied mind, rather than committing to a Spiritual Path that will grant eternal Peace. If we do not venerate some form of God, , in our own unique way ...if we do not make time to worship the Great Spirit which is the Eternal Victory-us Light. within us ...we cannot claim the Divine gifts which are our primordial inheritance. Why? Because as the negative forces move us in a soul-less direction, they are separating us more and more from our Highest Path of Faith and Love as Beings of Light.

It is part of the master plan of evil forces to sway us away from the simple basic recognition of the Spirit World and our Soul Wisdom. In the history of the evolving Earth, there have been times when the dark forces encroached upon the Sacred Intelligence and this is currently one of those cycles. If you knew the huge variety of ways that evil manifests itself around you and the rest of the world, it would boggle your mind.

These Teachings will open up your mind to the possibilities of the many ways that the forces of Light and darkness can present themselves in your Life. The material you will be reading in this

14

book can help you and others around you by arming you with tools to decipher experiences that you previously thought un-explainable.

The first step towards maintaining consistent Happiness in your Life is to understand more of what goes on around you. The second step is to learn what you can do when confronted, attacked or influenced by the unseen worlds in a negative way. The next step is to DO THE WORK by practicing the rituals, prayers and energetic laws for Spiritual Protection. The final step is to remain Great-full by being thank-full for the messages you have received, regardless of the form they came in. For actually, it is the challenges and lessons on your path that have inspired you to put the Wisdom into practice…thereby finally healing your self.

Chapter 2

THE IMPECCABLE WARRIORS OF LIGHT

The Impeccable Warrior… lives in a conscious state…truly accepting and experiencing Life as a Sacred Being on a Sacred Journey… They know they are assisted by a Timeless, Compassionate Wisdom that whole-heartedly Respects and honours them.

Since the beginning of time, there have been Impeccable Warriors of Light in every spiritual tradition. These are the beings that choose to take FULL responsibility for their state of being and surroundings.

An Impeccable being chooses to learn from everything in their path. They choose to monitor their usage of energies with great vigilance. In this way, they do not allow themselves to be led into negative actions and reactions by the negative forces. They know the value of their Golden Energy and are fully aware it is highly sought after by energy vampires.

The Impeccable Warrior understands this precious Golden Energy is needed to fund their Life projects, ideas and activities. They fully comprehend that if they piddle their energetic funding away in ignorance, their energetic bank account may end up overdrawn when they need it the most.

Walking the Spiritual Path as an Impeccable Warrior is achievable by everyone. The Impeccable Warrior Respects and recognizes that other worlds exist beside them, whereas the masses walk through

Life with their eyes closed or only partially open. Most people learn a few spiritual principles and then lock themselves inside that box. From that point on, they no longer allow themselves to explore, contemplate and consider ideas outside the limiting parameters they have accepted.

Endeavouring to become an Impeccable Warrior of Light is the same goal as desiring to be absolutely free of all false understanding. The Impeccable Warrior of Light will not accept being bound by chains, bars and fences of narrow perceptions. If you choose to strive for Freedom, the question to ask yourself in every situation is this: "Do I wish to be 'right' or do I wish to be Free?" Do you want to feel you are "right" or do you want to be happy?

As with any science, the small minds marry an idea and then stand to the death on that thought, regardless of it being incomplete or obsolete. Whereas the great minds of the world, such as Einstein and Stephen Hawking ...are willing to explore, research and forever be open to new information. Their ego is not dented if they find there is more to the experiment or theory than previously perceived.

Remember, investing all your energy in "being right" robs you of energy you could have invested in becoming Free...a Liberated, fully Enlightened Being! Those who wish to be 'right' remain stuck in their limiting box of thought. Those who are pulled by the goal of Freedom find they relish becoming fully aware of the big picture of Creation and all that exists.

The Impeccable Warrior is not interested in attaching themselves to restrictive thinking just so they can boost their ego by feeling they are 'right' about every matter. The goal for them is to be FREE... free of the negative emotions, delusions, expectations and regrets that constitute the petty, limiting ego. The Wise Warrior is driven by a hunger for True Knowledge, for an expansion of awareness... not by that which further inflates their ego.

The Impeccable Warrior has come to understand that the Supreme Intelligence of this Universe is NOT limited. It is always beckoning us to open up to the greater realities existing in the many realms of the spirit world. By walking with their eyes FULLY open, the Impeccable Warrior does not get caught off guard...they are not surprised by the unexpected.

The Impeccable Warrior's mission on Earth is to whole-heartedly serve the forces of Light. They do this through their steadfast Devotion to the forces of Good and the Positive Spiritual Principles that support humanity's awakening. Whether that Impeccable being is a Shaman, Lama, Rabbi, Medicine Woman, Song Keeper, Healer or Priest…THE GOAL IS THE SAME!

Divine Mother refers to The Champions of Light as Impeccable so we understand the degree of Purity these beings reached. An Impeccable Being lives, breathes, eats, drinks and sleeps their Path. THE PATH LIVES WITHIN THEM…IT EMANATES FROM THEM WHEREVER THEY ARE…IN WHATEVER THEY DO. They don't just teach or preach it… it is a Way of Life for them. The Impeccable being can be a mother, father, schoolteacher, bus driver, accountant, beggar or any other position in society. The position one holds or any other outer appearance is not an indicator one way or another of someone's spiritual attainment. You may have met beings that hold titles or wear attire that might lead you to believe they are walking the Path of Impeccability, yet upon close examination it is revealed they are not living an Impeccable Life at all.

Impeccability becomes a part of us through utilizing Life's experiences to grind our petty ego to dust. One who commits to the path of Impeccability is committing to ending their stream of drama…the "suffering over the suffering." It is vital to contemplate exactly what I am imparting with this Teaching. As long as anyone is on Earth, they will suffer in some way. We come to the Earth plane to master our karmic lessons, which involve one type of pain or another, for our soul knows that by embodying on Planet Earth, we will suffer. Our whole purpose in re-incarnating on Mother Earth is to transcend challenges and then help others do so also…the goal of our experiences is to reach a point of Light where we no longer allow trials to separate us from our Light Nature.

Heroic Beings all suffer either from one thing or another, be it the effects of old age and illness, or the dark forces using the weak people around the Impeccable Warrior to create blocks and disturbance. So outer/surface suffering will continue to occur as the karmic seeds planted through past actions and past lives continue to blossom. However, by choosing to not "suffer over the suffering" the Impeccable being will not waste their Golden Energy in complaining, whining and wallowing in the 'poor me' syndrome. The Impeccable Warrior Of Light recognizes it is the dark forces who are plunging the mind into a world of regrets and feelings that involve sentiments such as, `I should have/would have/could have'.

An Impeccable Being firmly holds the attitude that all matters All Ways work out for the best. They are able to see how all 'seeming' suffering brings forth some form of blessing and they discern what that blessing is, through application, prayer and contemplation. In this way, they are at Peace with their adversaries and obstacles. They see challenges and blocks as their 'friends' who assist them by pushing them to excel to a higher level of consciousness and IN THIS WAY, THE IMPECCABLE BEING IS ABLE TO MAINTAIN INNER Peace, IN THE MIDST OF TRIALS.

The Impeccable Warrior of Light does not allow themselves to be utilized by the dark forces and therefore does not feed any negative energy. As soon as the Warrior Of Light senses any disruptive energy moving towards them, will immediately go into action, dissolving and transforming those forces attempting to glum onto them. By doing so, the Impeccable Warrior of Light is all-ways uplifting every thing and every one that crosses their path.

Know How The Negative Forces Work, Because They Know You!

The negative forces are supremely well trained in the art of war and destruction. Like all excellent Warriors, the forces of evil are also trained in the art and science of moving about without being noticed by their target. It is their goal to be as invisible as possible so that they can start their campaign of harassment upon you. Their aim is to avoid identification as they attempt to attack you in their unlimited forms.

However, the Universe is a Compassionate Universe and therefore there are signs that you can look for which will alert you to the presence of destructive energies. If you are Impeccable in maintaining a watchful eye and are immaculate in your protection practices, you will be able to quickly deflect all threatening forms and therefore sustain the high level of spiritual cleanliness that brings inner and outer tranquillity.

By knowing how the sinister energies of the Universe work, you can quickly identify their presence at all times. The negative forces know it is much more difficult to bring down someone who is willing to do the daily work of securing their work base, home and inner Temple.

As an Impeccable Warrior, be aware the dark forces will continually attempt to cast the net of laziness or forget-fullness upon you, distracting you with a flood of desires. They know that once they have ensnared you, it makes it easier for them to create havoc in your Life. Any suffering they can create anywhere furthers their mission of stirring the pot of human suffering.

Know this: The sinister energies of the Universe do know YOU! The first thing they do is scan you and immediately they know e-v-e-r-y-thing: how you think, your fears, your weak spots, your Strengths and your destiny! They take their assignment of your destruction absolutely seriously.

Do you take your success and protection equally seriously? All malevolent forces are admirable opponents and we can learn much from their dedicated discipline. It is wise to note their discipline and to Respect their accomplished warrior ways. Otherwise, while you are sitting in denial, they will bulldoze you and knock you over with their highly polished tenacity.

Therefore, let us give negative forces their due credit. They are totally determined and one-pointed to create suffering and pain in your Life. Every dark force knows you well... the dark side is watching you at all times. They study you so they can constantly find ways to penetrate your Spiritual Protection. This illustrates how well trained they are.

Are you as disciplined? Do you know when they are attacking your mind? Do you see them as they are sneaking into your energetic field and pummelling you with their propaganda, convincing you that self-destructive actions and emotions are acceptable to your spirit? To break free of these "sneaky whisperers", it is help-full if you create a list of all your negative patterns. Then write out all the justifications your demons have fed your mind, in order to wear down your discipline and create self-loathing within you. The more you are willing to take responsibility for having relinquished your power to energetic bullies, the more you will find you are able to expertly recognize the presence of ominous energies.

You now know that the negative forces know you very well…that they know what greatness you are capable of…and they want you on THEIR side. The more they can convince you to leave behind the Light-filled ways, the easier it is for them to brainwash you to watch television, for example, instead of doing your spiritual practices. The more doubts they can instil in you…the more distance they can create between you and your Angels/Higher-Self/Protectors… the more they rejoice!

Negative forces are excellent warriors--they consistently practice the time-proven warfare technique for capturing their prey. 'divide and conquer.' By producing a sense of separation between you and your God Source they cause you to feel small, weak, help-less, hope-less and angry. THEY want you to believe your God Source has abandoned you. DEMONS ARE LIARS. NOTHING THEY TELL YOU IS TRUE!

However, as long as you believe it to be true, the perspectives of the dark forces will colour your Life adventures on this Earth, as you continually full-fill your negative belief patterns. Each round of suffering brings additional pain…and the resentment to that pain then brings even more suffering! On and on it goes in a circular motion of endless torments. All the while, through your sadness, rage and anxiety, you are fattening the forces of darkness. By giving them your Golden Life Force day after day in one way or another, you make them stronger and mightier.

In order to live a power-full, happy Life, it is imperative to remember that your distress fills them with an ecstatic sense of power…so it is vital to choose TO NOT FEED THEM.

21

The following story illustrates this point very well:

A Cherokee Native American grandfather was teaching his grandchildren about the nature of Life on Mother Earth. He said to them, "A fierce fight is going on inside me. It is a terrible fight between two wolves. One wolf is evil—he is fear, anger, envy, sorrow, regret, greed, arrogance, self-pity, guilt, resentment, inferiority, lies, false pride, competition, superiority, and ego.

The other is good—he is Joy, Peace, Love, Hope, Serenity, Humility, Kindness, Benevolence, Friendship, Courage, Empathy, Nobility, Generosity, Truth, Compassion, Devotion and Faith.

This same fight is going on inside you as well as within every other person, too."

They thought about it for a minute and then one child asked his grandfather, "Which wolf will win?" The Elder wisely replied, "The one you feed."

OPENING YOUR EYES TO THE RADIANT BEAUTY AND YOUR SACRED DUTY

To understand negative forces, we must comprehend our role here on Earth and the Sacred Duty that walking on this Radiant Jewel entails. This planet is considered a Radiant Jewel within the many Galaxies and Universes.

The Wise Ones are absolutely aware it is the greatest pleasure and honour to take birth here on the Beauty-full, Flowering Earth. The Saints and Sages have revealed in countless scriptures and Teachings that it is not easy to be granted a birth here, as there is a long list of souls waiting in line for a ticket to re-embody here.

Regardless of whether you are an old or new soul, innumerable factors need to come together in just the perfect way for re-incarnation to be granted here. It may take hundreds or thousands of years for that window of opportunity to present itself and when it does there is great rejoicing on behalf of the soul.

Mother Earth offers us everything we could possibly need to live happily. While walking on the physical Earth, we have available to us marvels such as majestic mountains, lush green valleys, rejuvenating waters, gorgeous skies…opulent jewels, mouth-watering fruits, healing herbs and vegetables…as well as other exquisite creations. It is an absolutely awesome place to be…and be-ing here is definitely a reason for jubilation!

If we don't recognize this fact and cannot appreciate Mother Earth's innumerable gifts and abundant scrumptious sustenance, it is only due to ignorance of our Sacred Duty. For our Sacred Duty is to appreciate, to be Great-full and be fully committed to our assignment here. By being totally present here, we are able to receive and accept the Divine gifts that are All-Ways being bestowed upon us. We cannot be present if our attention and energies are all concentrated on escape, or our focus is on attachment to never returning to the Blue Jewel Realm.

The Earth experience is an amazing one; it is the place we come to for the sacred purifying process, giving us the opportunity to grow spiritually and know ourselves as creators. This is a marvel-us arena that grants us the profound opportunity to master immense spiritual principles such as Forgiveness, Compassion, Courage…Strength, Universal Love and Balance… while being surrounded by conditions which can plunge us into an abyss of illusion.

We come to this phenomenal playing field to experience the dance of the polarities, the cosmic battle between Good and Evil. Yet, we do not have to cry and wail our Life away. The discovery and refinement of these Virtues allows us to advance as spiritual beings to an elevated state of consciousness.

This experience of Life on Planet Earth is the most golden of all Golden Jewels. There is a song that says, 'If you can make it there, you can make it anywhere', and this applies perfectly to Life here on Earth! This is THE testing ground and it is THE highest opportunity to be able to be here and confront the karmic seeds we have planted over so many Life-times. It is the greatest opportunity to even have the chance to tackle and transform the many psychic impressions we are carrying around within us. When we realize how many beings wish they could be here in our shoes, we then perceive Life on the Radiant Jewel as a supreme blessing, rather than a curse.

While still in the haze of ignorance, many spiritual aspirants adopt the ill-advised stance that they know they will not be reincarnating on this Earth again. Others constantly broadcast their outlook of not desiring to ever again be born as a human on this Earth. This mind-set of theirs reveals that they have not fully embraced the Grace that is bestowed through a human birth. Unfortunately they will never graduate to the next level of their evolution with that attitude.

For example, if you are in the third level of studies in a certain school and you despise being there, you will not do the homework assigned in that classroom because you do not Respect the lessons that particular school is offering you. Through this disdain you will misuse your time in the third level, foolishly praying for it to come to an end, instead of applying yourself, appreciating and mastering what is being gifted to you. Day by day, the minutes in the third level studies would drag by until one day, everyone in the classroom would be granted a holiday. Ecstatic, you would feel that you were free! Free from the weight of those daily lessons that the classroom was imposing upon you! However, a vacation from school is just that--a temporary break from the duties--not a permanent release. So, is it any surprise that when school season resumes again, there you are…once more assigned to the third level!

Since you despised the classroom on your previous assignment, you did not do the homework. Having ignored the homework, you have to re-attend that classroom, over and over again…until one day you grasp that the way to graduate to the next level is to do the homework! Armed with this realization, you embrace the third level and the work that must take place there. By approaching it with a positive outlook, you no longer resist, so everything flows for you. Your brain is more relaxed and therefore assimilates knowledge faster and easier. Before you know it, you've graduated! Along the way, you were able to see the humour and benefit of your trials. Armed with a positive, receptive view of your adventures, you had more fun and found that time flew by.

Once you have mastered the success-full attitude necessary for victory in your present level, you are bestowed the opportunity to apply everything you have learned so far, in the next level! Through a stream of opportunities, you finally develop within yourself a high esteem for Life's homework, which allows you to prize the chances bequeathed upon you by the University of Life.

If you were not in resistance...if your Wisdom were already established within you...you would get down on your knees and thank all those forces that care so much about you and your soul evolution, for customizing the perfect classroom for you, with such perfect lessons.

Those beings that have reached Enlightenment praise the human birth and the invaluable time allotted to us here on the Radiant Jewel. If asked to volunteer for another Life-time on the Radiant Jewel, no Being who has reached the highest levels of Self-Love and Compassion for others, would ever say no to the Forces of Good.

Seva, which is self-less service to humanity is the most satisfying, enriching experience...and no being who truly Loves the Light, (as opposed to only talking about Loving it) would hesitate for a second to assist humanity in reaching its highest Balance and Wisdom.

When we can fully accept that which is gifted unto us...when we can identify the blessing in every occurrence and see the beauty in all that appears before us, THEN it is easy to celebrate Life on the Radiant Jewel. Beings who are able to maintain The Great Attitude (gratitude)...sing and dance their way through Life...for they see the scintillating Divine Creative Force forever birthing blessings for everyone.

Therefore, it is supremely valuable to 'get with the program' and live Joy-fully as an ecstatic being. Somehow, someway, we acquired enough Grace to be allowed to be here for a certain amount of time. Let us open up our eyes to the boundless beauty that surrounds us here and not waste one ounce of this wondrous gift by sleepwalking through it.

God's perfection is in all that appears around us. Once we see everything as God's perfect plan, we do not leak our Golden Energy by resisting the perfect lesson offered to us. We CHOOSE the viewpoint that all matters arrive in our hands in the perfect way and at the perfect moment. By seeing the endless string of perfection in all creation within us and around us, we are free from the weight of judgments, trepidation, anxiety and fears that hinder our ability to flow with God's perfect plan for our soul's further expansion. In this way, we are easily able to tackle our assignments with great Zest and sacred enthusiasm.

Are the weak able to help the suffering? No…there is not enough Strength to do so…for they are weighed down by their own issues. For example, if you were drowning, it would be difficult to save another drowning person, since your mind, body and spirit would not have the stamina and might required. To be of service in alleviating suffering, we must have Strength, Endurance and Stamina within us.

We are here to be Impeccable Warriors of Light. The sacred assignment we committed to when we agreed to incarnate on the Blue Jewel was to utilize everything around us to become Impeccable Warriors.

To become a Great Warrior, one must have Great Teachers and great adversaries as well. For only through the actual challenge are we able to take the Wisdom shared with us by the Teacher and find a way to make it work for us, in our own individualistic way! An Impeccable Warrior realizes it is vita. to UNDERSTAND their adversaries thoroughly. In order to be prepared for our encounters with them, we must know their methods of operation and comprehend how they think.

It is always wise to Respect the adversaries' strong points and pinpoint their weak points. If you are not aware of your adversaries' methods of thinking and operating you will never succeed, for they will always have the upper hand and be able to fool you over and over again, as they manipulate your energy.

God's perfection is in BOTH the challenges and rewards that appear before us. By walking through Life with this conviction, we are able to full-fill our Sacred Duty, which is to praise and enjoy Life to the highest degree. As we develop an unwavering Faith in God's perfect plan, we truly honour Life on the Radiant Jewel by Joy-fully appreciating every minute of it. This means staying in a state of Lightness during the times that appear to be 'trying', as well as the sweet cycles. We are able to do this when we maintain daily Spiritual Protection practices.

Our Sacred Duty is to DILIGENTLY employ the Positive Principles. By unswervingly applying them to every challenge, we insure our triumph on behalf of the Legions of Light. I assure you... all lessons contained within every drama are to be TREASURED. The drama is the stage for our martial arts tournament...and the struggles we encounter are the tests that will show what you have learned so far. In every bout it will be revealed if you are able to overturn the attacker or whether the assailing force knocks you down. The lessons we extract from each conflict constitute the Honour badges, medals of Courage and Wisdom staffs we earn and are awarded by the Forces of Light.

Therefore, our Sacred Duty is to refine the spiritual weapons Spirit has given us for the purpose of upholding the Spiritual Laws. Then you will experience being master of your own destiny and victim of none. The reward of devoting our energies to IMPECCABLE ATTENTION and INTENTION...is the soul-satisfaction that comes from relishing our walk on Mother Earth as Sacred Beings Of Light...on a Sacred Pilgrimage.

TREASURING THE GOLDEN ENERGY

Lack of Self-Love/Self-Respect is a common human syndrome. Regardless of the culture or country humans belong to, most people share a difficulty in honouring themselves, for they do not believe themselves to be a superbly wondrous God created Temple. The majority of beings have no comprehension of the phenomenal, mystical Energy housed within that Temple.

This astounding Energy is what we call Life Force. Only a rare being is deeply aware of what those words truly mean, as the bulk of humanity has become jaded to the magnificence of this Celestial gift we call Life Force. It takes Energy to do anything, anywhere, anytime. It takes Energy to move our bodies, to generate thoughts, launch a rocket ship, dream and create cars, buildings, shoes, computers, furniture and the rest of Creation! All these things originate from the 'mind', but it takes Energy to drive and operate the mind. Where does the mind get its power to be, to think, to imagine? The answer is the Golden Energy!

This Golden Energy which is referred to by countless other names throughout this world and innumerable other realms, is known as Shakti in the Vedic scriptures of India and The Holy Spirit in other traditions. The Shakti/Holy Spirit is the Golden Energy that births and powers all Creation. Only through this Golden Energy does the spark of Life exist and solely through this Shakti/Holy Spirit can that spark of Life ignite anywhere in the Cosmos.

It is therefore because of the Golden Energy that objects and realities are able to materialize. Through the power of that same Shakti...Universes and Galaxies must at some point dissolve. Energy, Energy, Energy...the key is to become conscious of your relationship with The Golden Energy.

The power that humans carry within them is far more potent than nuclear power. What if you wholeheartedly believed you carried a power within you that was greater than nuclear power? How would you use it? Mother God/Father God's ability to birth, maintain and dissolve all realities also exists within you. The Shakti/Holy Spirit has been placed within every one of us, empowering each soul with this awesome ability to create, maintain and dissolve worlds.

How do we do this? Through our choices! An ancient Teaching states, "The world is as you see it," and the Impeccable Warrior of Light is fully aware of this and lives with this awareness. My root Guru, Swami, 'Baba' Muktananda would often say that in order to instantly change the world around us we should change the eyeglasses we are wearing.

How true, if you put on pink glasses the world becomes pink. If you tire of pink and desire to live in a purple or electric blue, you simply and immediately choose to put on the appropriate lens. If you wake up to find the day is gloomy and gray but you put on golden-tinted glasses the world immediately changes for you, appearing brighter, doesn't it?

We can do this energetically, without having to buy the tinted sunglasses...just replace your perspective. Instead of perceiving something as a gloomy occurrence, replace it with a positive vision. Thus, if you don't want something to exist in your world any more...

by opting to make changes…you dissolve your present existence and move yourself into a new reality.

Likewise, if you are happy and content and then allow the negative forces to convince you to choose destructive actions, you can suddenly find yourself outside the gates of your previous Heaven. The power of your thoughts and the power of the ENERGY that you infuse those thoughts with, can create or destroy any perceived realities you focus on, moving you from one world to another. As we select what to believe, what to sustain and what to let go of in our Life, we are constantly birthing, maintaining and dissolving the world around us.

The Golden Energy enlivens all it is directed towards. There is an energetic Teaching that states, 'Wherever your attention goes…your energy flows'. Likewise it is true that wherever your energy flows your attention goes. An Impeccable Warrior Respects the Golden Law that ATTENTION AND ENERGY TRAVEL TOGETHER. To walk as an Impeccable Warrior of Light you must understand that your Golden Energy gives Life to any thoughts you focus on. In so doing, you can make wise choices and vow to maintain a positive point of view on all your Life situations.

DREAM THE BEAUTY-FULL DREAM, NOT THE NIGHTMARE

Another Golden Law is 'If you can perceive it, you can achieve it'. If you elect to invest your Golden Energy in envisioning your Golden Dreams…and then proceed to feed it Golden Energy through self-effort, you can witness its manifestation in your Life. You have the God-given gift to choose…so vote to use your Golden Life Force for 'dreaming the Beauty-full Dream', by opting to focus on your positive goals instead of your fears and worries.

What kind of world you will live in tomorrow, next year, or in the next Life-time, depends on the thoughts, visions and inspirations you are selecting today! What we construct with our Golden Energy this very moment, will affect us down the road. Many people let the dark forces consume them with negative images of bad luck, ill health, pain-full relationships, and so on. If you choose to live this way, as

29

you entertain these scenarios, you are 'dreaming the nightmare'.

Whether you realize it or not, you never have the luxury of utilizing your Golden Life Force casually. Every seed planted will move towards blossoming with every moment that passes. Unless you start tending your garden with a fierce Devotion to its radiance, you can easily find yourself over-run with weeds. The Impeccable Warrior of Light decides to invest their Life Force wisely, by choosing to build their Life as a testament to the Spiritual Principles of Beauty, Balance, Joy, Wisdom, Courage, Faith-fullness, Strength and Devotion to God/Spirit.

To walk as an Impeccable Warrior of Light, we must regard the Golden Energy, the Life Force, as Sacred. For as long as we fail to even contemplate the supreme value of that Holy Gift and Power, we will not be able to esteem the Golden Energy and protect it.

The Impeccable Warrior is fully aware that the negative forces desire to steal this Holy Gift. Consequently the Wise Warrior will consciously choose to remain alert at all times, to the endless schemes the conniving dark forces use to snatch Golden Energy from the un-prepared, unsuspecting weak ones. *Do not let this make you paranoid*, for a paranoid warrior is the perfect candidate for failure. Instead this Wisdom should inspire you to heightened levels of astuteness and responsibility. This is a necessary awareness, for to walk the path as a Brilliant Being requires that you safeguard the Golden Energy and utilize it with the utmost Respect, Vigilance and Wisdom.

WHY AREN'T WE TAUGHT THIS?

The negative forces have all-ways pushed for humanity to be in… and stay in…denial of what the Body Wisdom is communicating. As I have said, NONE of this is new. Hatred, jealousy, envy, war, greed, dishonesty, fear, viciousness and all other negative traits are behaviour patterns that have been in existence in every age. Wherever meanness and cruelty are present, there exists the Force of Evil that has created that ugliness. All people living in negative states of any type were good beings before being overtaken by evil spirits/energies. Hence, all cultures have rituals and prayers for protection.

Dark forces have eternally worked at obliterating acceptance of and Respect for this Golden Knowledge. Throughout the cycles, after many attempts to disrupt and topple the Natural Ways of Wisdom, they always succeeded to various degrees. For example, in recent history, thousands of years ago the negative forces succeeded in the destruction of the Goddess Temples and Goddess Wisdom. In the last five hundred years, we have seen the dissolution of countless Indigenous cultures such as the Mayan, Aztec, Aboriginal and Northern Native American. The list is too long to mention them all.

These dark forces have cyclically sought to destroy the cultures that honour the forces of Nature, Respect the Mother Earth, Her healing herbs and healing ways. All these Indigenous cultures were based on communicating with everything around them. They recognized that everything is alive, breathing and communicating with us. They had prayers, rituals and a ceremonial manner of inter-relating with the Moon, Sun, Stars…animals, plants… Ancestors… and the Lords/Forces of the Land.

The Ancient Wisdom ways, which are based on living in Harmony and Respect for all, promote the connectedness of all Life. It is this realization that the negative forces continually seek to wipe off the face of this planet.

If you are new to this way of thinking, you may still wonder why this connection is so threatening to the negative forces. The answer is this: to be consciously connected is to be whole. A fragmented being experiences suffering, whereas a whole being is a Balanced being and KNOWS they are HOLY. To be connected means to know that we belong to a cosmic family such as Father Sky and Grandmother Moon. When we live cognizant of the Cosmos as our home, we feel our link to the Sacred Sites and points of Natural power that enhance our Life Force such as Oceans, Rivers, Mountains and Deserts.

We communicate with the sacred elements of Wind, Fire, Air and Ether, knowing we depend on them. We comprehend that all these forces, and more, are always present to assist and teach us. Therefore we interrelate with these forces knowingly, Great-fully and wisely, understanding that they are just as alive as we are.

Knowing this instils us with a great empowerment to live a magical, mystical Life as reverent Beings. The Impeccable Warrior … lives in a conscious state…truly accepting and experiencing Life as a Sacred Being on a Sacred Journey…They know they are assisted by a Timeless, Compassionate Wisdom that whole-heartedly Respects and honours them.

In modern society, most people are fascinated with their existing connection to other realms. Yet they continually turn against the unseen world, convincing their self to ignore the link between them and the multitude of interrelating dimensions.

It is not just the Indigenous cultures that have experienced a loss of their right to address those surrounding worlds in a Sacred Way; every one of us has also been deprived of a more meaningful connection with the True Reality. We see this in the case of Indigenous traditions that may not have had their ancient Wisdom wiped out by conquering forces, but rather had the Wisdom Ways eroded through the infiltration of the western society that worships technology over Spirit and Nature.

The Indigenous Wisdom and the 'old country' ways have many wise warnings and remedies to keep us physically, emotionally and spiritually strong. In past ages, the Elders prepared the children to succeed in carrying out strong radiant lives by teaching them of the vast realities that live side by side with us. They did not teach them to deny the existence of the spirit realm, but instead shared with them a Spiritual Path, which acknowledged the many entrances to the spirit world.

They trained the children regarding the many types of dangers that could appear in dealing with spirit realms and the guidelines of protection that had been tested and proved by others before them. The Wisdom of those who had successfully dealt with the spirit world was imparted through plays, writings and oral stories. In this way, they taught them the Path of Courage, Insight and Transmutation, which is the Path of the Impeccable Warrior.

The Impeccable Warrior knows that once they have opened up to the subtle aspects of Life, they have paved the way to receive the profound Wisdom of the Universe.

The Western World may question Life in our Galaxy or elsewhere in space, however all Indigenous traditions have Creation Stories which place their roots in Cosmic points of origin such as Sirius, the Milky Way, Pleiades, the Morning Star Venus or other Planets and Stars. When we fail to honour our Celestial Roots we become easy targets for further manipulation by the forces of darkness.

Although it is part of the collective soul-evolution of the human race to have witnessed mass destruction of endless Indigenous Wisdom Teachings, we need to re-call that every one of us has roots and those roots lead back to times when people naturally used herbs, sacred sound, rituals, sacred Ceremony and other energetic tools and techniques for healing and protection.

KNOW YOUR SOURCE OF PROTECTION: WHO IS YOUR SOURCE?

When people share with me their spiritual problems, I usually ask the following: "What is your path? What spiritual practices do you maintain on a daily basis? Who do you consider your Protector(s)? Who do you have Faith in? Whom do you count on?"

We are easy targets if we walk this Earth as motherless and fatherless children. As much as possible, at all times, you must know who your Divine Team is.

I all-ways urge the person to go deeper into their spiritual practices to connect with this team of Divine Protectors. If you do not have any spiritual practices or are not committed to a particular Spiritual Path, then I highly urge you to start 'shopping around' for the perfect path for you.

To do this you can experiment with different paths by attending programs sponsored by various groups and traditions. Even if you don't find the path that is perfect for you right away, you will still gain from every group. If you don't resonate with the overall philosophy of the organization, each experience may still expose you to at least one technique or Teaching that will assist you in forming a spiritual alignment to your Mother God/Father God and all Protectors assigned to you.

LA LA LAND:
FEEDING GROUND FOR THE NEGATIVE FORCES

Many people in the spiritual community walk their Spiritual Path in a very 'la, la, la', floating manner, spacing along, not taking responsibility for establishing a strong solid foundation for their spiritual being and Life. Hiding behind the 'it's all good' lax attitude allows them to avoid taking accountability for their energies and choices.

It is imperative to grip the value in becoming solid, grounded and strong. By floating in a cosmic cloud the spiritual seeker fails to deal with the negative energies that have latched on to them. Anyone with a discerning mind can look at an ungrounded person and see their lack of stability. The manipulative energies of the world are quick to seize their frailty and utilize it to create an ever-flowing stream of imbalance, fogginess, weakness, lack of commitment and overall hazy grip on the realities surrounding them.

In the same way that they are blind in recognizing a clear-cut path in this material world, they are also oblivious as to their truest and Highest Destiny. Clarity, perseverance, Fortitude, vigour and Dedication are Virtues, Sacred Qualities that reflect a potency of mind and Strength of purpose. Inhabitants of the 'la la' world may have passion and be big dreamers, BUT the influences of the negative forces block their follow-through.

The Impeccable Warrior of Light has mastered both a heightened sensitivity as well as a practical, grounded posture. This powerful combination enables them to 'walk the talk', say what they mean and mean what they say. By being fully present in every moment they are able to Respect all creation through their focus and commitment to each moment, whether that relationship is with another human, Mother Nature, Father Sky, the cosmic realms or other aspects of Life. The Impeccable Warrior of Light interacts with Balanced and harmonious conduct due to full awareness.

Know that when anyone allows themselves to live in a state of illusion, it sends out party invitations to the negative forces to do what they do best, which is to come on over, settle in, possess and disrupt! And once they are there it is party, party, party time!

Therefore, choose to be cognizant of all energies around you and within you and the disguises those forces use to prey upon and live through you. By being on the Earth at this time, you have the opportunity to Master the techniques of protection for your mind, body and spirit. Working towards the highest potential for your own lasting Happiness and that of humanity must start NOW, not tomorrow.

THE ETERNAL BATTLE OF THE SOUL ESCALATES

A battle for our souls has been ongoing throughout the eons, however now the battle has reached a point of escalation unseen before in Mother Earth's history. Everything we have undergone as a collective soul has now brought us to a pivotal moment of choice.

We have evolved through ages upon ages of being showered with Grace. We have been sent one Realized Being after another. We have seen beings embody upon this Earth and use the ancient spiritual principles to raise their vibrations and transcend human suffering. Buddha, Jesus Christ, my Gurus and the Teachers of other paths have all illuminated for us the Spiritual Laws that purified and uplifted them to Enlightenment. All the Great Beings who have appeared here on Earth have been encouraging us all along to master the Golden Laws of Goodness. They inspired us to leave behind the petty ways and to embrace the Path of Wisdom. They have taught and shown us how to live in Harmony with the Celestial and Earth Forces.

Repeatedly we have been given endless examples and Teachings of Liberation via the Work of Saints and Masters from countless traditions. Like any wise parent, our Divine Protectors know that we have reached the stage where we should now be able to make positive choices towards a positive future. Every parent has to give the child some tough Love at times to wake the child up and accelerate the child's growth out of its stagnation…and this is the point of choice we now face.

Imagine a Heroic Being who has evolved through many Life-times and now finally has the opportunity to manifest the 'victory of all victories.' Naturally, at that crucial moment, any fear or darkness left in the Heroine/Hero would surface. At the same time, because they are on the verge of Triumph, all their Protectors would be doing everything possible to help them succeed on behalf of all that is Good. In the same way, if you were running a marathon and had reached the last leg, you would be bombarded with voices in your head telling you that you cannot make it, but at the same time there would be scores of spectators all cheering for you to reach the finish line.

Anytime we reach a crucial point of choice, a huge portal opens up so this battle for the soul can take place. This is exactly what is happening on Mother Earth at this time. A unique portal is now open, allowing both dark forces and Legions of Light to flood this plane, with each camp influencing us more than ever. The malicious forces connive fiercely to entice us towards lower vibrations, whereas the Divine Protectors defend us as They cheer us on towards Enlightenment and Peace on Earth.

This is the time that has been prophesied by many traditions. Prophets, seers and Spiritual Paths have spoken of, written about and referred to this unique moment in our spiritual evolution. Our evolutionary path, and the choices we have made along the way have brought us to this amazing and crucial point.

Since it is THE MOMENT...the moment of all moments, the karma of all karmas and the choice of all choices...the stakes are the highest they have ever been. This means that WE, and the choices WE make, represent a tremendous prize for whichever side we choose to align with.

At this time there are vast, unfathomable Light forces streaming forth to assist humankind...there is also great danger as the dark forces are making their desperate, frantic efforts to keep us all in a state of suffering...by extinguishing the Light that is expanding. Both Light and dark forces are pouring forth in record numbers. They are both making their presence known in a very dramatic way, as each side beckons us.

We are indeed living in a time of miracles...however...it is imperative we be aware, that at the same time...we are also being confronted with great deception. In order to be immune to the hypnotic powers of the forces of evil, everyone…especially ministers, priests, nuns, healers, psychics, intuitives and channelers…must become aware of the endless subtle methods the forces of darkness use to gain our Trust.

THE SECRET IS BALANCE, FAITH, STRENGTH AND LOTS OF LOVE

The secret is balance and full awareness. While enjoying Life on the Beauty-full Flowering Earth, we should keep our eyes and ears open at all times, to know what all the forces around us are up to. FULL AWARENESS is what the Universe is asking of us, so we can accurately relate to the worlds around us.

Are you paranoid when you drive an automobile or operate any machinery? No, but to avoid accidents, you do need to be aware of your vehicle and all the traffic around you, don't you? It is the same with this knowledge. The idea of being responsible for the manoeuvring of an automobile or operating a train or aeroplane might be daunting at first, but with practice you grow in confidence and AWARENESS.

If you are not a professional aeroplane pilot…what is the difference between you and someone who is? TRAINING! The trained individual is confident in skills they practiced and polished. If they had not applied themselves to the training, they would not be able to easily handle such a large vehicle. It is the same with mastering the Laws of Spiritual Protection.

When you were a child, crosing the street was a tremendously dangerous endeavour, but with experience and practice, you developed a Self-Confidence that supported you in the spontaneous, intelligent reactions necessary for a safe crossing.

By going through dark periods personally and as a collective spirit, we learn from all negative situations that SPIRITUAL PRACTICES MUST NEVER BE TAKEN FOR GRANTED. For little by little, bit-by-bit, negative energies eat away at our sacred Harmony, Co-operation, Willingness, Devotion, Dedication and Purity. Before we know it, we are no longer our Luminous Self… one day we discover we have degenerated to a mere 'shadow' of our previous Loving, Balanced, Courageous Self.

The good news is that all experiences Strengthen us and through getting 'lost' along the way, we learn much. In dealing with the invisible worlds that reach out to you…you can develop rock-solid Faith in your spontaneous reflexes, techniques and skills…to help you deal with and transform anything that crosses your Path!

Chapter 3

CHOOSE WISELY – YOU CANNOT SERVE TWO MASTERS

It is up to each of us to hold a reality in place that stems from conscious positive choices...choices that show we are ringing true with our soul's Highest Destiny. On the Mother Earth plane...you have the choice of what type of circle you will be a part of...a circle of endless triumphs or a circle of chronic pain.

If you lived in a big city, you wouldn't leave the doors to your home wide open. If you did, you could end up with good visitors, but you could also end up with some disruptive guests. It is the same with our energetic field. Just as we lock our home to protect our environment and our valuables, it is important to close the door to negative energies, letting them know we are off limits to them. This also includes closing the door to those voices in your head that goad you into being angry, jealous, insecure, fear-full, depressed, mean, or violent.

Your good actions feed the Positive Forces, which sustain the Universal Energies of Kindness, Beauty, Love, Harmony, Sweetness, Honour, Compassion and all other sacred Virtues. Your negative choices feed all negative energies, which then have more power to in turn Strengthen the Universal Force of Evil.

This is why it is so important to vote wisely at every moment, with every thought, with every breath, as to what you wish to support in this Universe. It is not just up to the Medicine People, Lamas, Saints and Shamans to live a pure Life...it is your Sacred Duty as well.

The Universal Energies of Goodness need each one of you to

feed them if you and humanity are to succeed in living Prosperous, Happy, Valiant and Balanced lives. The Compassionate Energies need everyone's vote as to what kind of world we decide to live in. It is up to each of us to hold a reality in place that stems from CONSCIOUS positive choices…choices that show we are ringing true with our soul's highest destiny.

It is our Sacred Duty to CHOOSE to be protected and by doing so CHOOSE to transform and uplift the negative energies, by electing to see the Good in everything! RE-MEMBER: it is the Sacred Duty of the sinister voices to ATTEMPT to convince us we are victims of destructive realities…and it is OUR duty to refuse to follow evil forces down any dark path.

It is OUR duty to say "NO!" to them, to banish them. It is OUR duty to HAVE Faith IN OUR Divinity and remain focused on the Positive. It is OUR duty to transcend…to rise above all tough circumstances…to not let any negative perspective glum unto us, so we can SOAR in Life. You can't fly if you have bags of sand, rocks, baggage or heavy garbage attached to you. .

The truth is that if we choose to feed the Radiant Energies, the instant we move to do so, we have already succeeded spiritually; we have rung true in that testing moment. Soul Triumph is what it is REALLY all about, ALL-WAYS.

Hence, choose to leave behind feelings of victim hood—banish and replace all beliefs that things do not work out for you. When you find yourself thinking those kinds of thoughts, or ANY negative thoughts, recognize it as the voice of vicious forces that are trying to possess you bit by bit. Keep your Temple clean by ordering them out and disintegrating them the minute you recognize their presence.

YOUR LIFE IS NOT YOUR OWN

In today's society we often hear, "Live your own Life…be yourself!" This guidance is misinterpreted and used as an excuse to choose to indulge in a life-style of self-centredness instead of being aligned with the Higher-Self.

To be a Wise Impeccable Warrior you must live this Life with the understanding that you embodied on this Radiant Earth to SERVE. We are all Divine INSTRUMENTS. Instruments are created to be utilised…and at every single moment of your Life you are allowing yourself to be implemented by either positive or negative forces.

You are automatically serving one of those camps by aligning with certain ideas, feelings and beliefs. The million-dollar question is: WHOM are you aligning with? WHAT are you endorsing through your thoughts and emotions?

All suffering comes from thinking that your Life is your own. Why? Nothing in the Universe is free. *Everything that is gifted to us has a price, a responsibility that goes along with the package.* The God Perfect Intelligence allowed you to take birth on Mother Earth so you would full-fill a special purpose. Do you know what that is?

You came to Earth with a mission and as long as you do not recall what that is, as long as you do not recognize the Golden Path that you came to walk, you will carry around the fragmented energy, mind and body of a spiritual orphan. Erroneously believing you are alone on this Earth Pilgrimage stems from not remembering that specific Protectors have a karmic agreement with you, to guide and protect you. When you decided to come to Earth, certain Guides, Celestial and Earth Forces contracted to work with you as a Divine Team. YOU ARE NOT ALONE! They will guide you to complete your mission, and do your part in uplifting humanity.

You have a Sacred Team and your Life is pledged to them, in the sense that you made an agreement with them, before you were born. They are counting on you to do your part and are waiting for you to full-fill your Highest Destiny. You came to the Jewel Planet to serve…to work on behalf of your Higher-Self, Sacred Team, Humanity and all Creation. Your Divine Purpose is to serve God/ Spirit/Good in expanding the Light here and now!

In Life, most people go through one disappointing adventure after another, as they seek a Unity that seems unattainable. They run from one experience to the next, jumping from need to need and desire to desire…buying one material thing after another…tasting dish after dish of food...involving themselves in a string of relationships...all of which is simply an indulgence in an endless stream of attempts to experience a sense of true and absolute belonging.

The soul hungers for the homecoming, for the embrace with the Higher Forces that guide its Life here on Earth. But due to ignorance, we try to satisfy this hunger through material, emotional and mental means, instead of giving ourselves to Spirit and Spirit's master plan for us.

What you think you want and what your spirit wants are too often, two different things. When you start making choices according to the inner guidance of your Spiritual Team and not your ego (the ever-craving mind)...then you start living the Golden Life. Once you start walking your Golden Path, you choose to act instead of react, by tuning in and asking, "What does God want me to do in this case?"

If you feel a pull to make a change or a move, instead of letting the mind consume you with worry or debate, you pray on it, asking, "What is my next assignment? Where do my Guides want me to live? Does this action make my soul happy?"

When you start aligning yourself with your Life purpose, with your Higher-Self, instead of the petty personality, you experience Peace. Many people come to see me, who seemingly have so much more material wealth than I do...yet I am happy and at Peace and they wish they had what I have.

Once you accept that you belong to God and God belongs to you, you will not casually allow negative energies to create distance between you and your Spiritual Protectors.

Once you vow to develop an invincible Self-Love, Self-Respect, Faith and Wisdom, then even during challenging times you feel Great-full...because you UNDERSTAND what is really happening...you know the rules of the game that you chose to play here on Mother Earth and fully comprehend what is truly at stake at all moments: YOUR SOUL!

FREE WILL

Do you have to walk in awareness and protect yourself? No. We all have what is wrongly addressed as 'Free Will'. Just as in everything we do in Life, we always have the choice as to whether we wish to take the bumpy road or the smooth road in Life.

If we choose to go sailing in the rocky ocean on a flimsy raft, without any training, without a Life preserver, wearing a suit of lead, that is our choice! Are our Protectors happy with that choice? In making that choice, are we helping Them as they strive to help us succeed, or are we making Their work more difficult? And most importantly, who implanted that idea in our consciousness? Who or what convinced us to plunge into such dangerous conditions, in such a Life threatening way?

As you go beyond the thoughts to see where those negative, Life-destroying thoughts come from, you will begin to see how easily you are manipulated into disrespecting this sacred and supremely valuable gift called Life.

The question is this: is your 'Free Will' actually free to choose, when negative forces are already attached to you or using their sneaky ways to influence you? Who is actually doing the choosing? IS IT YOUR WILL OR THEIRS?

Free Will is also not free from another viewpoint in that every negative action must be paid back…it must be paid for somehow, either immediately, or down the road. The Universal Law is: for every action we perform, there is an equal or greater reaction that we set in motion. Remember, there are no secrets in the Universe and our every move is noted both by the negative and positive forces. No one ever really gets away with anything. Our actions today not only affect our tomorrow, but Life-time after Life-time of tomorrows, so the more we protect ourselves, the easier and more natural it will be to make positive choices.

Every time that we make a Life-enhancing, soul-expanding choice we are feeding the Universal Energies. Each time we take an action that is filled with Courage, Love, Respect, Balance, Beauty, Sweetness, Goodness, Wisdom, Kindness, Compassion, Clarity,

Faith and Devotion, we are feeding those Energies so they can augment and amplify to continue to support humanity.

Due to the Law of Grace, your Courage and Self-Love gets multiplied and goes on to serve many others who will be in need of these qualities. If you decide to be reckless you are feeding the Negative Energies of Disdain and Disrespect in the Universe, which will then go to feed those qualities into humanity.

By choosing to feed the Positive Universal Energies, we infuse the Universe with the Divine nature of Happiness, Zest-full Gusto, Effervescent Joy, Purity, Harmony and Regal Resplendence, opening the door to waves upon waves of increasing Grace. These Grace Waves then flow onward to benefit and liberate all Creation from any limitations. Every positive choice is therefore a Cosmic and Earthly Victory causing jubilation among all the Compassionate Beings and Forces.

NO PAIN, NO GAIN

Do Martial Arts students have to do the exercises that will Strengthen them? If they are content to have poor skills and remain beginners, they do not. No one can physically drag them and force them to do it. However, if they wish to become a Champion they do. If they wish to have the finely tuned moves to be victorious in each match, and move up the ladder of accomplishment, they do. They can allow themselves to be manipulated by negative forces and choose to be sloppy, lazy or cowardly, but by choosing this, they will not develop the skills, Strength, clarity, sensory perception and Intuition they need to full-fill their hearts' desires to make progress and hit the mark.

It takes training, attention and Dedication to succeed at anything and spirituality is no different. If we choose wisely, we will know what our soul wants of us and likewise what the negative forces want of us. By doing this we will choose to break the chains of bondage and utilize our Golden Energy in the wisest manner.

The Impeccable Warrior of Light sees that, contrary to popular thought, we are not here to do as we please regarding the Universal

Spiritual Laws. Of course, we can live in that false belief, because it is all-ways left up to us to choose. However, until we live by the Golden Teaching that WE ARE HERE TO SERVE GOD, we will continue to suffer.

In order to discern the Highest Path and wisest actions, the Impeccable Warrior asks: "What does God want in this moment? What do my Angels want from me in this situation?" Instead of focusing on what the little petty ego wants, it is wiser to question, "What do my Spiritual Protectors need me to do, so that I may live in my most Peace-full existence...and in this way reach my Highest Destiny?"

If we wish to travel upon a smooth road, then we DO have to accept the homework, become knowledgeable and develop techniques that we have great Faith in, which we practice on a daily basis. This becomes our protective shield helping us ask the right questions...hear the true answers...and tap into the Courage within ourselves to follow through on our sacred assignments.

WIN ENOUGH BATTLES AND YOU WIN THE WAR

Will you win all the battles? Not on the surface, perhaps, but if you strive for the Impeccable Path and honour the Positive Principles, you do triumph in every battle.

When you are working for the upliftment of others, it may seem as if you don't all-ways win against the negative forces. There may be times when those who are controlled by the darkness cannot choose the Light and it may seem as if you cannot wrestle them out of the grip of the demons that are holding them hostage. In such a situation you must never give up. Keep doing your prayers and when that soul has accumulated enough Grace, enough Love, they will be able to make positive choices.

Your daily work helps move them towards that position of Self-Respect. Remain Faith-full that Good Work never goes to waste. The ones you are striving to defend may seem to grow in consciousness at a snails pace or worse, but they are moving. PRAYER ALL WAYS MOVES ENERGY. It is impossible to not move them, it is just a matter of degrees and a matter of whether anyone can actually detect the forward movement…but even if it is microscopic, it is taking place!

Do your best to win the battle, but if it seems you are defeated, focus on winning the war. If you NEVER GIVE UP and never surrender to the dark forces, THAT IN ITSELF IS ALREADY A VICTORY.

DAILY AWARENESS

Most people shower everyday. Imagine if you didn't. What if you went years without showering? You would stink horribly and there would be a thick crust of dirt on you. In the same way, since the vast majority of people don't cleanse themselves daily of the foul vibrations they pick up, imagine how encrusted they are of all kinds of negative energies. This does not necessarily make them a bad person of course, but it does make them an easy target for more negative forces, since they are already allowing "bad" company to live in and around them.

Often deeply sensitive, sweet people are the most affected and infected. Since the energetic law is that 'birds of a feather flock together', one negative energy invites two more and then those two invite eight more, so that you end up with a crowded discotheque full of degrading forces. A downward spiral keeps building as they start to control you more and you are able to control them less! As they grow in power, they accelerate the tearing apart of your Temple.

However, when you cleanse yourself and your home each day… and you connect with your Angels and Protectors through your prayers and offerings, then it is easier to have a strong aura, mind, body and spirit. All of which will supports you in driving out the present ominous energies and blocking future wicked forces.

If you care about yourself, you nourish your body with healthy food each day, so the positive elements can protect you against disease and the hardship that occurs due to illness. In the same way, you must keep up your spiritual Strength and vitality by cleansing the energetic field around your mind, body and spirit of all debris the vile forces have deposited upon you.

Remember, they will try to move you away from your inherent Light nature…into the darkness, as much as possible each day. If you let them, before you know it you find you are no longer inspired to do your altar work, prayers, offerings, songs, rituals or whatever practices connect you to your Divine Source of Light. Negative energies can infiltrate your Life in such subtle ways…they are so sly that you may not even perceive those little ways in which they are chipping away at your spiritual discipline.

Without you realizing it, they will slowly nudge you little by little into complacency and a false sense of security, where you find you suddenly have the perfect justification as to why it's acceptable to do your Spiritual Work 'later'. You might succumb to such thoughts as, "*I'm too tired*" or "*I'd rather watch television*". You may even justify it with such 'reasonable' excuses such as wanting to do your spiritual practices when everyone has gone to sleep, telling yourself you can then do it with more attention.

In this way you set yourself up perfectly only to discover that you don't do it once everyone has gone to bed, it doesn't work out the way your mind rationalized it would and days, weeks and months go by without you giving yourself or the house the protection it needs.

I remember three examples of this, and in each example the people involved in this syndrome had all undergone previous training on Spiritual Protection and Shamanism and considered themselves knowledgeable on this subject. Even though they 'knew' how important it was, little by little they had fallen away from maintaining their circle of protection.

One woman shared that her intuitive daughter told her on several occasions that they needed to smudge the house. Yet, each time, the mother replied that they were in a rush, that she wanted to cleanse it later when she could do it thoroughly. The little girl recognized that the dark forces were blinding her mother to how desperately the house needed the cleansing and felt an overwhelming urge to protect her family. After a fist fight erupted in their home, the daughter went ahead without her mother to cleanse the space thoroughly and upon seeing this, the mother finally woke up to how layered her house was with malicious invaders.

In the second woman's case, I noticed hardness had begun to settle in her face, voice and personality. At the same time, I witnessed that she was distancing herself from her practices more and more each day. I did many prayers for her to wake up. Later on she shared that during that time period, her three year-old child had been asking her every day if they could do the house cleansing mantra. But the mother would consistently reply that they did not have time to do it thoroughly and that they would do it at a 'better' time. Is there such a thing as a 'better' time to rescue your self from drowning?

My teacher Don Jacinto trained me in the Mayan Sacred Therapy the western world calls Soul Retrieval. In Mexico and South America it is known as a Limpia, which literally means 'cleansing' but is considered to mean 'Spiritual Cleansing' (for further information on this technique see Chapter 8: Mayan Soul Retrievals).

One day, a gentleman who had been trained in Shamanic ways for many years came to me for a Soul Retrieval Limpia. He believed he needed a thorough cleansing because he felt an evil presence stalking him. He is a strong man, a healer who does hands-on healing and has a successful practice. During the session it was confirmed he had entities attached to him. I asked him if he knew how to protect himself and when he responded he did, I was surprised. I asked him how it was then that he wound up in this condition and he replied that he could not remember exactly how or when he had stopped maintaining his protection shield.

From these examples you can clearly see that the destructive forces will convince you that you do not need to be consistent in performing your daily practices. If you are not paying vigilant attention, you will not even notice the lax attitude slip in.

ANYTIME YOU SEE OR FEEL illness, weakness, hardship, etc. move into your surroundings, you need to get to work and cleanse and fortify your mind, emotions, body and spirit, if you do not wish to go on a domino-effect downward slide.

Years ago, when my student Swami Durgadas was then known as Victory Ray, he one day found himself feeling ill with flu-like symptoms. He had been on a very positive roll and all of a sudden he felt as if all his Life Force had been drained from him. It took him a few days to realize the attack was so strong that he could not lift himself out of that condition through his normal practices and was wise enough to know he now needed concentrated Grace and called us for an immediate Mayan Soul Retrieval Limpia.

Intuitively, it had already been revealed to me that his normally heroic state of mind had dropped a few notches, for he is an excellent student who strives to pay sharp attention to his surroundings. I asked him why he had allowed himself to be derailed for even those couple of days. He admitted that a cloud had settled in his mind. At one point he found himself questioning whether he wanted to recover from his illness and due to his hesitation to quickly respond 'Yes!' he detected his lax attitude as the signature of the malevolent forces.

When he became aware of the seductive negative wave that was descending upon him, he snapped out of his deluded mind state and called in for the Soul Retrieval Limpia right away.

Swami Durgadas strives to hit the mark every time as an Impeccable Warrior of Light and for this reason he was not willing to become a casualty. For once you are in a weakened state...it is extremely difficult to dig yourself out of the hole you have fallen into.

Once in that condition, it is best to get help from those who are experts in these cases. However, daily vigilance will help you avoid pitfalls.

As we go through the following, let us keep in mind the age old Teaching, "Every dark cloud has a silver lining." If we get attacked or possessed by some destructive force, looking at the situation from the big picture, we see that within the challenge is the opportunity to learn something of value in the process...and thanks to the episode we emerge stronger, wiser and now have experience we can draw on to help others.

So whatever the situation, look at it as a special training your Higher-Self chose to enroll you in. Maintain your focus on the fact that you did so because you had confidence you would succeed in the end! Even though danger can be daunting, all peril gives us an opportunity to build spiritual muscles.

Does protection build our spiritual muscles? Yes, in the same way that a daily physical work-out will help you build physical Strength, your daily time in your practices gives Strength to the spiritual qualities such as Faith, Perseverance, Dedication and Positive Power...all of which boost your connection to your Spiritual Protectors.

Once we reach a certain level, do we stop our regimen? No, it is vital to continue to increase and fortify your spiritual muscles, for the more power-full you become, the bigger an opponent you are entitled to take on. Just as a weight lifter earns the right to attempt to lift bigger weights with each level already accomplished, the more superior the opponent you do battle with, the more accomplished you become by wrestling with them.

In weight-lifting, the athlete will encounter resistance from the weights and undergo a sense of momentary struggle, but in the process of all this the athlete is developing mightier muscles...it is the same with the spiritual weight-lifting you have been engaging in.

It is noteworthy that you never hear a weight-lifter whining about having to graduate to heavier weights and you don't hear of a runner or swimmer complaining because they challenge themselves to go further. If a runner is accustomed to running six miles they will happily push themselves to go further and last longer! But most people don't have that kind of attitude towards their daily obstacles. Why? Because, they allow the self-deprecation demons to implant a 'poor me, look at how I suffer' victim mentality.

To be an Impeccable Warrior of Light, you must NEVER allow negative forces to rob you of Enthusiasm and Appreciation for the adversities of Life. For through your own custom-designed hardships you will cultivate Nobility, Confidence, Endurance, Humility and Compassion for others. Each battle you survive purifies your soul, gifting you Knowledge and a sense of spiritual accomplishment.

Of course, to promote spiritual vitality within yourself you must take spiritual vitamins, which are the rituals, prayers and offerings you make to your Spirit Team. You must face your daily workouts with relish when encountering negative forces that attempt to impede your Happiness and Success. Enthusiasm, Gusto and Ecstasy are all sacred qualities that are excellent allies for transcending negativity!

From everything I have witnessed I feel that psychic intruders often have an advantage over the spiritual seeker because the dark forces are 100% committed to their mission of creating chaos and confusion! They are well organized and will apply themselves with the greatest ruthlessness....stopping at nothing.

Most humans are not as committed. Humanity is not determined to defend and preserve its Happiness, Harmony, Prosperity, Wisdom and Health. Humans tend to be care-less and half-hearted about their mission, which is to preserve the Goodness in their lives and throughout the Cosmos.

Yet, in spite of their lack of Confidence and Determination, humans have access to The Great Remedy known as Grace. Divine Grace can conquer and dissolve any evil, no matter how great it may seem. We simply need to pray for that Grace to manifest...when we invoke it with the greatest ardour through our spiritual practices, it will be delivered unto us.

WHY DON'T WE CALL ON GRACE MORE OFTEN?

If we have this amazing Grace available to us, why don't we call on it more often? The answer is, because we easily get side tracked by TOO MANY things. The negative forces create an illusion in our mind and we become convinced it is the true reality.

We are often like the bull that keeps charging the red cape instead of going after the source of his torment, which is the bull-fighter. It is the bull-fighter that keeps waving the red cape in front of the bull over and over again, to distract the bull long enough to inflict pain and eventual death!

In the same way, we suffer, allowing ourselves to be tormented mentally, emotionally and physically, blaming the romantic partner, friends, childhood, parent, child, employer, government, transportation system, the clerk in the store and countless others. Only a rare being dives beyond the surface irritant t. un-cover the truth…that it is the dark forces that plant negativity in us and on our path…in order to steer us towards negative actions.

While we are obsessed with angrily and emotionally chasing after the red cape, we do not address the bull-fighter that is controlling the cape and lives on to continue torturing us with negative beliefs, attitudes and Life-styles.

The real problems in our lives are not the job, money, relationship or health issues. All of these surface obstacles are just serving as flashing lights to alert us that we need to acknowledge the presence of negative spirits, entities and energies in our Life and the lives of others.

By becoming thoroughly familiar with the many ways these insidious vibrations can leak into our existence, by being disciplined in casting them out, we free up our energy to call on Grace with more fervour.

You all-ways have a choice as to whether you spend time with pain and suffering which begets more pain and suffering, OR to spend time in contemplating and invoking Grace which then floods more Grace upon you. On the Mother Earth plane…YOU HAVE THE CHOICE OF WHAT TYPE OF CIRCLE YOU WILL BE A PART OF… AN ENDLESS CIRCLE OF TRIUMPH OR A CHRONIC CIRCLE OF PAIN.

It's a cyclical process…the more we call on Grace, the more we protect ourselves from destructive forces and the more protected we are, the more we remember that abundant Grace is available to us all-ways and the more we invoke it with immense ardour.

HOW DO WE ADDRESS SPIRITUAL HOMEWORK?

If a situation appears in our lives we must ask what the Energy of the Universe seeks from us. Why has this combination of factors materialized in our Life? Why us and why at this moment?

The Universe is a perfect place, therefore if something comes into OUR lives, instead of someone else's, there has to be a perfect reason as to why. Once we figure out the 'why'…'why us'…and 'why now'…we can create the solution. If the perfect answer does not come to you right away, don't feel dis-heartened, just keep praying with great Determination for the perfect sacred intelligence to be present within you to clarify and comprehend. Your prayers and rituals will bring forth the perfect action and then you can experiment with the solutions you intuit. Do not allow your Determination to fall-ter at any point. If the first experiment is not the complete key to success, your ongoing prayers will somehow continue to bring you what you need to transform any energy. Grace will solve any puzzle and unravel even the most intricate web intended to trap and entangle you.

Remember that no 'torture' is meant to go on forever. Every lesson is only in your Life for a certain amount of time. How long it will last is determined by numerous factors, including your self-effort, karma and Grace. Once you master the lesson, you no longer need that particular challenge. You will graduate from that classroom and be allowed to leave that battlefield.

Will that be the end to challenges? No…however, some will be small and easier to handle, while others will require more from us to overcome them. Do not allow the trials encountered on your path to crush your spirit…You are a Sacred Being on a Sacred Journey and your Holy Quest is defined by the attitude with which you face up to your stream of trials.

We must remember that we did not come to Earth to cruise or skate along without spiritual responsibilities. We came here to WORK…and work is SACRED…for in applying ourselves to the task at hand and conquering the lesson…we gather much knowledge that is invaluable on our journey. We came to Mother Earth to learn how to transform energy, how to take the apparent reality and transmute it by filling it with Light.

Once we make Peace with the fact that we did not reincarnate just to lie in bed and eat bonbons all day, we will have a more enthusiastic attitude about tackling the homework at hand.

NO ONE EVER EARNED A BLACK BELT IN MARTIAL ARTS BY SITTING AROUND EATING BON-BONS AND WATCHING TELEVISION ALL DAY. If a situation is in your Life, then it is there for you to deal with it and triumph!

From one perspective we can see that negative forces are actually Compassionate towards us, for they have revealed themselves to us by creating pain-full situations in our Life. Because of the pain, we are now aware that something is out of Balance and that we need to bring it back into Harmony.

The Impeccable Warrior of Light develops an attitude toward their dilemmas that allows them to see everything as a spiritual opportunity to master a Wisdom Principle. The Wise Warrior understands that any spiritual homework that is ignored will just keep knocking on their door until it is addressed with the spiritual solution that is required.

Like the Martial Artist, we can never develop and fine-tune our power movements unless we practice. And in order to practice, we must walk onto the sparring mat. Each time it seems we are beaten, we are not..IF...we learn something of value that we can apply towards our well being in the future.

Re-member...with every triumph...we earn the right to take on bigger opponents. Do not let this intimidate you, for even though they are larger than the ones in the past, you will find them to be easier to handle, because you now have a stronger confidence in your skills, Protectors and The Light.

Later in our spiritual development, we are able to see that each episode or adventure on our path motivated us to call on the Spiritual Lineage of Master Teachers, Angels and other Spiritual Protectors who are there to all-ways guide us towards victory. By observing how our Spiritual Guides respond to our petitions, to our invocations for assistance, we learn to comprehend the language of Grace.

The language of Grace is mysterious at times. We need to pay great attention to how the Universe is communicating with us. We need to recognize the signs, symbols and the many ways in which our Angels and other Spiritual Protectors are sending us messages and inspiration in our daily lives. It could be in the way that a candle flickers, a cloud is formed, the wind picks up or a specific bird flies by. The answer to our questions may appear through a magazine article or the title of a book that synchronistically crosses our path. Spirit might talk to us through a friend who 'just happens' to unwittingly say something that totally clarifies our question.

A man once shared with me the story of how God delivered his spiritual name to him. He had asked his Spirit Guides what his new name should be. As this man was watching television, inwardly his mind was totally consumed with this question when suddenly a character in the movie suddenly shouted, "His name shall be Arjuna!" Upon hearing this, he felt chills over his body and he knew beyond a shadow of a doubt that this was the name he was to use for the new phase of his Life.

Another illustration of the intricate way Grace blesses us involved a woman who came to see me for a Soul Retrieval Limpia. During the consultation, she mentioned that she felt displaced because the spiritual group she had been working with for many years had pushed her out of the organization and she could not understand why. She felt she had contributed in a large way towards the church's growth and found herself in deep anguish over the perceived betrayal. My Spirit Guides revealed that it wasn't the spiritual organization that was pushing her out of her old routine; it was the Universe, which wanted her to move on to other work. She understood this and later attended the Impeccable Warrior of Light Training Intensive to solidify her connection with her own Guides. She understood that in order to vanquish any disparaging inner or outer voices, she would need to intensify her spiritual practices and cultivate unswerving Trust.

In the course of the Intensive, she shared with the group the accuracy of the Teachings my Guides had given her. She told that one evening she had seen a fund-raising commercial on television in which an African woman was appealing for assistance in feeding the homeless orphans of Africa. As she was viewing the program she felt as if the woman on the screen was gazing directly at her. At one point, she heard the African woman say, "We need your help; you must help us right away". As she heard this she felt the woman zoom from the screen directly into her heart, igniting within her an all-consuming desire to respond immediately.

The program was offering free videos of the infomercial, for those interested in becoming fund raisers for the mission and the woman called the phone number to request one. When she received it, she was shocked to see that the woman that had appeared before her eyes and entered her heart so dramatically was not to be found anywhere in the program!

The Universe can communicate with us in a million different ways. It is up to us to become familiar with this part of the Spiritual Path and master the Language of Grace. Upon doing so, you will discover that the Universe is always listening and likewise always responding to you. Then you will have the conviction that Divine inspiration is available in abundance, to help you soar like an Eagle.

The language of Grace will give you the Wings of Light to soar above all your troubles and the Love of your Protectors will shine forth a beacon of Light to guide you safely along The Way.

NEGATIVE FORCES CAST A CLOUD OVER YOUR MIND: TWO EXAMPLES

A student of mine experienced the clouded mind syndrome in the following way: The negative energies has been building up for years, caused in part by the energies of the building she was living in and partially by issues created due to personality differences between her, her husband and her mother-in-law. She found herself in a constantly angry and frustrated frame of mind. They had all been living together for eight years and had experienced the same issues arising repeatedly.

Since we are living in a time when everyone is being pushed to master their karmic lessons, she found herself becoming increasingly irritated by everyone's shortcomings. Her basic nature is that of a perfectionist and therefore pushed for everything to be carried out according to her demands. The Anger Demon and its cousin, the Demon of Impatience had taken firm residence in her mind and due to their presence, she could not perceive that everyone else was already catering to her. She found herself shutting down more than ever, feeling that there was no hope of any real change. She found herself becoming convinced that it might be best if she and her husband went their separate ways.

Her husband decided to fight the negative forces by increasing the prayers, mantras and spiritual dance that formed his spiritual practices. The more spiritual work he did, the more it irritated the evil self-destructive forces within her and one day when he said that he had not been able to do his daily prayers, she said, *"Good! That means MY prayers are working!"* He and I agreed that this was not the strong, upbeat Loving person we both knew, so I encouraged him to press on with his Spiritual Work in a creative, intelligent way in order to rescue the real her from the demons controlling her.

It was clear the best strategy was to not let her know he was offering prayers for their well-being, yet continue to apply the pressure on the malevolent energies to vacate his home and his wife's spirit. I shared with him that I had noticed the day before that a huge cockroach-like bug had crawled on her picture that was sitting on my altar. Also, after I had done a remote Soul Retrieval Limpia for her, the candle that was burning on the altar started a fire, which has never happened in all the years of using candles. It had been sitting in a bowl of water and 'should' not have happened, but it did. All these developments were simply signs alerting me to the serious degree of possession she was experiencing.

Earlier on her husband had requested daily remote Soul Retrieval Limpias for her spirit and therefore I continued petitioning Grace for her each day. He began spiritually cleansing the home, showering her with Love and Compassion, while increasing his prayers with greater Zest and Determination. In days, she found herself in a much more positive frame of mind and her husband was then able to relate to her the battle we had been waging on her behalf.

Later, she explained that the issues she had with the people around her had been triggering constant anger in her, with the fury growing to such a point that it had consumed her. My reply to her applies to everyone: When we are doing our prayers regularly with great vigilance, the Love streaming from the Forces of Compassion and Wisdom is able to REACH us. Due to the infusion of Divine Love, we in turn are able to interact with the world in a calmer manner and create positive solutions to our daily challenges, instead of reacting in anger and disgust.

If we are perfectionist types, as she is, our daily smudging (cleansing) and other spiritual practices help us meet blocks, delays and what seems like lack of Cooperation, with greater patience. By taking refuge in Grace, we develop within us a philosophical approach, driving away rash behaviour. We are then able to make wise choices and avoid self-defeating behaviour.

However, when we allow the sinister energies of the Universe to re-move us bit by bit from our inner centre of Peace, Hope, Bliss and Loved ones...the forces of darkness succeed in creating an illusionary huge gap between us and the Light. Before we detect it, we have driven away the Angel of Harmony and pushed away our Loved ones. No one is as 'perfect' as we would like them to be and when the demons that despise Unity begin to brainwash us...they convince us that we do not need the people around us...and that we should discard them.

It is the malevolent spirits that encourage within us the feelings of impatience, disdain, doubt, intolerance and an overall lack of Compassion for others. They fill us with notions that WE are right and everyone else is wrong, or that others don't really care about us...in this way they foster within us negative behaviour.

In beings that need to communicate their feelings more, they create a desire to shut down. In those who are already too quick to fire verbal missiles, they foster an attitude that thrives on confrontation.

With the help of disruptive forces, a marriage can be destroyed in a second. In a heartbeat harsh words can be spoken that are not truly meant, stubbornness and pride can set in, the heart can harden and before you know it, you are separated! Unless there is an increase in spiritual practices to change the whole vibration that has set in, the home Life, the partnership and any mutual Cooperation is headed for total destruction.

She understood when I instructed her that the next time she finds mutual Respect, Support and Cooperation eroding in any of her relationships, she should increase her prayers and altar work to dissolve all psychic encroachers and birth a higher vibration. I reminded her that the higher frequency brings with it a new reality with the Positive energies she calls forth in her prayers.

Of course, now that the cloud of forget-fullness had been lifted through her husband's good work and the Grace bestowed by the Soul Retrieval Limpias that were administered, it was easy for her to see that the solutions I had given her were NATURAL, WISE SOLUTIONS. After all, if you become physically ill and you are on a downward spiral, you go to a health practitioner and apply additional remedies. In going for help, you add more positive measures to whatever you are already doing.

If you are not committed to a daily health prevention program and find yourself becoming ill, the dis-ease alerts you to the fact that you need to take action…you do need to put some health-building program into place. It is the same way with spiritual un-easiness, which includes any kind of suffering…All obstructions to your balance and Happiness must be addressed immediately.

Spiritual practices unleash a flood of Self-Esteem, filling us with Love for others. Through steadily aligning with the Light, miraculous improvements in our attitude take place. When we are able to appreciate Life as the wondrous adventure it is, we are able to value the sacred opportunities it brings us. Our Light Attitude fills us with Faith that Spirit's Creation is indeed a perfect one. It re-awakens us to the Wisdom of changing the way the world appears, by changing ourselves.

The letter she sent me a week later is excellent testament to the Power of Prayer:

Dearest Peace Mother,

This morning, I went to a friend's place and chanted the Maha Mrituynjaya Mantra 108 times. It was very soothing! I dedicated my chants to you for all that you have done for us in the past year! Thank you! Thank you! Thank you! I Love you very much. For now, my husband and I are going to be using the above chant, as well as the Gayatri Mantra, chanting it in front of the kids so they learn from our actions, in addition to benefiting from the sacred words and vibes!"

As I shared with her, the Teaching that states 'The family that prays together, stays together' holds immense truth. When the whole family works together toward defending the home front, it invokes a strong shield of Protection over the family, the group Harmony and each person's Prosperity.

The second example of the clouds the sinister forces cast is that of a couple who had contacted me because the husband was being attacked on the mental, emotional and physical level. Before contacting me, he had been experimenting with quite a combination of techniques and gadgets to rouse his Kundalini (his spiritual energy).

The Kundalini (Spiritual Energy) within us must be awakened and stimulated as we open up spiritually, however it must be guided with the highest Wisdom and care. This subject is dealt with in more detail in my upcoming book 'The Shamanic Healing Art Journal'... however; there is also much information all-ready available to you these days, both in books and on the internet. My root Guru Swami Muktananda Paramahamsa spoke at length about Kundalini experiences in his autobiography 'Play of Consciousness'. My Heart Guru, Gurumayi Chidvilasananda has also written books on the subject, as has one of Her Ashram's Swamis, Swami Kripananda, all of which are available on the Siddha Yoga website bookstore.

He had begun to use an electronic device that is advertised as a meditation enhancer. Use of that gadget and a combination of other many factors, overloaded his energetic system. His circuits, known as meridians and nadis, were suddenly overloaded and blew up. He then became overly sensitized and could not sleep or rest comfortably, feeling and seeing an onslaught of demons attacking him every day and night. His attempts to sleep were filled with endless nightmares and he became too fatigued to work.

His wife arranged with the Sacred Peace Center for me to administer some Soul Retrieval Limpias on him. They resided in another country, but rather than performing the Limpia by remote means I suggested the sessions be done on the phone, in order for his spirit to hear my voice and be soothed by the vibration. Their response was that since he was so sensitive, he could not tolerate the vibration of the phone, and therefore would not be able to hold a phone. They asked me to please work over his spirit, by working on his behalf at my altar.

After a few remote Soul Retrieval Limpia prayers carried out at my altar over his written prayer request, he was recovering well. Still, I felt that in his case, he would make faster progress if I could speak with him. I still felt strongly that he needed to receive the full impact of the vibration in my voice and so I suggested a speaker-phone.

They reacted incredulously. "How is it that we did not think of this before?" they asked themselves! Indeed, isn't it amazing that it took so long to think of such a simple thing?

This man is trained in Shamanism and during the Mayan Soul Retrieval Limpias he's had, he has often been told by my Guides that he is meant to do more Shamanic ritual work, which he all-ways agrees with. But after the second phone Limpia, my Guides directed me to tell him that in order to do power-full Work, he himself would need to become stronger and this applied to all levels of his being. They revealed he had allowed himself to get out of shape. I pointed out to him that an Impeccable Warrior needs to provide Spirit with a Temple that is perfectly fortified and prepared for anything that might happen and anything that might be asked of him.

In his case the message was clear that he needed to begin physical workouts to Strengthen the vehicle, so his Guides would have a sufficient vehicle to work with. After this, he did begin an exercise regime and in doing so, he realized he had undergone a mild heart attack before contacting me. Being a strong, determined and sometimes-stubborn man, he had chosen to ignore this possibility, until the Soul Retrieval sessions removed enough clouds from his Wisdom Mind, enabling him to see clearly what was taking place. His wife wrote that she could also see how profoundly the Limpias had lifted the clouded vision. She wrote:

"Dear Peace Mother,
This past week we have been smudging the house daily. I felt the sinister energies were thick in the bedroom so I put more effort into

clearing that space and now it feels much better. I do not feel any negative energies coming from anything inside or outside the house but I will continue being vigilant. My husband is looking better and feeling stronger. He has come to the conclusion that he did have a heart attack in July although we're not sure whether it was before or after the Kundalini syndrome. This could explain his slow progress and explain why he got so weak. He also realized that his blood is too thick so he's taking aspirin, fish oil, gingko and vitamin E to help thin the blood. This has all been in the past week. I believe he was in denial before this time. Perhaps now he'll make faster progress. It looks like the negative forces were really clouding his vision. I believe all your prayers have made the difference, s. big thanks to you and Divine Mother and all the Angels and Saints."

This is why it is wise to cultivate Grace at every opportunity. You never know when you might get zapped by conspiring forces, but we have seen time and again that even if a deep haze does befall you, if you are blessed to have sufficient Grace in your karmic bank, seemingly out of nowhere a solution can appear.

Grace bestowed to this man recognition of the other ways the forces of evil were clouding his intelligence through forget-fullness. I asked the Sacred Peace Center to send him a list of questions about his activities before and after the psychic attack, knowing the answers would confirm my suspicions about which energetic laws he was not adhering to. Through the questionnaire and his honest replies, I discovered that he had been accepting gifts from someone who wanted to possess him and those evil cords were playing havoc with his Golden Energy. This next segment of his story leads us into the next chapter which covers the myriad ways deceptive energies use to enter you mind, body, home and soul.

Chapter 4

THE MANY WAYS NEGATIVE ENERGY SNEAKS IN

Although many positive helpful energies can channel through us, the sneaky ones can also come through, pretending to be good forces, giving us powers and making us feel good, to win us over. The negative forces know that by pretending to be a positive force, they can get the people to drop their defenses and in this way sneak in. The Impeccable Warrior understands that all items have energy attached to them and that by allowing an item to descend upon the body or enter the home/Temple space they have accepted the vibrations that article has been infused with.

The saying "Beware of gift horses" stems from the story of the Trojan War, in which the Trojans could not break down the excellently protected fortress of the enemy they were warring with. So they decided to trick their enemies into allowing them to enter. They did this by building a giant stunning golden horse, but unbeknownst to the enemy, it had been hollowed out and filled with an army of invaders. As they were receiving what seemed a generous gift, they were actually inviting an attacking force into their home base. By disguising the attack as a kind gesture, the Trojans found a way to get across the normally impeccable defence of their enemies and stage a surprise blow upon them.

Along the same lines, think of the story of Sleeping Beauty. A wicked sorceress gave the Heroine Sleeping Beauty an apple in a seeming gesture of Kindness. The apple was actually full of poison and Sleeping Beauty fell into a coma-like deep sleep that lasted for years. Remember what you have already learned…evil forces are extremely cunning and intelligent. What better way to attack the unwitting than through a 'gift' or kind gesture?

CORDS: DO NOT ASSUME THAT ALL GIFTS ARE GOOD FOR YOU

Not every item given to you by others is actually good for you. It may have been programmed to harm by the person and there are cases when an item itself carries negative energy. In the early days of my training, while on Pilgrimage in Mexico, I was moved to order a box full of Jesus Christ statues. This particular image of Jesus is very much revered and considered especially miraculous. The statues were handled by several different people and boxed up. Upon reaching our destination, the Shaman and Priest accompanying me opened the box and were shocked to be blasted by a whirlwind of wickedness. These Christ statues somehow became infused with the darkest energy you can imagine, which lurched at us.

It is possible that they became loaded with such evil energy by being housed in warehouses where they also keep black magic items, for many people who sell statues and Spiritual Protection tools, also sell black magic supplies. It is common for practitioners and vendors to treat the sale of these items as a business, where they supply people whatever they want, with total disregard to how that person may use it. The vendor does not care if someone intends to kill someone with black magic. The vendor mistakenly believes they are absolved from any karma by being the peddler of such evil pain inducing items. There are other vendors and practitioners who themselves practice the dark arts. Whenever I have sensed the presence of black magic demons in some "spiritual", "New Age" and "mystical" bookstores, my perceptions have later been confirmed by employees and members of the community who have long known of the owners' dark practices.

For these misguided people, it is all "business as usual" to store and sell items that a Light worker will utilize to call forth healing, side by side with articles that will be implemented for evil purposes by black magic junkies. In the case of the Jesus statues, however it came to be that they wound up reeking of darkness, they were beyond salvaging and I had to take them to the ocean and surrender them to The Great Mother Healing Waters.

In another case, I was asked to do Soul Retrieval Limpias for a man who was deteriorating rapidly and most definitely headed for death. After the Limpias, he immediately began recovering, but not as dramatically as I felt should be the case. I prayed on it, asking Divine Mother to reveal to me what was holding up his healing progress. After receiving Divine Clarity on this, I was guided to let him know that there was something in his home causing the slow recovery. I knew it was at least one item and that likely there were many.

I instructed the man's spouse to begin with the first step, which was to smudge the whole house from top to bottom with sacred smoke, cleansing it thoroughly. This helped somewhat, however I could sense there was still something evil present there and therefore advised the man to go to the next step, which was to perform a detached energetic inventory of the house.

By detached I mean putting aside sentiment while checking into the vibrations emanating from every article in the house, since sentiment often causes us to keep things that our energetic field is reacting to negatively. Many times when we are given gifts, we do not want to appear rude or feel that we are unappreciative, so we keep items even though somewhere inside of us there is an alarm that keeps going off every time we walk by the item, see it or think of it. I find that whenever my attention is repeated. drawn to an item, it means I need to investigate the trail of energy further.

In other cases, people who seem nice enough or "so sweet" can give you gifts with intentions layered into it. They might have envy towards you, or secretly wish for your relationship with someone to break up so they can take their place. It's good to remember the fairy tales, where the evil witch or wolf masquerades as a kind old lady who first befriends the Hero/Heroine, but then offers them a poisoned apple or attacks them in some other manner.

The Forces of Evil will often send a messenger and that messenger will not alert you to their presence by wearing a sign that says, "Hey! I am here to destroy your Health/Happiness! Look at me! I am evil!" YOU have to sense the energy around an item and if YOUR gut feeling/inner voice, registers any misgivings, listen to it! DO NOT DISREGARD THE VOICE OF YOUR Wisdom MIND... DISCERN YOUR DOUBTS.

There are not always hard and fast rules on these matters. An item might be a bit loaded but if you put it on your altar and transmute the negative charge with prayers, smudge and/or sacred movement, you can re-birth it into a good energy. However, sometimes this process may have to go on for a long time before it is all-right for you to use the item. Or it may never feel good to you.

The only way to know is to listen to your inner Wisdom and STAY DETACHED. When we are attached to something, we will allow ourselves to be confused by our desires and sidetracked from clearing out any item that is detrimental to us. You may find yourself thinking, "This is so Beauty-full! I can't let go of this!" or "I've always wanted one of these," and our mind's voice will get in the way of the True Voice, which is trying to warn us!

I am given many Beauty-full gifts. Some things I am sure I do not wish to keep and I discard as soon as possible. If it is not clear as to the vibration a gift carries, I put it on my altar until I get a message. The message may be that it is for someone else who has yet to show up to receive it, or it may be that the gift is for Divine Mother and is meant to stay on the altar, as an offering. If you are not sure about the item, place it on the altar and this way it will become more and more charged with positive vibrations.

Twice I was given Shamanic protection items that are considered to be of great power, by the same person. Since the person who gave them to me had a romantic interest in me, I felt they might try to access my energy or manipulate my feelings for them through the items, so I put them on my altar and left them there for a long time. Periodically, I would ask my Guides if it was safe for me to wear those talismans. If I still received an energetic "No", then I would question whether I should give the amulets away...and if so...whom were they intended for? The Spirit Guides would respond that the talismans were meant to stay with me until further instructions were given, but they weren't yet charged enough. Since I did not have any attachment to them, I was not overcome with desire to wear them and I was willing to be patient for as long as necessary.

Only when the items energetically communicated with me, notifying me they were fully charged and ready to be implemented, did I begin to use them. It turned out one was meant for me, but the other was for The Oracle Of The Light, Shree Dayananda's protection. Clarity prevails and confusion dissipates when we listen without any desires clouding our Wisdom.

A woman attending the Impeccable Warrior Of Light Intensive shared an experience with a man who had 'gifted' her a necklace in order to energetically cord her, since he was romantically interested in her. Although he had not asked her if she would accept it, he boldly went up to her and placed it around her neck, telling her he wanted her to have it. Immediately, she felt that she should not wear the necklace and took it off.

Whenever her mind was overcome by self-destructive forces, she was flooded with thoughts of putting it on again. She would begin to wear it, but as soon as she did…she once again heard an alarm go off. She wisely removed it and set it aside, although she was not clear as to what to do with it until she attended the Intensive.

She was relieved to hear that not only was it acceptable to discard any gift given to you, but also in cases where you feel someone is attempting to tap into your energy, it is the wisest thing to do. It is highly recommended to discard any items you sense have been given to you in order to 'cord you', in order to place hooks or inroads to your energy. For more on cords, read the following section on 'How To Cut Cords'.

While performing a remote energetic scan I once did for a health practitioner, I was told by my Guides that the man and his partner were not clearing the energy in their office as they would to the energies of their home. When asked about it, they confirmed that somehow their vision had been clouded and they had not been relating to their place of work with the same caution they were applying to their living space. Yet, numerous people were entering the business on a daily basis, certainly many more than ever visited their home, so if they had been in an awakened state of mind they would have readily addressed the daily inflow of mixed energies within the business.

The fact that these are basic practices of Spiritual Protection… that he is trained in the Shamanic Ways…yet was not able to have the necessary awareness to protect himself properly…should alert us all to the power of the clouds that can descend on anyone, at anytime. The Impeccable Warrior of Light fully understands the absolute necessity for daily energetic inventory of all items. A constant clearing and daily invocation of the Light, Goodness and Protection for your space and everything within it, is always essential.

Since this is such a Compassionate Universe, the dark forces are all-ways picked up by our radar. When we are not paying close enough attention…if we are not willing to Respect the validity of the message…and the important warning it is trying to give us… we disregard it. We convince ourselves to block it out. However the alarm keeps going off as a way of trying to wake us up to the danger that is present around us. Sometimes when we disregard the buzzing and ringing alarm, Spirit will then send us the message in countless miraculous ways…via dreams…our totems, cloud formations or friends, to name just a few.

Whenever I have my attention constantly pulled to an article, I know I need to see with my Intuitive Vision and listen with my higher senses. Often times I find that the item that continually calls out to my attention, needs to be removed from my Life.

Of course, an article can also be charged positively and also be trying to deliver a message. I discern whether the signals I am receiving are good or negative, by asking, "How do I feel about this item? What is it that I am feeling in response to this item/person?" I check in a detached way as to what the article is evoking from me. As I have mentioned before, you will not be able to do a true reading on what is transpiring if you are attached to keeping the item because of some sentimental reason. But if you are willing to see and hear the truth, the truth will surface…it will reveal itself to you in one way or another, and set you free!

There are endless manners in which articles become implanted with detrimental energies. In some cases it is due to a person programming items with harmful intentions. In other scenarios the person gifting or selling you an item, may not even be aware that the article either came to them already negatively charged... or somehow became imbued with toxic vibrations while in their possession. The following stories exemplify how gifted items can have injurious effects.

The first demonstration of this involved a female student of mine, and a man who was an accomplished dark sorcerer. When the student met the dark sorcerer, he instantly set his sights on her. She was a vibrant, intelligent and Joy-full person, who had a strong will and was able to attract Prosperity very easily. She had an excellent career and well established financial security. He was struggling on all levels, practically home-less and penny-less. When their paths crossed, after only a few minutes after meeting her, he immediately told her he was in Love with her. From then on, he proceeded to cord her through poetry that he faxed her every day. Then he Strengthened and multiplied the cords by insisting that she needed to have his artwork on all the walls of her home.

He sent her boxes of paintings, which she unwittingly covered her living space with. Whereas in the beginning she was not sure how she felt about him, after he flooded her with these energetic cords, she found herself wishing to have him move into her home. He was pushing her on this heavily, as well as persistently bombarding her with suggestions to study with him instead of me. He was intent on separating her from the Teachings and would tell her she could accomplish so much more if she joined forces with him.

Deep within her, some part of her knew she was being manipulated and so she consulted with me about her desire to accept him as a partner. I asked her to review everything she had been taught about cords, reminding her that the thoughts she was having...and the choices those thoughts were leading to... might not even be her own...but rather *his will* imposing itself upon her. It was so easy for everyone around her to see how much this dark sorcerer needed her essence, Strength and vibrancy.

His body was deteriorating and he had problems walking as the dark forces within him consumed his Life Force. She naturally carried within her a bright ray of Love, Enthusiasm and Inspiration that he desperately needed in order to feed his withering body. The darkness had been taking a toll on his body, he was constantly in pain and nothing worked out for him, leaving his Life on a steep decline. By the time he met her, the dark side had completely taken him over, convincing him he had no other options open to him other than to leech onto her Radiance.

The evil forces knew he, their host body, would soon expire without a new source to siphon energy from. They had drained him of any Light and now the dark force of evil intentions was on the prowl for fresh, strong sustenance. The darkness living in him, knew there was no hope for going on, without high powered Golden Energy/Life Force such as hers.

Months later, a friend of the woman shared with me that she had seen her and could not believe it was the same person she knew. She looked depleted, pale, drawn and had aged greatly in such a short amount of time. Unfortunately, this news did not surprise me. As we have already covered, entities and demons enter through the energetic holes within us and if not eradicated will lead us down ruinous (ruin-us) paths.

Before this ever happened, it had become clear to me that the big hole, the looming weakness within her was relationships and her sexual energy. She had a very high sex drive and she had not been full-filled by her previous partners, so she was desperate to have yet another man in her Life, who could possibly satisfy this need within her. I had observed this frailness in her energetic field, as she desperately flung herself at any man around her.

Because she was so needy, it was easy for the dark sorcerer to enwrap her. Did she have karma with this person? Yes, this is why she felt the attraction. Sometimes it can be an initial or an ongoing attraction. But did she have to choose what she chose? No!

THE SOUL YEARNS TO CHOOSE POSITIVE REALITIES... ANYTHING ELSE WE ACCEPT IS COMING FROM THE DARK SIDE.

Why? To de-rail us from our Highest Destiny! The more intensely we are controlled by the willingness to fall from Grace...the more we need to pray and pray and pray, with all our might, for Spiritual Protection. We must invoke Grace with every particle of our being, for the dissolution of the pain-inducing karmas. There is a saying that states, "Love is blind", but the correct Wisdom Teaching is: Lust, attachment to beings and outcomes, greed and desperation cause blind spots. They all blind our Wisdom, definitely causing suffering through impairing our judgment.

An accomplished Medicine Woman was sharing with me how difficult her husband could be at times. I pointed out to her that she was the one who had chosen him...that no one had forced her into the relationship. She began to laugh, expressing that choices made due to raging hormones can indeed lead to much drama.

We all have human bodies...we all have karma with other people... and we all have choices to make regarding every relationship that crosses our path. This is precisely the reason we need to absolutely dedicate ourselves to cultivating Grace. In such situations, only through Grace can we somehow re-gain our Golden Mind and uphold our commitment to Goodness, Purity and Soul-Victory.

The next example of curses disguised as gifts involves our friend from chapter Three, who had the Kundalini Syndrome attack. For easier identification, we shall refer to him as 'Z'. When 'Z' was in a haze of forget-fullness that was sponsored by the vile forces clouding his mind...he was not responding as well as I expected to the Soul Retrieval Limpias he was receiving. He was then instructed to do an energetic inventory of his home and we followed up by questioning him as to what he had discovered during that process. *He responded that he and his wife had removed items from the house and he could feel the difference, with a vast increase in the amount of Light registered.*

We proceeded to do another Limpia and during it I received a message from my Guides that there were still items in the house that had negative energies attached to them. I asked him if there might still be articles in the house that had been given to him by others and he responded affirmatively. At that moment the cloud lifted and he realized there was a woman who was trying to possess him and she had been gifting him many ceremonial artifacts, such as masks.

Once the haze dissolved, he knew exactly whom it was that was plundering his energy.

We actually always know who is trying to harm us. Our soul knows what they are doing, however when the dark forces cast a veil of deception upon us, we find ourselves going along with the surface reality instead of discerning the true energetics taking place. In this case, because of the spiritual cleansings he had received... and other practices he had implemented to maintain a high level of Purity within him and around him...he was now able to make a commitment to scrutinize afresh all items in his home for unwanted vibrations.

I share these stories with you to illustrate how you can become aware of the ample ways people can tap into your energy and control you. Now we can discuss cords and how to sever them.

How To Cut Cords

I shall share with you two easy techniques. Initially, you must sense where in your physical or energetic body you are corded. It could be the third eye, throat, heart, solar plexus, or sexual organs. If you Trust your inner knowing, you will know where someone has placed hooks in you. Once someone has cast their hook into you, they will continue to tug on your energy. The Good News is that once you have identified the area you can cut cords in one of two easy ways.

Technique 1:

Envision silver energetic strings extending from your body and imagine you have radiant, potent scissors in your hand. Now use those all power-full scissors to CUT those energetic lines running from your body to someone or something else.

After you have severed the cords, it is important you also reel in your energy lines, as you should never leave any strings dangling from your body. Each time you cut the energetic strings in front of one of the areas of your body, say silently or out loud, "I cut this cord and reel my energy lines in!" Making a motion similar to reeling in a fishing line…reel in your end of the energy line. Then you can bless and release the person by simply stating, "I bless and release you."

If you feel the person who has corded you is harm-full, you can remove them from your Life by adding statements such as "You are now gone, gone, gone from my Life! Let there only be Peace between us."

You are invoking Peace between your spirit and theirs and this is paramount. For regardless of what someone has seemingly done to you, regardless of the ill you perceive they performed against you… the whole Higher Purpose of the experience was for you to master all emotions and reactions brought on by that entire episode. To stay in blame would be to discount the supreme perfection of your Soul Lessons and the growth they are bequeathing unto you.

It is vital to recognize that removing someone from your immediate physical reality RARELY removes the people from your energy field as well. As an example, let us imagine you banish someone from your immediate reality through affirmations or prayers, with the result being they re-locate thousands of miles away from you. Even with so much physical distance between you, you would still find yourself entangled with them and your mutual drama, with recurring thoughts of them…drawn to constantly re-call the pain or hardship of the relationship.

I realize it can feel supremely challenging to see your experience with them as a blessing in disguise. Yet, the Impeccable Warrior lives by the Wisdom that no matter how much distance you put between you and your challenges and tormentors, if you continue to feel anger, hurt, resentment or bitterness from the experience, you have failed to truly free yourself from those energetic cords. Cutting those cords is up to you and is actually your Sacred Duty, for your soul desires to be free of the illusions that bring continual suffering.

While you continue to leak energy over any memories, the negative forces remain very much in control of you…and YOU are assisting them in this process of bondage. It is supremely important to affirm, "Let there only be Peace between us", as only when there is Peace WITHIN YOU, will you be able to move on.

As long as there is no Peace in your mind and heart...even if your perceived antagonists are far away...anytime you allow the demons of Discord to replay the scenes of conflict in your mind over and over again...you are still energetically tied to them and to the past.

By entertaining inner hostility, even if the adversaries you have physically broken free of, if you have not mentally and emotionally broken free, then you have not energetically broken free. While that which you feel caused you hardship, may no longer be in your Life in physical form, the clashes will continue because the mind continues to flash scene from the past which disturb you, infusing your energetic field with that negative vibration.

These scenes of challenges then broadcast this frequency of dis-balance from you to the world around you, and of course, someone else, who matches up perfectly with that frequency will appear in your Life to create a similar torture for you! The affirmation, "Let there only be Peace between us", establishes that energy of release, detachment and therefore Freedom, layer by layer...so you CAN wipe the movie screen clear...and experience a NEW reality. Practicing at cutting cords and replacing them with detachment and serenity...will one day enable you to manifest a reality where you have mastered that lesson...and CAN, FINALLY, after many Life-times, move on. Isn't that fantastic!

Technique 2:

Imagine you are a warrior with your sword in its sheath on your back. Reach back, draw your sword and let it drop in front of you with lightening speed, at once cutting all cords attached to you. As you are slicing, give the command, "I cut all cords and draw every particle of my energy back into myself."

Technique 3:

If you wish, you can use a high-tech for collecting your energy lines. Simply visualize a button somewhere on your body, such as your shoulder or wrist, that you can press which immediately draws all the energetic ends in. With one touch they all come flying in! ZIP! I prefer to add sound effects to the commands, and if you do too, then use whatever commands and whatever sounds empower you. ZOOM is another English language power word.

You can go further and make it totally clear that you are unavailable to any negative forces by making statements such as the following in your mind or out loud, "I am not available to you! I belong to the Light! All my energies belong to the Light! Get out now! I order you to leave in the name of _____.. When you take refuge in whomever you have Faith in, your Protectors are immediately present. By invoking them, they are there energetically, standing with you to fight off any type of psychic attack.

DANGERS OF TAROT CARDS, OUIJI BOARDS AND CHANNELLING

Anything such as Tarot cards, Ouiji boards, channelling and other similar practices, create portals which are opened when you participate, allowing perfect opportunities for the forces of evil to enter. Remember: when you open a portal, unless you really know how to guard it, anything can come through. The malevolent forces are expertly devious to begin with and will take advantage of any opening into your Life.

If you do work with the cards, always pay attention to how the energy feels around you afterwards. Do you feel uncomfortable in your house? Pay attention to anything unusual that happens, or appears. You are dealing with living forces that can seep in. Just as dust comes in through the tiniest cracks, so does negative energy. It's not about being paranoid...it is about being intelligent and observant.

Tarot:

Many people have experienced terrifying episodes with evil entities while working with the cards. Unfortunately, there are many books and teachers on the mechanics of working with the cards but very few ever teach you how to thoroughly protect yourself while opening these portals. Recognizing the power of the portal opened by these cards, I feel anyone who sells cards or books on cards without warning and educating the buyer, is committing a sin.

They are responsible for gross negligence for they are tossing the unprepared to the wolves! Where is the Compassion in that? And why do they not warn people? Greed is their motive--they do not want to "scare" anyone from making a purchase. It has become all about commerce…their purpose in Life is to promote sales, instead of Wisdom. Training is crucial in operating any heavy equipment and so it is with these types of instruments.

Card decks are often treated like a game, or toy, something to do for entertainment. If you are going to shuffle cards, pick cards, do a spread, or anything with them at all, you should first put in place some kind of protection.

The upcoming chapter on 'Protection Tools and Guidelines… Cleansing Ingredients and Amulets' will give you a long list of time-honoured ingredients you can use to create protection. You will also need to say prayers, mantras or a statement of intention, so the message is sent to all Forces as to the boundaries you are setting. These affirmations, prayers or rituals need to make it clear WHO or what you belong to…WHO OR WHAT you are committed to…and WHICH energies or beings you are available to OR NOT available for. Some examples are:

"I am encircled and protected by the Violet Flame!
I am surrounded and protected by the Angels and Archangels!
I belong to the Legions of Light and no negative force is
allowed… to EVER be present within me or around me!
I call forth the Legions of Light, all Compassionate Masters and
Protectors to be present
and defend us against all evil, today and All Ways!"

A student of mine is often overwhelmed by the constant storm of negative thoughts and images that flood her mind. She shared with me she was planning to begin working with cards and I gave her a stern warning. I clearly let her know that I did not recommend she get involved with Tarot cards or use any playing cards for any purpose at that time. I explained to her that if she could not even handle the energies that were already attacking her viciously on a daily basis, she certainly should not be opening up dangerous portals. I felt if she did play around with these sensitive gateways, the forces could destroy her.

After receiving those Teachings, she chose to work with the Medicine cards instead, which have animal symbols on them. I considered them to be less dangerous, although all forms of divination open portals and are therefore an opportunity for dark forces to disguise themselves and enter into a relationship with you. It is natural for the Soul to desire to expand it's Intuition, but if you build up Strength first and continue to fortify your Protective Shield, then you will not be destroyed by anything that tries to attack you along the way

Ouiji Boards:

This is a favourite of evil forces and I don't recommend for anyone to use it. As far as I am concerned, you are just asking for trouble when you engage with these forces. I am appalled that they sell this item in game stores for anyone to 'play' with. STAY AWAY from this and engage in chanting, meditation or prayers instead. All these positive endeavours will kindle your Kundalini and therefore Intuitive Vision without putting your Life in the hands of Evil powers.

Channelling:

You must be very care-full, watch-full and attentive of feelings and signs when channelling. You need to truly know whether the beings channelling through you are good or negative and this requires great discernment.

Although many Positive, help-full energies can channel through us, the sneaky whisperers can also come through, as they disguise themselves as benefactors. Their method of seduction is to give us powers and feed our ego…in this way they win us over. Dark forces know that by pretending to be benevolent, they can get people to drop their defences and in this way creep in.

If you are channelling negative forces, although they may give you candy in the beginning, by giving you powers and feeding your ego, their true purpose is to poison you and kill you as soon as possible. They will eventually destroy you and will proceed on their path to your destruction by affecting you in your weak areas.

Someone once asked what I meant by the word 'destroy'. I mean destruction in all possible ways. Destructive forces are programmed to begin chipping away at one area after another of your Life. They will begin their attacks in the areas that are the weakest. If your weak area is your body, they will start with that...beware...they don't stop there.

After that, they continue their march into other areas of your Life. They may go after your Prosperity, then destroy the Harmony in your relationships or sabotage your positive projects. Do you understand now? The following petition that was sent to me is a perfect example of this.

"Dear Peace Mother, I'm asking for your help. Starting last March, I was taken over by a force that I thought was good for me at first. Now, I'm no longer 'channelled through' like I was before, but my Life has been destroyed. I'm subjected to terrible pain on a daily basis, depression and anxiety, which caused me to have a nervous breakdown, lose my job and my home. I now have to stay at my mothers' house, far away from the community I Love and miss. I'm not able to function and it's hard to survive."

I proceeded to do remote Soul Retrieval Limpias to clear away the entities that were attached to her. After receiving the first couple of Limpias she wrote:

"Thanks so much for the Limpias. My condition is improving. Most of the really bizarre symptoms are gone. There are moments now when a Peaceful feeling comes in. It feels like there is a benevolent force working with me, although when the depression hits I can't always feel this force. I am praying constantly and I am very grateful for your prayers."

In this case, I recommended for her to repeat the mantra, Kali Durge Namo Nama continuously, along with any other prayers for protection she may know, as well as calling on the Violet Light for another layer of protection. Even though she is being showered with Grace through the Soul Retrieval Limpias, **she must also continue to cultivate that Grace through her self-effort.**

If your legs are your weak area, then even though the negative energies might give you the power to channel great information, you'd have more and more problems with your legs and eventually perhaps even lose them, or the use of them.

I once met a woman who was a classic example of this. She channelled the spirits of those on the other side and from what I observed, she was not grounded, not protecting herself enough and due to so many sinister energies attached to her already, definitely no longer ABLE to shield herself enough. She had several car accidents in which her legs were hurt and was close to losing one of her legs to gangrene. She lived in a fantasy world where everyone she met absolutely Loved her. But upon meeting those that she felt adored her, it was discovered that none of them wanted anything to do with her again, since her ungrounded-ness presented many problems wherever she went.

Her relationships and finances were all a huge disaster and sadly, she was addicted to "channelling"…she could not recognize she was opening portals and engaging with spirits, without setting up the proper boundaries.

CLEAR ALL ENERGIES AFTER PSYCHIC OR HEALING WORK

May everyone learn from the unfortunate ones who have fallen on the battle-field. Their weak example should motivate everyone to all-ways clear out the sickly/stuck/confused/tormented/evil energy that is removed from others, after having contact with them. It doesn't matter if you interact with people in person or speak to someone on the phone—anytime you come into contact with someone, whether in a general way, or after applying any psychic/healing work, it is wise to clear yourself and your space of any negative vibrations attached to them.

For example, after every Soul Retrieval session, I cleanse the rattles and cloths that I use in the healing session as well as the chair the person sat in and the whole space once they have left.

When you are concentrating on something or someone, their energy is present with you. When the Soul Retrieval session is done via the phone I also cleanse anything that I have used in the session, as well as the space in the healing room and the rest of the Centre. Depending on how serious a case it is, I will adjust the amount of cleansing and protective precautions I will take.

As we have established before, a person may cross your path that is kind, gentle and considerate…keep in mind that even though they are an overall Lovely person, this does not indicate they have no challenges. Remain aware that any suffering they are undergoing is caused by disruptive forces they carry with them…and take precautions because energies can easily hop from one person to another like any infectious dis-ease.

When you allow people to come into your home for any reason, via any avenue, be it in person, over the phone, Internet, mail, third eye or radio, their energies are crossing yours… and there is bound to be remnants of their energy left behind. You inherit chunks of energy, to varying degrees, from all the company you keep.

IF YOU OPEN THE DOOR, ANYONE CAN COME IN

An Impeccable Warrior never loses sight of this. They do not assume that doorways allow only good forces to come in. For example. in the traditions of India, as well as many other spiritual paths, before Ceremonial Work commences, the Priest 'binds' the directions. Binding means they cast out harm-full energies and set up protective parameters, through certain rituals and mantras. They summon the Divine Protectors to be present, to guard the energetic doors they will be opening and keep out evil spirits, so the sacred Work will flow harmoniously for everyone attending, without any obstacles or obtrusions.

A true teacher warns people not to become enamoured of spiritual powers. In the Vedic Scriptures of India, spiritual powers such as the ability to materialize objects, to channel, mind-read and other psychic abilities are called siddhis. Don Jacinto called them 'mayas', which is interesting because in the Vedic tradition the word 'maya' means illusion. Don Jacinto also made it very clear that he had no need for these 'mayas' since he was only interested in being an instrument for the highest and purest Healing Light.

All solid paths report that many a student on the Spiritual Path has gotten stuck, due to addiction to ego-feeding powers. Once enthralled by the powers they believed made them special and important, these individuals never went on to become Enlightened. They never pursued Liberation from the Ego, which is the lair of all demons. The seduced mistakenly felt their work was done when they received their powers from the dark side. Now satisfied with themselves, they remained contentedly entrapped by powers sponsored by the force of Evil, disguised as a beneficent force. All my teachers warned their students to avoid this illusory pitfall on the Spiritual Path.

I have indeed met a stream of people who had numerous beings appear to them and channel through them, all of which seems to be a good occurrence. However, upon a close examination of the person and their ego we see they are not able to commit to Impeccable Purity. Through their inability to maintain unwavering Faith and Strength, through not holding themselves consciously accountable to the path of Impeccability, it reveals they are hosting deceptive company. The forces channelling through half-baked individuals are NOT a Divine Force committed to guiding the seeker to Balance and True Happiness.

Why will the negative spirits try to destroy you? As we have revealed before, they live to cause you suffering and then feed off your misery, for they live on the negative emotions that are generated by humanity. The more you suffer the fatter they become.

An Impeccable Warrior feeds the forces of good and starves the negative forces by being fully aware at all times and choosing only to be a vehicle for the Highest and the Purest Force. The Cherokee wolf story I shared with you earlier sums it all up perfectly.

Once a student of mine wrote that she had been having one dazzling cosmic experience after another with the most glorious fantastic visions of Divine Mother. Night after night she was filled with anticipation of falling into her dream state, telling Divine Mother how much she looked forward to yet another vision. She did not remember to bind the directions, setting up protection all

81

around her, and she did not state that ONLY Positive energies were allowed to interact with her.

One evening, instead of the usual type of visions, a horrifically dark energy pounced on her, pinning her down and grabbing her by the throat. She later told me it felt like the vilest of the dark demons and she had never been so terrified in all her Life. In spite of her fear, due to the power of her daily practices, she was able to collect herself enough to shout out prayers for protection, calling on Jesus, Divine Mother Mary, Kali and Durga to help her. The demon force did dissolve and the experience left her much wiser as to how the sinister energies can sneak in and surprise us.

The Impeccable Warrior remains mind-full that the negative forces are all-ways trying to get their "foot inside the door" in a myriad of ways. This Wisdom Teaching reminds you to recognize that when you open yourself up without installing your Protectors to guard you and the space around you, your openness creates an available channel for the forces to flow through. Let us remain aware at all times that they are rude and self-centered. They don't care if you have not invited them--it is their impeccably vicious nature to use every ounce of their being to squeeze in through any opening, even if they haven't been directly invited.

HOW CAN YOU DISCERN WHICH ENERGIES ARE BENEVOLENT AND WHICH ARE MALEVOLENT?

You do this by constantly putting them to the test, by asking them to commit to the Light, or to pledge themselves to Mother God/ Father God, Goodness and Compassion.

Whenever any energy is flowing through you or others, you can qualify those vibrations by saying, "If you are not from the highest and purest Light, I order you to leave!" There are many ways to test them. For example, you can also say, "If you are not committed to the greatest Love and Compassion for humanity, I order you to leave! I am only available to the highest and purest energies!" Another simple statement is "If you do not Love and Respect me, I order you to leave immediately!

Your commitment must be towards your Highest Good and in the same way, you must insist that any force that is not present to shower you with Love, must vacate the space within you and around you. In order to reach your Highest Destiny, your Life should reflect that you are becoming spiritually stronger by associating with your True Guides. The truly pure Guides are not in your Life to encourage you to be petty or drown in smallness. They are committed to assisting you in the purification that must take place and they are present to help you re-call your Divine nature. Real Guides help you to become an Impeccable Warrior of Light by fostering a solid foundation within you of Self-Respect, Dignity, Serenity and Compassion for others.

I once heard of a woman who began to hear voices telling her that she was one of the "chosen ones". In the name of being one of the 'chosen' ones they instructed her towards many self-destructive actions. These out-of-body entities were engaging in sexual activities with her and encouraging her to allow her Life to become extremely chaotic.

Holding her increasingly spell-bound, one day they told her that she must full-fill her destiny as a 'chosen' one, by leaving her house and driving her car at dangerously high speeds, in order for her to be present at a certain location by a specific time. They further instructed her that when any Law Enforcers tried to stop her, she should ignore them. She was not to stop for any reason, they told her, for they needed her to be at the designated area at the exact time ordered.

Because of the tremendous speed she was driving at, naturally, the Police did attempt to stop her, repeatedly telling her to pull over. However, in keeping with instructions from her 'guides', she ignored the traffic enforcers and refused to heed their commands. In the end the police were forced to set up a barricade to stop her. The sinister entities continued with their evil work, once again inflicting destructive counsel upon her, urging her to run through the barricade. Being heavily under their influence, instead of stopping her vehicle... she broke many laws and ran through the Police barricade!

Needless to say, this resulted in her incarceration. She had been fighting a child custody battle before all this happened and of course, this event damaged her credibility greatly. Do you see how these voices were not instructing her to make wise choices but instead to disrupt the Balance of her Life completely?

This is a very tough area to discern on the Spiritual Path. It is not always easy to clearly see where something is leading you. For, on the path of Self-less Service, Purity and Enlightenment, admirable beings have also had to go through an immense variety of physical, emotional or financial losses. Yet, whatever is lost should be replaced with a greater Faith in Spirit's Positive Principles.

We know we're on the right path when all of Life's sequences result in an increased Strength and Faith in the Goodness of the Universe. All of my teachers were PRACTICAL Beings who had a Joy-full. sense of humour along with profound Devotion to serving humanity. They accomplished Their mission by uplifting all Creation through their own choices…by the example of the lives they led… and the many Compassionate actions they donated to alleviate the suffering of humanity. May these Teachings bring you further clarity regarding your path and the role of DISCERNMENT on The Path. The most important thing is to choose to stay awake at all moments… being aware of the times you tend to take it for granted that all voices are elevating voices…**Be willing to put your sources to the test!**

VISITORS: NO-ONE TRAVELS UNACCOMPANIED

It is necessary to always be aware of others' energies and how their vibrations influence their actions. Without being aware of it, some folks have become complainers, whiners, bitter, angry, envious, fear-full and jealous.

Jealousy-Envy is a mammoth energy that causes much suffering, both within the envious person and the target of their jealousy. It is so destructive a force that it is one of the Bible's Ten Commandments: Thou shalt not covet thy neighbour… (Exodus 20:17)

Often people are surprised that others would be jealous of them, their Life or possessions. The reason some people find it hard to believe that anyone would be jealous of them is that in their own eyes, they don't possess anything others could be envious of. On the Wisdom Path, we comprehend that jealousy, envy and judgments are a natural reaction of the impure mind.

Hence, the human mind is just doing what it instinctively does… to re-act. Since the mind is directed by the negative forces attached to it… a being may not even be aware of WHY they re-act a certain way. However, it is imperative YOU KNOW that whether someone is sending you energy consciously or unconsciously…energy is still being zapped onto you…and your energetic body will register it.

It is common that after the physical visitors leave your home, they will leave some energetic visitors behind. In the same way that visitors bring germs and bacteria into your home, or an email can bring a virus into your computer, most people carry some kind of negative energy, for these energies are attached to them. Once they bring these spirits to your home, that visiting spirit may decide it likes your home better and would rather be attached to you than the host they rode in on.

In the same way that people with issues can bring confused or anguished forces into your home, there are beings that leave your home full of the blessings, Light and Peace they carry within them. In India and Mexico it is the custom to invite Holy Beings to visit one's home. It is considered a great honour to have one's home blessed by the radiant force of Compassion, Wisdom and Grace that exists in the Holy Being's presence. With this knowledge the host/hostess knows that the Holy Being might not visit for very long but they consider it an immense privilege just to have the Holy Being set foot inside the home.

We must remember that everyone is emanating a vibration. At all times, you are providing a home for invisible beings (energies) within you and around you and they are emanating a particular frequency to everyone and everything in the Universe.

Those who are able to see and hear those frequencies are able to be fully aware of whom and what is actually present. An example is the Realized Being who walks accompanied by the spirits of Their Lineage…which would be the spirit of their departed Teacher…the Teacher's Teacher and other Masters connected to that Lineage. It is those Compassionate spirits who are actually working through the Holy Being and those who meet the Saint can feel the higher frequency of Peace, Love, Inspiration and Purity that reside within the Holy Being. Everyone who comes in contact with such a being is affected by the radiation of Goodness, by the Bright Light that is streaming from the Pure Being.

The same energetic law applies to the opposite, where any attached dark forces would emanate a foul, disturbing or fear-producing vibration. As people walk on their Spiritual Path, as long as they continue to embrace negativity in any form, it will provide an opening for more sinister entities to latch onto them and live with them.

When someone comes to visit your home, they could be the sweetest person full of good intentions and possibly also performing many good actions in the world. This Goodness within them is due to the Positive Forces travelling with the being, however if the seeker still has big holes in some area of their Life that they have not yet healed, it is indicative of some type of negative presence that accompanies them as well.

It will vary from person to person as to how much invisible negativity they will leave behind in your home. For this reason I highly recommend that you always do a big smudge, a big smoke cleansing of your home after your company leaves. In the same way that you would be shocked if you could see the germs left behind by visitors, you would also be surprised at the malevolent or mischievous energies they leave behind.

I once had a student, whom I shall refer to as 'J' who did not want to believe any of this. She organized a Peace Pilgrimage for us in Arizona in a community that was known as a haven for artists and healers. The majority of these beings were sweet, well-meaning floaters....beings who were floating through Life without any grounding. Within the community there were also others who were able to see and feel how they and others were constantly being manipulated by the dark forces of the area and the karmic inner demons each person was carrying.

When the Impeccable Warrior of Light Spiritual Protection Intensive was proposed for an upcoming program 'J' felt the subject of dark forces would frighten her friends. She felt her fellow residents would not be open, and that they could not cope with the subject of Spiritual Protection. Actually, it was her inner demons that were blocking this vital training from reaching others. As was demonstrated later on, there were many who knew they needed the tools this Intensive would provide them and had been praying for such Wisdom to come to them.

After I left the area she proceeded with her spiritual unfoldment and continued to develop her psychic ability by attending many workshops and classes. Along the way she started to work with the pendulum and she learned to use it to measure the positive and negative energy in the spaces around her. She later shared with me that she was astounded at the high amounts of negative energy her friends left behind whenever they visited her. I give her the Teachings on smudging regularly and she felt great relief to know there were spiritual antidotes for dissolving the traces of negative forces left in her abode or car. Now that she had found a way of identifying both the negative energies and the level of their intensity, she was motivated to uphold the discipline of quickly cleansing the entire house after her guests left.

No longer afraid of the subject matter of Spiritual Protection, by the next year she was begging me to return to Arizona to teach this Intensive, both for her sake and the sake of the her community. Now, she realized the vast majority of them were also too unaware and therefore, unguarded. For more methods and ingredients for protection see Chapter 7: Protection Tools and Guidelines.

BLACK MAGIC

When well-meaning people think of the subject of black magic, they immediately envision someone else carrying it out. Visions pop up of a gypsy, or a possessed, confused person dealing in such dark practices. However, it is vital to every soul on Earth to accept and acknowledge that black magic is actually carried out by the majority of the human population, in one form or another.

It is time you wake up to the full scope of both of these aspects of black magic. The first aspect is CONSCIOUS manipulation. There are those who are consciously committed to the dark side and so actively embrace black magic in a purpose-full way, driven by inner demons such as envy or vengeance and a desire to control others. It is wise to discard disbelief and accept that yes, there are so many people around us whom you would not suspect of practicing dark arts, yet they do so regularly. Like any addiction, it has become a way of Life for them.

Within this group there are two kinds of individuals: those who do their own dirty work in order to control others and those who mistakenly believe that by hiring or convincing someone else to carry out the black magic absolves them from sin.

The second aspect of the dark science is the one that the seeker rarely contemplates, yet is the key to Enlightenment: those who engage in black magic UNCONSCIOUSLY. In order to progress spiritually, each seeker must take responsibility as to their unconscious support of black magic. For although most people are not aware of it, the fact is that every time you have a negative thought about a Loved one, friend, stranger or even yourself, YOU are engaging in "black magic". Energetically, any negative thought you entertain thrusts a wave of slime, arrows or missiles at the object of your focus.

As Impeccable Warriors of Light, we must understand that both thought and emotion are "energy in motion". When you express negative emotion towards others, you have set in motion an army of negative energies towards the unaware individual. Depending on the core desire within your thought/emotion, you have sent that person a wave of sludge, or a black cloud to encircle them. Envy and jealousy have power...our words have power...and our thoughts and visualization have power to impose upon others our harm-full visions. When we engage in negative visualizations, we are contributing towards their downfall. The decline we push unto them can end up being bad luck, physical pain, emotional suffering and other types of distress.

It is therefore important to understand the consequences of your thought...word...and deed. The Universal laws of cause and effect are extremely predictable. Projecting negativity onto others in whichever form, incurs negative karma upon the individual, for in so doing you are inflicting limitations upon others, regardless of whether it was projected consciously or unconsciously.

Spiritual Protection is therefore a NECESSITY, for it is the lower human nature to engage in "black magic" by projecting our negative thoughts and judgments towards others. And let us remember, most people are doing the same towards us!

The only solution to prevent you from projecting negativity on another and visa versa is the following:

a)   Constant Prayer Work raises your own frequency thereby making you strong despite the negative energies being thrown at you. A higher vibration brings about more Clarity, Protection and Sacred Wisdom.

b)   Use the tools of Spiritual Protection and create your own method of daily cleansing of your aura. Master the following concept: The negative thoughts that pass through your mind are NOT your own. They are sponsored by dark energies influencing you. The source of your negative reactions could be dark energies that have latched unto you, projections from someone else or negative forces in your environment.

When you remain aware of this every time you feel the urge to emanate destructive vibrations towards someone, you will not give sinister energies the opportunity to take you down a dark alley with their usual tricks. No one can force you to receive something that you choose to not accept. If you do not claim those negative thoughts as your own…and All Ways banish them from your immediate space and from all beings everywhere…you become a purifier of negative energy in the world.

Through this practice you move from being entangled in negativity to instead serving all beings in this world and all other worlds. Great merit is earned from this simple act, which then brings forth a shower of Grace to help you dissolve the obstacles on your path. By remaining on the Positive Path, your actions burn up negative karma and further open the doors to the solutions you have been calling forth.

c)   The Impeccable Warrior of Light's duty goes even further; when you see somebody else projecting negativity knowingly or unknowingly, you must do what you can to bring to their attention the consequences of the negative karma they are inflicting upon themselves and the suffering they are causing another due to their unconsciousness or ignorance.

d)   An Impeccable Warrior of Light practices vigilance over themselves each day, so that they do not project negativity on to others, due to lack of unawareness. Therefore it is important to review your thoughts, emotion, word and deed everyday and see where you hit the mark and where you missed. Whether you hit the mark or missed it, re-member to raise every experience to the highest vibration, contemplating it through a CONSTRUCTIVE lens. At every moment, whatever happens within you and around you, be aware of your motives and actions, but do not engage in either self-deprecation or tainted pride. Just take note of it and learn something valuable from it.

One of the reasons people experience enormous transformation and increased good fortune after receiving Soul Retrieval Limpias, is the shower of Grace bestowed upon them, which quickly dissolves huge amounts of psychic debris, cords and obstacles that have been projected to the person by others. Any layers of projected darkness that we do not clear out then spawn further negativity in our lives in the form of doubt, insecurity, anger, impatience, discord, hostility, hardening of the heart, health imbalances, deterioration of Prosperity and much more. Each Mayan Soul Retrieval Limpia floods the seeker with Light, cleanses the aura, and enforces a protective shield around the being, increasing Strength in the spirit of the person. Once the spirit is re-generated, everything else can improve. When your spirit is strong it is easy to be in a Great-full state, full of Gusto and Positive Determination.

ENERGY VAMPIRES

Have you ever experienced being around someone who left you feeling absolutely drained? Whenever this happens, it is because you have allowed your Golden Life Force to be siphoned from you. Some people drain you of energy by involving you in their drama, stories, confusion, hostility, self-pity, stress, sadness and so on.

Everyone knows at least one person who has an endless appetite for attention. One version of this syndrome is the being who constantly evokes advice from others but never acts on any of it. They may seem sweet and kind-hearted, but they wear you out for they are firmly entrenched in their own self-centered Universe. The Impeccable Warrior is able to observe the situation through their Wisdom Eyes and discern this person as a bottomless pit of neediness.

Another syndrome is the person who does not verbalize their pent up feelings and by keeping their thoughts to themselves, engage you energetically. Their silence is shouting at us, evoking from us attention. Through their silence they draw everyone into expending immense amounts of energy to draw them out, to make them feel included.

Some people are energy vampires without realizing it, while others are absolutely aware of how they are sucking energy from others. The ones who do this knowingly have powers they have accumulated from past lives and are experts at zapping people, cording and draining them.

Whether or not someone is conscious of being an energy vampire, they are still possessed…and being used by a negative force to steal your energy…so the demon they are carrying is constantly fed.

It is your Sacred Duty to learn how to disarm them and protect your Golden Energy. You can do this through the basic Violet Light technique, where you immediately call forth a shield of purple Light all around you. Simply invoke the Violet Flame to protect you against all negative forces. As you envision it continuously blazing all around, you can use the declaration, "I AM BLESSED and PROTECTED perfectly by the Violet Light."

When you feel someone has hooked you with energetic cords, you can cut those cords with the assistance of the techniques given in the previous section titled "How To Curt Cords." It is through these cords, these energetic lines that the vampire will be drawing on your energy.

Another technique for defence is to visualize reaching out and seizing your energy that has been stolen, bringing it back into the area it was stolen from. If you feel it was taken from your heart, reach out and grab it and bring it back to your heart, depositing it there. You can do the same with the solar plexus. You will know if energy has been stolen from there by the sensations you will register in your stomach area. The same goes for your sexual areas…you will know when any person or spirit is manipulating your sexual energy to empower themselves.

With this technique of taking back your power, you can either imagine it or actually perform the physical action of reaching out in front of you to take back your power, then bringing it back to the area under attack. Reach out to the left if it is a memory you are tapping into…where your power was stolen from you in the past. If you are experiencing flashes of someone stealing your power in some future scenario…you can reach to the right for the future.

Worrying about the future, as well as any other fear-related visions, are signs you have given your power away. I recommend that every time you catch yourself relinquishing your power through future-related worries, immediately reach into the future and grab that power that you just gave up and re-claim it, bringing it back into your self.

If you are able to, you can also use the other techniques shown in the 'How To Cut Cords' section, such as snapping your finger three times or using your sword to cut those energetic lines. Regardless of what technique you use, do it with full commitment and let the energy vampires know you are serious, ordering them with full force to get their slimy hands off your power! Otherwise you are an unwitting accomplice in the theft of your own energy. An Impeccable Warrior guards their Golden Energy as they would the most priceless jewel.

Tv, Radio, Images, Words, Thoughts

Whether we are referring to television, radio, newspapers, magazines, books, internet, video or computer games, they ALL carry waves of energy to your world, body, mind, home and spirit. Be aware that when you are watching, listening or somehow focusing on something, you are actually inviting those energies and thought forms into your home and being. Today's society bombards you with a much higher percentage of negativity than images of Beauty, Harmony, Peace and Triumph of the human spirit. Society will tell you repeatedly that you need to participate in the media's campaign of pessimism, violence and ugly degradation.

The only reasons for involving oneself in negativity are

1) to utilize it for educational purposes as to the nature of negative/evil forces and
2. as an inspiration to increase one's prayers. As disruptive forces cross your path, they can serve as a reminder of what issues need the attention of your spiritual transformative work.

Once an image has reminded you of the existence of a particular suffering, you take it as a message to go to your altar, focus your prayers and begin the upliftment of that limited reality immediately.

Other than to enhance your knowledge of evil's past and present strategies, I do not believe you have to immerse yourself in the swamp of gloom, whether it is generated by the media, institutions, organizations, your negative neighbour, family or friends.

Once you begin to examine clearly the after-effects of negative surroundings, you will notice that such encounters leave you feeling fear-full, psychically attacked or rattled from the exposure. I once knew a couple where the husband would watch one violent movie after another. The wife was very sensitive and it affected her greatly. He did not think it was affecting him, but the accumulation of violence and ugliness did show through to others in his behaviour. Year after year of immersing himself in the turbulence of torture, meanness, cruelty, and vile language, this kind-hearted man became easily irritated by everyone and everything. He became very short-tempered, rude and mean. At the peak of his possession, his home became infested with rats, which are signs of the presence of sinister forces.

Many people think nothing of watching intensely violent or ugly scenes, such as scenes of torture, cruelty, abuse, pandemonium and so on. Those demons that possessed the character in the script to do those ugly things are projected into your home, body and spirit, to find a host to live through. Therefore, I highly recommend that you choose wisely as to what you and your family allow into your physical and psychic space. This will require vigilance and making conscious choices. Notice that even while you or your children are enjoying family-type entertainment, you often find that television networks will bombard you with loud commercials that contain cruel, creepy, chilling images and vile language.

Apathy is no substitute for Spiritual Protection. Therefore, if you do not have your protective shield on during any visual or auditory onslaught at those critical moments, you can find the energies represented in those disturbing vibrations attaching themselves to your home, body, mind and spirit. I recommend that you immediately call in your protective shield by snapping your fingers or clapping three times, for example, and order all negative forces out. I also recommend that whenever you and your family are focusing on any lower vibration thought form or image, you should only engage in it as an Impeccable Warrior of Light. This means knowingly protecting yourself and dissolving all darkness that will attempt to project itself onto you.

Once I was being interviewed and the interviewer shared the following case:

Her son asked her to watch a show she normally considered too dark to watch, but she had wanted to spend some bonding time with her son, so she agreed. The scenes were bothering her, for she is a very sensitive being. When the episode was finished, she went to stand up and screamed in pain. She couldn't get up! There was such intense pain in her legs that she had to lie back down. When she shared this with me, I told her I felt sure her legs were her weak spot and asked her if my statement was correct. No surprise to me, she answered that they were.

As I explained to her everything that I have shared with you so far in this section, the whole experience made sense to her. It is my opinion that violent, dark, rude or obnoxious images should only be watched in a very purposeful way and always with your protective shield up.

Whenever I reach a new country, at some point of my stay, I choose to do a quick channel surf of the local television programs, to see what the locals are immersing themselves in. But I do not need to remain focused on the vile, stupid or vicious for long. A quick glance tells me all I need to know and because I Respect myself and I treasure my Life Force, I do not squander any Golden Energy. I will only invest it with sound reason and for a higher purpose and therefore I will remain focused on any image only if I feel it will help somehow serve humanity for me to do so.

Rarely, but occasionally, if I hear from others that many people are watching certain dark programs, I may view a part of a program that has a story line about negative forces, in order to witness the attack of the dark forces upon the collective consciousness. In the process, I do not take it lightly and I am not sloppy in my approach to it. I am watching it for what I need to learn from it and protecting myself throughout the program.

For example, when I was flying from Los Angeles to Melbourne, the airline showed "The Lord of the Rings" and I wasn't sure whether I wanted to be bombarded with some of the images it contains. The Oracle Of The Light, Shree Dayananda had seen the movie and told me that certain images of the evil beings had left her feeling nauseous. I checked with my higher guidance as to whether it was wise to watch it at that time, since my physical body was fatigued from the long flight. My Wisdom answered that I should watch it so I could protect the other passengers who were not taking responsibility for what was being projected unto them.

The Impeccable Warrior does not deal with such images casually, so I did watch it, but in a fully conscious way. Whenever there was a scene that portrayed any form of evil I would snap my fingers three times and call out not only for my safeguard, but also for all of humanity's protection from sinister forces. Even though I chose to put myself in that classroom while knowing I would be bombarded by menacing images, I was on my guard to cast those forces out and dissolved their effect immediately. Since I was aware there were many other passengers watching the movie who were not shielding themselves, I called out for their defence, as well as the protection of the rest of the world.

BOOKS, MAIL AND EMAIL

The same principle applies for the contents of books, since they carry a vibration stemming from the writer, the person(s) who handled it, the power of the words written within it and the subject matter itself.

Out of all the people who may have touched a particular item, the energy that you will tune into the most would be the energy that is the strongest. Whoever has the most powerful vibration, be it positive or negative, is what you will register in your energetic body.

Everything is loaded with the vibrations of the person who sent it and those who touched it along the way. Even if you do not smudge every piece of mail each day, you can just smudge your whole house each day so that any vibrations that snuck into your space are transformed.

Here is an example of how energies can slip in seemingly unnoticed. I say seemingly because the body is always picking up what is going on around it. The mind, however, will try to discard the true reality through rationalization.

One night before I went to bed an e-mail came across with a prayer request where someone was asking for protection against several individuals that she felt were filled with evil entities who were trying to destroy her and her family. There was a very heavy energy that came across with that e-mail and I did snap my fingers three times while I was reading that message to place a protective shield around me. I was very aware of the need to protect myself and Sacred Peace Center from the energies attached to the person's name. I immediately wrote a prayer request for the petitioner and put it on the altar. I had already smudged the house and all the prayer requests on the altar prior to receiving this message, so I decided to take a chance that it would be all right. However, shortly after that I heard something that sounded like heavy breathing outside the window, which had a very strange quality to it. I became very still so as to fully identify it.

While I was repeating my mantra in my mind, I waited to see if it would go away. However when it wouldn't stop, I clapped my hands three times very loudly and with Zest made the sign of the cross in the air in front of me. I called for protection in all the directions calling on Kali, Durge, Tara, Ixchel (Mayan Mother of Medicine, pronounced Ish-chell), Tonantzin (Aztec Goddess, the Virgin of Guadalupe), Jesus and Quan Yin. I then started singing in a booming voice the mantra Kali Durge Namo Nama. It then subsided and I went to bed. About three in the morning I was jerked out of a dream state to hear the words of an inner voice saying, "there is an evil presence here". I continued to lie in bed observing the energy in the room, just quietly taking stock of what might be happening and I realized that my feet were buzzing with electricity, which is one of the ways my body Wisdom speaks to me.

Whenever my feet begin to vibrate with energy it means I am picking up a strong negative wave that is floating through my space or the surrounding area. I decided to turn on the big Light, since bright Light gives the negative forces less room to play around in. After doing my prayers in bed, I normally put my rosary on the left side of my pillow and after I tuned in to the message my feet were confirming, I noticed that my rosary had somehow wound up on the right side of the bed.

With focused Determination, I took my rosary and proceeded to repeat the mantra, Kali Durge Namo Nama, once again calling in protection from the East, North, West, South, Sky, Earth and the Sacred Temple of the Heart. I continued to call for the dissolution of all negative forces anywhere and the liberation of all beings so that they might be able to enjoy their lives in Peace and Harmony. At some point the energy shifted enough to where I knew I had full-filled my Sacred Duty by disintegrating that evil presence and I gave myself permission to go back to rest.

When I was younger, I had one sleepless night after another, experiencing fear because I did not have any tools with which to identify and vanquish negative waves. Now, with my training and initiation as a Peace Shaman, I confront every particle of evil knowing it is my duty to defend humanity by transforming the endless waves of darkness that circulate in the Universe. Because of this, I still rarely get to rest much, as I am constantly picking up on the negative forces. It is a perfect system designed by the Perfect Universe, where I am forewarned, so I can take action on behalf of humanity. Armed with the Impeccable Warrior techniques, I no longer fear the dark side, for I know it is the nature of the Light to be victory-us.

However, since I am committed to the Path of Impeccability, I am all-ways AWARE of what is attempting to enter my energetic field. I cannot transform something wisely if I am not aware of its existence and its intensity level. The same goes for you. If you experience fear, see it as a sensing device that alerts you to the presence of evil, but then discard the fear and the disruptive forces that are triggering that fear in you.

ALCOHOL, MEDICINAL DRUGS AND HALLUCINATORY DRUGS

When I was a young girl, many of my friends were involved in using mescaline, LSD and other harsh drugs. They attempted to lure me into partaking of these very popular substances and I asked myself if this was something I wanted to do. A voice within me said very clearly, "Do not take chances with your mind, do not endanger your path". Somehow, due to Grace, I chose to listen to that voice in spite of the immense peer pressure.

I was also surrounded by a youth culture that indulged in smoking of marijuana and large amounts would be put in my hands. Again,

I asked myself if this was something that I wanted to do. I found myself questioning my self as to what type of existence I prayed for each day. The realization dawned upon me that as far back as I could re-call into my childhood…my quest and main objective in Life ha. all-ways been to walk my Path fully conscious.

Even as a tiny child, my focus was all-ways Impeccability and my attention was fiercely focused on finding ways to become more alert and absolutely awake. I could see that the smoking of marijuana and ingesting of other drugs that were floating around me, caused people to go into a world of haziness and dreamy-ness which did not appeal to me. It was quite evident that when these worlds were entered, the person lost their sense of control over their destiny. Thanks to Grace and my Spiritual Protectors, that was enough to alert me and let me know that path was not the one for me.

We can see the face of evil clearly evident in today's prevalent presence of alcohol and drug addiction. Very few people have a strong enough protective shield where they can ingest mind-altering substances and not pay a price. The more sensitive you are, the more this especially applies to you. By indulging in alcohol and other mind-altering substances…including prescription drugs…holes are created in your aura that attract and allow more entities to take up residence in you.

Sometimes we see the immediate effect of a mind-altering substance. For example, some people become ugly and violent, others become sloppy and lewd, while still others become weepy or depressed. We see people of all ages, especially the young ones… succumb to the voice of evil that brainwashes them into taking refuge from the emptiness they feel, by plunging into drugs or alcohol. In other cases, it may seem certain people can handle drinking, recreational or prescription drugs, as it is not as easy to perceive the negative influence those substances are drawing in. Still, whether the effect is evident or not, know that both alcohol and drugs project you into another world.

The question is: are you a prepared and savvy traveller? The truth is most people are not. It is destructive, wicked energies that encourage anyone to catapult their spirit into the abyss of the unknown without proper guidance.

Why would anyone choose to become involved with potentially ruinous substances? Very simply, a sensitive person travels through Life as an exposed nerve. They experience Life's dramas in an intensified way. Unlike the thick-skinned person, who does not take everything so seriously, everything affects the sensitive being to an exaggerated degree. The overly sensitive Soul feels that the pain they see manifest on Planet Earth is tremendous…they are driven to find a way to block it. At this point, the Soul has two choices: take refuge in narcotics, which would then anaesthetize them from the harshness and pain they experience in their realities; or they can take refuge in Grace by embracing a Spiritual Path which can deliver to them the Tranquillity that comes from walking an Impeccable Path. To the weak-willed person, taking numbing substances seems to be easier path, but in the end, it is the most difficult and dangerous.

Of course, it seems very clear to the non-addicted person that drowning your sorrows in numbing substances is not the answer. You would think that the person would automatically choose the Spiritual Path since that is what the soul is yearning for. Yet, after seeing the downward spiral they are being led on, why do people continue to do it? Because once again, the bad company in their energetic field is calling the shots, pushing them to make one pain-producing choice after another. Some people will remain addicted their whole lives, but others will escape the clutches, often through a dramatic spiritual experience and go on to live a Life of Devotion to their destined Spiritual Path.

I once knew a man who was a Beauty-full caring being, a sensitive, Loving soul who never hesitated to extend a helping hand to those who asked for his help. This kind-hearted being could not control his self enough to stay away from the drugs his negative "friends" were involved with. Even though his wife and parents threatened to disown him, he continued in sometimes selling and regularly taking drugs for fifteen years. One day, after a weekend of drug activity, he was sitting in his living room in a stupor and he saw demons appear before him who were trying to drag him to the hellish regions. That experience woke him up and after that he became a committed member of his church, embarking on a Life of Self-less Service to his family and community.

Of course, once he embraced the Spiritual Life, he realized this was what he had been longing for all along. Since he hit bottom and was rescued by Grace, he has remained Faith-full to being fully involved with his church and worshipping community. By nourishing his soul instead of destroying it, he is now radiantly happy in his new Life.

In this man's case, many power-full people who had Faith in their prayers were praying for him for all those years. When someone is not able to escape the clutches of evil habits, one thing leads to another, as with each intake of a mind-altering substance, the holes in the aura become bigger. As the aura becomes torn and tattered, the shield of protection is dissipating and the further one gets lost in that dangerous world of injurious spirits. Imagine that the word gets out on the street that there is a party going on that anyone can get into. Before you know it one bad friend invites three, three invite nine more and those nine invite eighty-one!

This is the way it also works with entities, demons and other worldly attachments. As the crowd of negative voices grows, those malicious energies proceed to convince the person to forget the Sacred Ways and to instead continue to indulge in self-destructive behaviour. We can see this in the ongoing suffering of the Indigenous cultures that were conquered by western society and then pressured, tortured and seduced into forgetting their Wisdom Path. The percentage of the Indigenous population that is addicted to drugs or liquor is staggering. Everyone suffers from these brutal substances and in today's society we see the same symptoms of spiritual amnesia that the Indigenous communities are suffering from.

The Aboriginal culture of Australia and other Indigenous groups recognize that their ancestors were purposely given large amounts of grog to intoxicate them into a state of defenceless-ness. While in this stupor they were easy to sway into forgetting their Ceremonial Ways. Once the dark forces separate someone from the practice of steady spiritual practices, it is easy for evil to move the being into amnesia of the SOURCE of their Strength and power.

At this very moment, the present generations are seeing record percentages of addiction and ruined lives among their people. Once you give in to the seductive negative forces, you become locked into a vicious cycle and what holds true for the Aboriginal community holds true for everyone who ends up in this position.

On the one hand, the forces of darkness are holding them in bondage through addiction. While being held hostage by the sinister habit, they also suffer because their soul longs for the Peace that comes from living a holy and vibrant Life. Since the Indigenous culture carries within it an inherent sensitivity to Nature and the other worlds...the alcohol they quickly became addicted to...swiftly plunged them into a downward spiral. On top of that, since they are so sensitive, it has been difficult for them to extricate themselves from the grip of this evil.

The sensitive Soul yearns to experience oneness with God. The disparity between this yearning...this vision of what Life with God-oneness would be like...and the pain-full reality they perceive on Mother Earth...creates in them a desire to escape by any means.

We have already discussed that the negative forces have scanned everyone and know their make-up very well, so they stir the pot and urge the person to seek imaginary comfort through either numbing substances or through suicide. Eventually, it is all-ways suicide that they are pushing everyone towards. The drinking and the drugs are just a way of creating a downward spiral in the quality of Life so that the person will become totally overwhelmed with negativity and decide they cannot go on living.

However, there is all-ways the other choice, which is total commitment to a Spiritual Path. It doesn't have to be with any particular religion or group, but it does have to be a COMMITTED path, so beings can Strengthen their connection to their Spiritual Protectors, whoever those may be, and the evolution of the Purity of the soul.

For the sensitive person, there can be no middle ground. There is no middle choice. They are too sensitive and must take refuge in something to help them cope with the challenges in Life. Their refuge will either be the dark path or...'The Path Of Light'. They will either choose to plunge into a stupor that allows them to superficially block out the harshness of Life and forget about the meanness, cruelty and ugliness they see around them in the ongoing world events. Or they will choose to ride the boat of Grace across the rocky ocean of Life. There are countless beings that chose the path of numbness, but since they had somehow accumulated enough Grace in either this Life-time or another, at some point in their suffering something happened to divert their path towards the Light. At that critical moment, they were able to grab the Life preserver ring that was cast to them and they embarked upon the path of committed spirituality, instead of remaining in the mire.

Understanding this, you will be able to see the Goodness of the soul of those alcoholics and drug addicts you know or meet. When we look beyond the drug or alcohol induced personality and see who is really there as the original personality, we see a good person with a big heart.

Upon examination of their Life path, we find they encountered experiences that overwhelmed them. A person prone to any degree of addiction...is someone who feels Life is too hard, too ugly and too heavy to manage. Due to a weakness within them, they are not able to summon enough Strength within themselves at crucial moments to remain Faith-full to the Light. They have not yet accumulated enough Grace, so they are not able to commit WHOLEHEARTEDLY to a Spiritual Path and instead choose to travel the harder path, for years or perhaps Life-times.

Some people will argue that they are not addicted, that they just use mind-altering substances for recreation. By tuning out the ensnaring logic of the dark forces, we can easily see that due to the influence of those attached entities that are dedicated to the unhappiness and eventual destruction of these beings, these people are choosing THAT negative path as "recreation" instead of a more wholesome one.

The same person who thinks they are choosing to go into a careless mind state for recreation, yet does not see it as dangerous... is able to make wise Impeccable choices for their Life-style once entirely FREE of the influence of these injurious forces. Liquor, like tobacco, should only be used as a ceremonial OFFERING and not for recreational use.

Lastly, there are people who justify smoking marijuana. These individuals are misguided into thinking it is not a drug and mistakenly believing it is not destructive. When I hear this, I know full well it is the voice of an evil spirit talking through them.

In these cases, that conniving presence has hypnotized them into ignore-ance. I have met many such beings that sought help from Sacred Peace Center and received swift relief from the Mayan Soul Retrieval Limpia and I can tell you that everything we have shared in the Teachings on addictions applies equally to marijuana. It is supremely addictive and those who partake in it find they cannot go very long without being dragged back to their routine visits with this substance. The ever-increasing opening that each puff of this substance creates leads to more addictions in Life, more negativity and more unhappiness. It is especially seductive because the users can continue to function 'normally', however, if they were able to be honest with themselves, the users would see that it inhibits their progress in many aspects of their lives and fills them with self-loathing. The soul knows this is a destructive pattern, and as in all other repetitive detrimental behaviour, the soul longs for Purity and Freedom from the self-induced bondage.

In some Indigenous cultures, there is sometimes the tradition of initiation through hallucinogenic substances. However, this was and is all-ways done with the supervision of a spiritually advanced Teacher who commits to watch over you while you journey into the other worlds. They act as your guide and protector during the whole process. It has never been treated as a casual undertaking and it was not done for recreational thrills but instead, as part of sacred training into the Higher Mysteries.

Some people, however, are so deeply possessed by slick talking entities and will continue to justify to themselves and others, their usage of marijuana, peyote or other substances known for being used in ceremonial ways, by claiming that they are doing it as a way to get closer to Spirit. They have been brainwashed by the dark forces into believing their usage of these substances is part of their "spiritual" path. Upon examination of the energetic field of such a person, it is very clear to me that their substance usage has fragmented them. They are not whole and many things about their lives reflect that they are not whole. They have allowed the sinister forces to convince them that their actions are full of Wisdom', however to the objective observer, it is graphically clear they are not.

This path of false reality is an extremely dangerous path, for each experience with these hallucinogenic drugs is a roll of the dice. It is like playing Russian roulette. You never know what's going to happen each time you spin the revolver. Imagine spinning a revolving door, which accesses infinite pathways into other realms. The reality…is you have no control over who is going to come through this immense portal that has been opened. Real Shamans and other Impeccable Warriors of the Light know this, while amateurs are still in dangerous denial.

I once did a Soul Retrieval Limpia for a woman, 'K', who came to see me because she had witnessed a demon popping out of a friend of hers. 'K' had been in the habit of ingesting peyote and offering peyote to anyone who was going through a tough time. She naively believed that the mind shift they would experience could only benefit them. One day, a friend of hers was very depressed and 'K' gave her friend the hallucinogenic peyote. This triggered a demon making its presence known in a horrifying way before 'K'. Her friend started to race through the house, hopping up and down and actually bouncing around the room, while exuding the stench of the sinister force. 'K' had no idea what to do in the face of the disastrous turn of events, except to pray to her Spiritual Protectors while all this ensued. After her friend raced out of the house, 'K' was left in tears, feeling that some or all of this energy had entered her.

Afterwards, she found herself continually crying, filled with fear. Due to Grace, I was in her area at the time on a Peace Pilgrimage and she listened to the inner longing to contact me for a Soul Retrieval Limpia. She found out the hard way that using mind-altering substances is not fun and games. It is an exceedingly serious undertaking…and once again should only be done when a Master Teacher, Shaman or Spiritual Guide has instructed you that this is part of your training…at THAT particular stage of your evolvement…

Anyone who encourages you to embark upon such a dangerous voyage MUST pledge themselves to your protection and safe journey…taking full responsibility for watching over your physical and spiritual bodies while you journey. Do not settle for empty words…they must be able to deliver…they must have the sufficient Strength, Wisdom and Compassion to protect you impeccably.

Lastly, we should not be longing for these experiences. If we are not ensnared in attachment to these experiences, then we shall be able to discern if the person promising to protect us can actually do so. YOU MUST BE ABLE TO SEE CLEARLY who around you is strong and aligned with the Light and who is just full of talk.

NEVER ENTRUST YOUR SOUL TO A FRAGMENTED INDIVIDUAL. ONLY A GENUINE MASTER WILL CARE FOR YOUR SOUL AS SOMETHING PRECIOUS BEYOND DESCRIPTION.

The Impeccable Warrior is fully aware that they must have their senses fully intact at ALL times. They would not purposefully leave themselves vulnerable to surprise attacks by drugging themselves into a hazy consciousness through any kind of means. The Impeccable focus is on higher awareness, higher alertness, higher Wisdom and recognition. Indulging in alcohol or drugs in any un-ceremonial way without impeccable supervision can only lead to disaster. Why would anyone wish to endanger their mind, body and their soul? The Impeccable Warrior doesn't engage in soul endangering actions.

Beware of the manipulative forces of evil, which never tire of chipping away at person's will power, until they convince them that taking mind-altering substances is a 'cool' thing to do and an action that will have no negative repercussions.

The slick voice of foul energies will pour forth many a propaganda about the benefits of ingesting these substances. However, the truth is, every drop of narcotics ingested pushes us away from Grace, diminishing Balance, intoxicating our Purity and soiling our spirit.

I have been blessed to be granted many amazing gifts by Spirit, which allow me to do Divine Mother's Miraculous Work. I credit my Teachers for EVERYTHING. For only through their Grace, Love and support of my path, have I been able to triumph over dangers and challenges.

It has been my experience that Life will present to you plenty of hardship and dangers, so there is no need to go looking suffering, through foolish behaviour. All of my Teachers were Impeccable Warriors and none of them asked me to take a single mind-altering substance. They were all committed to the Purity of the body, mind and Spirit, and the principle paths for spiritual quantum leaps were:

* Studying the Wisdom Teachings
* Making abundant sacred offerings
* Steady Seva (Self-less Service)
* Regular, disciplined meditation
* Constant repetition of the God's Holy Names through Constant Prayers and Chanting
* Sacred dance
* Peace Ceremonies
* The cultivation of Devotion to one's own spirit

Through these practices I experienced countless cosmic visions and revelations. My dream state was overflowing with constant other-worldly experiences and I therefore instruct people who desire thrills to MEDITATE AND CHANT GOD'S NAMES. In your meditation, you can have cosmic experiences galore and you can spare your finances, body and spirit the costly expenditures.

HOLES: PROTECT YOUR WEAK SPOTS

It is of vital pertinence to self-analyse and to be honest with yourself as to what your weak spots are. For this is where you will be attacked first. We have already established in the section titled, 'There Are No Secrets in the Universe' that negative forces scan you to find openings, to find holes into which they can lodge. How do you recognize your weak spots? It's simple; they are the fears and imbalances you carry within you. For some people, their weak spot might be their mind, for others their body or spirit. This will show up in examples such as an obsessive perfectionist mind, pain-full relationships, illnesses and material or spiritual poverty.

If you were sexually abused as a child, your weak spot would be around your pelvis, in areas such as your hips and legs, along with issues of Trust. If your weak spot is your Spiritual Path it may show up as fear of God, fear of surrender to your Path, lack of Faith and lack of spiritual discipline. If your weak spot is lack of Self-Love it can show up as relationship addictions, insecurities, lack of Self-Confidence and general feelings of not being worthy of Love. These self-destructive perceptions result in a hardened heart and they push away intimacy, Kindness, tenderness and Cooperation.

Your weak spots have their roots in your past Life karmas. This often sets up scenarios in your childhood where you experience deep fear, therefore creating an opening for a dark force to enter into you. For example, if you experienced soul insecurity in the form of poverty, sadness, terror, isolation, repressive-ness…any version of emotional/mental/ physical abuse…this sparked anguish or desperation in you and thereby sent out an intense frequency of pain to the Universe.

The negative forces are just waiting to pounce on anyone and whenever you emanate a negative frequency such as "I fear", this signals the negative forces that you are vulnerable and easy to take over. The negative force will often appear as a voice which basically says "I am your friend, let me help you… I will help you cope…do this, act in this way" and so on. These entities become our 'coping' mechanisms and the way we manage or view Life.

On the one hand, these 'coping' mechanisms do help you cope with high stress/pain. However, because they are entities that are lodged within you they are also a block to your perfect Balance and Serenity. The obsession, anxiety or insecurity will not allow you to truly be in Peace and is like a huge flag or a neon sign that says to other entities and negative energies, "Here's a great landing spot, the landing strip is right here!" This is how the negative forces know where to go to attack you. Imagine your insecurities and dis-balances as being like a huge airport signalling for plane-load after plane-load of psychic terrorists to land and use you as their home base to battle from.

As a result of this invasion some people experience being overly disciplined, over-responsible, overly caring, anxious and depression-prone, over-compensating, people-pleasers, people-haters, overtly weepy and sentimental. Others become ungrounded and spacey; drifting off into escapism such as deep sleep anytime their path seems challenging or depressing.

Still others deal with Life by not feeling Loved no matter how much is given to them. The negative forces attached to the being create ALL of this. When a 'hungry ghost' is attached to you, no matter how much wealth, Love or success you have... no matter how attractive or well known you are, you are still left feeling as if it is not enough. This is where sexual, material, physical and emotional addictions and insecurities stem from. The key to liberation is to assess your own weak spots and take FULL responsibility for the protection and healing of those weak areas through the techniques that are given in this book and any others your path may lead you to discover, which are helpful.

For more knowledge on how holes produce physical suffering see the section on 'Aches and Pains'.

Chapter 5

LEARN THE SIGNS – IDENTIFYING & DISSOLVING GHOSTS, ENTITIES & DEMONS

We must all ways remember we are sacred sparks of the most Radiant Light. This is your true nature! Any image or thought crossing your mind screen...which obscures this brilliant nature of yours...is a signal alerting you to the presence of evil.

How do you know when you are 'possessed'? When you feel: unhappy, un-inspired, angry, depressed, frustrated...resent-full, resistant, inflexible, spite-full, uncooperative...envious, jealous, unsupported, calculating, scheming...disrespect-full, overly driven, obsessed or un-balanced...in any type of pain or sense of victim-hood.... This is only a partial checklist.

There are many ways demons can lodge themselves in you. Dark forces are the voices that justify negative choices and behaviour, or make you feel guilty, small, unworthy, tainted, not good enough and in lack. They use you to add confusion, despair, anger and sadness to the Earth plane by embroiling you in all these emotions and reactions.

You can identify the presence of sinister forces by self-destructive images that flash across your mental screen, or thought patterns and behaviour that are out-of-Balance and out-of-Harmony with the Spiritual Laws of Peace-full living. The key to spotting them quickly, before they establish deep roots in your Life, is to observe everything that crosses your mind screen. Know that only negative forces plant negative images or thought in your mind...self-loathing, deprecation or arrogant egotism is never sponsored by the Forces of Light.

Any negative thought form is actually the voice of evil talking into your ear. It is vital to realize your friends, family and the rest of humanity go through the same scenario--their negative behaviour also stems from the negative forces attached to them. When you maintain this awareness you can stop blaming your-self or others for the constant stream of ensuing negative actions.

Of course this does not mean that we allow the negative behaviour to go on unchecked or uncorrected. The purpose of spotting the negative forces is so that you can immediately stop them from influencing you or your Loved ones and in this way, avert suffering and pain. **Most people mistakenly believe that they are their thoughts.** You can free yourself from wrong-full feelings about who you are and what you perceive yourself to be when you remember that the thoughts that cross your mind screen are simply a reflection of the energies around you. The negative forces will all-ways attempt to contaminate the mind by whispering ugly, dirty, perverted, weak, deceptive, sad, shameful, victim-like thought forms into your Divine instrument: the Glory-us Mind of Light.

We must all ways remember we are sacred sparks of the most Radiant Light. This is your true nature! Any image or thought crossing your mind screen...which obscures this brilliant nature of yours...Is a signal alerting you to the presence of evil.

You must not believe the defeatist. You must not believe the deprecating 'self-talk' the sinister forces are trying to program unto you. They want you to feel ashamed. Forces of degradation and depravity desire for you to feel tired, addicted, depressed, unworthy, angry, frustrated, a victim and separate from your true Divine nature. They hunger for you to believe that you cannot succeed at your great visions and dreams. They desire for you to cry, wail and feel that nothing ever works out for you. They want you to see the seeming imperfection in others, Life and the Universe. Their aim is for you to feel tainted, weak, resentful, bitter, sad, insignificant and powerless!

When you accept their mind-corrupting techniques, you have allowed them to succeed. It is the nature of evil to keep attacking you by filling you with these self-deprecating notions. But once again, this is not who you truly are and to be an Impeccable Warrior, you must never take on the negative qualities that they are trying to impose upon you. DO NOT BELIEVE THEIR PROPAGANDA! REJECT IT! An Impeccable Warrior all-ways chooses to break free of Soul-belittling bondage!

How do we break their spell? By refusing to listen to their low vibration chatter and instantly casting them out. Here are some simple ways to do that:

1.   Snap your figures three times and make a sign of a sacred symbol, such as the cross, either over you or in the air in front of you. If you or your child cannot snap your fingers, you can also clap your hands three times. This should be done with a sense of power and commitment, not in a weak way. Show you mean it! Everything we use in spiritual work has an inherent power, but we give it more power by doing it with great Gusto and flair! So when I make the sign of the cross in the air in front of me, I end my motion with a fling of my hand into the air sending forth a powerful energetic wave. The snapping sound has power, making the sign of the cross bestows its power and the energy we back up the action with infuses the exercise with potency. All of this, along with our Faith in the protection available to us as Divine Beings, enables you to drive out negative influences. Children and people who are naturally dramatic find this easy to do!

2.   I am neither Catholic nor Christian…however I am often moved to use the sign of the cross for my protection as well as the defence of others and in binding a place against attack. The cross symbol is a universal primordial symbol for protection and wholeness, which was utilized eons before the Christians and Catholics adopted it in their practices. You can use any symbol that fills you with the sense of protection. To me, the cross is a symbol that shouts to the dark forces, "Stop! Hands off! This is Sacred Ground and I am off limits to you!" This ancient symbol declares you are unavailable to dark forces and tells them, "You have no right to be here!" World traditions have other symbols they utilize for the

same purpose and you can adopt those symbols in addition to or instead of the cross. Whichever symbol and words you implement should convey the message that you belong to the Divine Forces… that your home, mind, body and spirit is a Temple for the Light. Make it clear to malicious energies that you are only available to the Compassionate Forces of Good and that malevolent energies are forbidden to enter or stay in your mind, body, spirit, home or land.

    3.   Order them out by giving a simple and direct command such as "Get out! I order you to leave in the name of _____!. You can command them to leave in the name of any Light Being you have Faith in, whoever you feel you can count on for protection. For example you can take refuge in Jesus, Mary, Buddha, Kali, Durga, Tara, Shiva, the Ascended Masters or any other being or Divine presence that brings you a sense of empowerment and Peace. This can also include Celestial Forces such as 'The Divine Power of Love', "The Legions of Light" or 'All that is Sacred and Holy'. For example, you can say, "I order you to leave in the name of God's All-Powerful Light!" or, "I belong to the Light, I choose the Light, if you are not committed to the purest Light, I order you to leave now!"

As you make sacred defence a part of your Life, you will find you are naturally drawn to respond to attacks immediately by issuing your commandments of protection, snapping your fingers and making protection symbols over you or in front of you.

Once you understand that dark thoughts are not your thoughts you will no longer invest your precious Golden Energy in those negative images. You will no longer claim those false limiting pictures as a decree of who you are. You will instead see them as harm-full illusions that foul energies are spinning into your mind. By learning the many ways in which dark forces will strive to confuse you and all humanity, you will no longer be manipulated into self-destructive behaviour and reactions.

Armed with knowledge, you will more easily detect the appearance of vile forces in your thoughts, emotions and body. You will begin to realize that whenever they are near you or in your surroundings, some type of sign or sensation will alert you to their vicious presence. You will no longer get caught up in their hate-full projections and mistakenly accept it as a judgment of your innate Goodness and Purity. The key to Happiness is to live in this new awareness, which frees you to Love yourself as a Lovable, Beauty-full, Light-filled child of God. Once you cast off the shadow that had been flung upon you by dark forces…and refuse to let them enshroud you any longer…you can proceed to live Life to your highest Divine potential, every day!

ACHES AND PAINS

There may be moments when you will feel as if you are being pinched or pushed. At times you may feel as if you have been beaten up, sore or achy even though your physical activity does not warrant those reactions. You may also feel a sharp pain all of a sudden. The negative forces cause this and it is an alarm that a sinister energy has just crossed your path.

Remember, negative forces attack your weak spots. For example if someone has been sexually abused as a child, they would tend to feel pain in their hips or within the womb when been attacked by negative energies. If the dark forces cause you to feel as if you carry the world on your back, your upper, middle or lower back will be where you will feel the pressure of the attack.

Whenever you feel under psychic assault is important to wear a band of gold around your hips. Gold underwear can also be utilized for protection. For outer-wear you can wear gold or any of the colours of the rainbow. Stick to Strength-giving colours. Stay away from dark brown, any shades of grey or black. Only a few people are strong enough to wear the dark colours and make them work for them.

At different times of our growth, there will be particular colours that will attract negative forces into our bodies in the form of aches and pains. For example, if you are already experiencing aches and pains, in most cases it would not be wise to wear red either, as it can intensify the pain. Although red represents Life Force and energy such as seen in healthy blood…it is also a flag that attracts attack. Hence, the bull-fighters use a red cape to antagonize and hold the focus of the bull. Note also that red automobiles are known to receive more speeding citations than other colours! Red is an exciter and provokes reaction and hostility as well, so if you are striving to heal or relax, it is not a wise hue to surround yourself with. Although there can be exceptions to this, that is the general rule of thumb.

In some cases, the result of psychic attack will produce physical symptoms that are recognized by the medical profession. On the other hand, many people experience aches and pains that cannot be explained by the medical community. Either way, the FACT is that if you have a weakness in your body, when the negative forces attack, they will aggravate that area. So if your weak links are your knees or your shoulders then the psychic attack will highlight the frailty and cause pain in that area. Aches and pains can also reveal additional specifics of the energies causing the suffering. Back problems, for example, can be a sign of people talking about you behind your back, envy, judgments, jealousies, burdens, guilt, money issues ... or any other form of lack of support.

Time and time again I see that when we dissolve some or all of the demons that are attached, there is instantly a new reality for that person. I have seen the Spiritual Laws in action as I observe a stream of people from all walks of Life healed by the Divine Work we offer at Sacred Peace Center. Although people come to us carrying torment caused by such an immense variety of physical symptoms, as soon as the Soul Retrieval Limpia was I performed over them, the person's protective shield was Strengthened. As an intense shower of Divine Mother's Grace was bequeathed by their Spiritual Protectors and mine...a. immense infusion of Light/Grace/Spiritual Protection took place, power-fully blasting out the demons lodged in the karmic holes.

Each time I witness this, I find that the person before me actually feels something jump out of them, often times as their body reacts with a sudden jerk. In one case, I was doing a Limpia over a woman who was diagnosed with lung cancer. Of course, the attached entities were pushing her to continue to smoke, even though she could hardly breathe. On top of that the spite-full demons had been fuelling bitterness within her to the point where everyone else in her family viewed her as a cold-hearted, self-centered, tact-less and mean person. During the Soul Retrieval session she asked if her sister could stay in the room and permission was granted. While doing the Mayan Prayers over her, I saw a hideous entity lunge at me. After we finished, the sister asked me, "Did you see what I saw? I saw a demon jump right out of her and run out of the room during the session!" I acknowledged that I did indeed see it and explained to her that I sometimes see the entities while at other times I sense their presence.

SEEING SHADOWS

We all see shadows out of the corner of our eyes, zipping by, however people often dismiss what they have seen…telling themselves it's a figment of their imagination. But those shadows do exist…and you and everyone else has seen them. These are spirits that will hide in dark spaces, such as closets, cupboards, attics, under beds and in basements. The question is: who are they and what do they need from you, in order to be released.

Sometimes when someone passes to the other side, their spirit may come to your home to say goodbye. Years ago my nephew, along with The Oracle Shree Dayananda, visited me. This was during a period in which Shree Dayananda and I were doing full battle with dark forces, as part of our training. As you can imagine, my nephew was plunged into a fast growth by living in the same residence. One night, he found his attention being drawn to the crack at the bottom of his door. He was able to see a shadow zip back and forth throughout the night. The next morning he asked me if I had been walking back and forth in the hallway in front of his room. When I told him I had not left my room all night, we knew we had a visitor. At that time we had quite a few 'visitors' making their presence known in different ways. One 'visitor' would not let me sleep. As soon as I'd close my eyes, an invisible energy would pull my right leg and jerk me awake. This went on for days, with me being awakened every few minutes, all night long.

Since I didn't know who it was and had not deduced if it was a positive or negative energy, I started sleeping out on the patio. I instinctively knew being outdoors, in fresh air with the sky and moon as my view, I would be charged with power and a heightened Intuition to provide me with clarity. Once I was sleeping in nature, I suddenly began to wonder if Don Vicente, a Mayan Shaman I had been in contact with, had passed away. He had been on his deathbed when I last saw him. I found out later that he had indeed been calling my name over and over when he crossed to the other side. He obviously had been trying to contact me to give me a message.

It is very important to say prayers for these shadows. Let them know that if they have a message for you to give it to you in a way you will understand. Declare that if they are negative forces they must leave. You can communicate many things to them in many ways, but the important thing is to make it clear that your house is a temple dedicated to Mother God/Father God and nothing negative can stay there. Let them know they have to move on to the Light and in your own way, call on the Light to illuminate their path and uplift them. Your invocation does not have to be complex, just say it with conviction. You can use prayers you know from the Bible or other traditions, such as the protection mantra, Kali Durge Namo Nama. By stating a purpose before beginning any prayer, the intention will deliver the prayer to the right mailbox, in a sense.

We recorded the Kali Durge Namo Nama Mantra to full-fill Divine Mothers Will that all humanity, especially children, have easy ways to call forth their protection and dispel negative forms (see back of book for ways to order this). Before or after repeating the mantra or prayer, make a statement such as:
"I call upon _____(Divine Mother's All Power-full Grace, God's All Transforming Light, the Violet Flame of Protection and Compassion, and so on) to come forth and dissolve any negative energies present.

Remove them immediately and uplift them to their highest destiny! I command them to go to the Light and leave me and this place in Peace!"

It is up to you as to whether you wish to just ask for their removal, or wish to also call for their liberation from the overall force of evil, from the darkness. Your commands will have more power if you contemplate as much as possible what exactly you wish to ask for beforehand. During your quiet moments of review you can receive Clarity on what you believe...what you have Faith in...and what you wish for these beings/energies who are stuck. By contemplating and achieving Clarity, you will be able to be one-pointed in your declarations to the Universe of Compassion.

A secret to empower your prayers, mantra, affirmation or declaration is to repeat it nine, twenty-seven or one hundred and eight times. But how much progress you will make in any one attempt will be determined by how thick, stuck or stubborn the energy is that you are trying to move.

There are some properties that are flooded with spirits who are trapped there because of the violent way they died. Wherever you go, there are areas that experienced battles, massacres, earthquakes, tidal waves, hurricanes, flooding, and other events in which groups of people were all killed at once. The spirits lingering there are still full of sadness or anger at their sudden death...or the particular way their Life ended. When you encounter large numbers of spirits, it requires a lot more work. Often times repeated work is necessary in order to move a large number of Souls to the Light. If you can feel energy in a location...by training yourself to pay heightened attention...you will develop the ability to see their energetic forms moving about. In one of my other books, 'The Shamanic Healing Art Journal' gives further Teachings on this subject.

PSYCHIC SERPENTS

In our physical existence and the dream world there are serpents that will chase you and bite you as well as benevolent serpents that can show up in your Life to give you positive messages. In the psychic world, negative energy can show up in the form of little black serpents. Those beings whose psychic eyes are open, can see them zip by as they slither on the floor, if they pay close attention to the signs around them at all times. Even if you cannot see them, sometimes you can sense them crawling over your feet or feel their bites. Yet, when you look, nothing will seem to be there. As negativity builds up in a place, the serpents multiply and in an extremely negative space, you can wind up with the floor covered with them.

One day a woman came to see me to discuss the unhappiness in her family's home. She herself was a tortured being, with many problems, anxieties, fears, and insecurities. She began to tell me about the home and her experiences of psychic attack there. After hearing only a little bit of the ongoing drama, I shared with her that I felt the source of the family's torment was due to the house being possessed by an evil presence. She admitted that she did sense a dark energy in the house and proceeded to tell me that whenever she fell asleep, she would experience small dark serpents wrapping themselves around her wrists, tie-ing her down. She would then not be able to move, as one horrible image after another appeared on her mental screen while she tried to rest.

A student of mine had a home that was over-run with psychic serpents as a result of the ongoing build up of negativity between himself, his mother and his wife. The constant arguments and general lack of Harmony kept those serpents breeding, yet up until he received these Teachings he was not able to acknowledge their presence. Up until the moment he accepted the Impeccable Warrior Of Light Golden Knowledge, he had been in denial on what he had been seeing and sensing.

After receiving the Impeccable Warrior of Light Wisdom, he proceeded to pay greater attention to everything around him and was then able to see the serpents out of the corners of his eyes, as they speedily slithered by. One day, he could feel that the whole floor was covered with their little black bodies. He used a house cleansing kit and when he returned, he sensed the place was littered with dead serpents. They had been there for a long time but only now was he able to perceive them.

The key to perceiving them is to remain awake...aware...and you can do that by praying each day to be able to maintain your Higher Vision. Pray to be an Impeccable Warrior of Light so you are EASILY able to tune in and sense everything that is taking place around you. This insight will allow you to make informed decisions as to what action is the most the appropriate for each case.

CHILDREN

Most children are powerful, magical, in-tune beings. So they come to this planet armed with most of what they will need to succeed in this Life. As a parent…you can help them most by re-minding them of the training…and tools available to them for dealing with the unseen worlds. They have already done this work in past lives and they carry the memory of it in their cellular body. Some children remember chunks of past lives clearly and others will remember more after they acquire further training. Either way, just as you had to confront dealing with different aspects of darkness…disdain-full forces will constantly be interacting with all children. By setting an example of vigilance, you are giving them the training they need to walk through Life fully aware. When you set the example for your children by Respecting your Golden Energy, you are gifting them the ultimate Wisdom with which to blaze a trail of the brightest Light wherever their Path takes them.

Child Abuse

Child abuse is an evil that has been present in most cultures for a much longer time than you can imagine. It has been prevalent in past ages and is quite rampant at this time on our planet. It is normally a generational issue, meaning that there is a history of it in the previous generation and the generations before. In our society, when we hear of someone molesting children or performing any other cruel or ugly action…you often hear people ask "What could have possessed them to do such a thing?" The fact that the word 'possessed' is used shows us that the generations before us understood that all abuse is the result of negative energies possessing someone and then using them to destroy Purity.

All molestation, infringement and abuse is the result of a power-full demon taking over someone, to steal power from another being. It is a karmic set-up and we will talk more on that in the section on

'Incest and Abuse'. Children come into this world already totally open, so they see and sense everything around them. They see spirits, Fairies, Angels and Spirit Guides easily, until enough grown-ups around them pressure the child to shut down their senses and ignore their feelings.

Since they are supremely sensitive, they see and feel both the positive and negative energies around them. If you watch a baby's eyes and pay attention to their facial expressions, you will see they are aware of the unseen worlds and the unspoken thought forms floating around them. Whenever I have performed a Soul Retrieval Prayer around or upon a baby, they giggle, gurgling happily and their eyes become wide open...as they bathe in Divine Mother's luminous radiance. Their faces reveal Soul satisfaction, showing they are bursting with delight at the sight of Golden Beings floating in the room. By remaining aware that your child could be an old Soul in a small body, you will re-member how important it is to listen to them, honour their feelings and insights.

Most children are pure and untainted, so they represent the purest power here on Mother Earth. The demons know that if they can taint the child's Purity they have broken the child's power-full spirit. The force of evil knows that children are living, breathing unconditional Love. Each child that can be torn away from the magical, mystical world of Light they live in and thrown into the dark world of fear, anxiety, self-doubt, and low self-esteem, is a victory for the wicked forces. When any kind of traumatic abuse occurs in a child's Life, it is the work of the dark forces that are attempting to rob the child of the sacred Trust of Life and God. It is the force of evil, attempting to convince the being to turn away from their Angels and Spirit.

Incest and Sexual Abuse

We have now covered that the demons possess people and then utilize them to break the spirit of the purest beings, which are the children. Sexual energy is sacred and is the power that propels our spiritual evolvement. It opens doors to Knowledge and was not meant to become an addictive activity. Sexual energy should be focused on experiencing one-ness with God...utilised for accessing the Pure

Ecstasy of our God nature. By engaging in it in a scientifically holy way, sexual energy connects you further with your Light Body.

When this energy is contaminated and associated with shame, it robs the child of this connection and propels them on a long journey to discard the shame associated with it until the day when they can re-connect firmly with Wisdom, Self-Respect and the Love the Universe has for them.

In the Vedic (scriptural) traditions of India this sexual/spiritual energy is known as Kundalini. The Kundalini energy is coiled at the end of the spine and proceeds to move up through the body's energetic spiritual centres (Chakras) as we engage in spiritual practices. The Life purpose of each being is to awaken and activate this sacred Kundalini. With each level or Chakra it is raised to…the more Wisdom becomes accessible to us… and the more the Universe within is revealed.

It is taught that it is dangerous for the Kundalini to be awakened within the human being too abruptly. When this energy is shocked by being activated at too young of an age it is said that the serpent-like Kundalini flips its normal position and becomes inverted. This then obviously causes an un-balance within the individual by over-stimulating this base centre. Because the base centre has been blasted open before the being has developed the awareness to deal with all the issues that go along with sexual activity, the child is catapulted into the world of desire, repulsion, shame, denial and confusion. So many pain-full experiences are set up for someone with this kind of karma. Through all this chaos, the demon forces are successful in robbing the child of its innocent connection to Spirit.

The shock, ensuing abuse, shame, fear and all other related emotions over sexual abuse is then imprinted into the areas of the body abused. The demons controlling the abuser and the Destiny of the abused, know that these issues will continue to keep the abused child's soul fragmented. Those clever dark forces are fully aware that this fragmentation gives the dark forces a Life-time gateway through which to enter and trigger angst in the being. Through sexual abuse, the harm-full forces then affect how the child later relates to relationships…sexual activity…their Protectors, the Light and Spiritual Path.

When sexual molestation of any kind occurs, to anyone of any age, it is an attempt of the dark forces to rob that person of dignity. It is a way of scattering the person's energy by humiliating them. This often leaves the child feeling rejected by God and the Angels, or infused with a deep rooted anger and resentment towards their Spiritual Protectors, while others are launched into a belief that they were being punished for the sins of past incarnations. By freezing someone in a pain-filled past, the sinister forces keep them from focusing on realizing their Highest Destiny.

Why do the dark forces do this? It is the nature of negative energies to steal power, to steal Goodness, to tear at Purity. The darkness absolutely hates The Light and all Purity. The purer something is, the more they want to violate it and the power of a child is the purest power. The dark forces do not want the pure power within that Soul to expand...evil knows as the child grows, any unhampered power will multiply and increase into awesome power, so they must crush the child's potential by stealing the very essence of the Soul's spiritual being. In doing so they have now distracted this child from the world of pure power...and cast them into a world of guilt, shame, confusion and overall darkness.

It is a perfect tactic for the negative forces to influence weak people to molest and abuse children. Obviously the intention of the negative forces is for the abused one to stay locked into a Life-time of anger, shame, blame and victim-hood.

The Impeccable Warrior of Light is cognizant that the ultimate victory is to unplug from the drama and bless and release the past. As long as we choose to hang on to the pain, we are never free of the past, for with each flashback, with each spark of self-recrimination or blame of others, we are re-living the hideous moment once again! Once we understand that everything in Life is a karmic set-up to help us master the lesson our Higher-Self created for us, we can accept that the abuser was simply playing their important part in our Soul Journey.

I realize that forgetting and forgiving the past can be difficult for most people. I promise you that when the Soul earns enough merit...and is flooded with Grace...anyone who was abused or an abuser...can and will release the past and turn over a new Leaf. Through Grace this can occur and once it does, the being can then serve humanity with immense Compassion.

Let us remember that the force of evil itself generates all negative behaviour. The abuser is also cast into a world of karmic repercussions as they have incurred karmic debt through their destructive actions. It is the driving negative entity that is propelling the abuser into misguided, vile, self-satisfying behaviour.

As an Impeccable Warrior we adhere to the teaching of 'no mud or blood on our hands'. This means that whatever you choose to do as far as righting a perceived wrong...should be done without hate, anger or sense of vengeance. We must at all times remember that we are never victims of any-thing or any-one and that all experiences in Life carry at least one blessing and usually many.

It is our spiritual home-work to recognize and appreciate the boons within the lessons that seem tough and harsh, instead of only welcoming conditions which are immediately pleasing to us. It is our Sacred Duty to pray for the upliftment of all those who have crossed our path in a seemingly 'good' or seemingly 'bad' way. In this way we "rise above" and leave behind that which attempted to lock us into eternal suffering through soul pain.

Any direct involvement with abuse is all-ways an experience that will have a tremendous impact on anyone. Such profound impact reveals that this is a major karmic lesson and discloses how imperative it is for us to master it once and for all. For this reason, we blame no one and hate nothing. The Impeccable Warrior of Light honours the Teaching that this is a perfect Universe where each person is in the perfect classroom at all times in order to receive the perfect Divine training for their perfect soul expansion.

This does not mean that anyone should tie themselves down on the railroad tracks and just sit there and wait for the train to run them over repeatedly. Let us remember that the point of existence is Mastery, not misery, not wallowing! The sooner you can blast your way through an experience, the better for you and for all of humanity.

Children's Protection: Listen To The Children

Since a child's Intuition is still firmly established it is vital to watch the children attentively and Respect their reactions. They are so pure that they 'see' or sense so much more than the adults around them. But if you condition them to deny their experiences, they will deny them. However, in doing so it will cause a huge fragmentation in their power and set them up for an onslaught of psychic attacks.

Because they see so much psychic activity around them, don't make them sleep in the dark if it bothers them. Let them have as much Light in a room as they need to feel supported and at Peace. I know many adults who still prefer to sleep with the Light on and I encourage them to continue to do so. By turning off the lights, it just gives the negative presence more Freedom to act up and create disturbances. In some cases this just makes it harder to get solid rest, whereas, in other situations a darkened space gives them full liberty to terrorize. Not everyone needs to sleep with a Light on, in fact some people sleep better in the dark. They are beings I call Cave Dwellers. Their whole being functions better on low lighting. Beings with karmic roots to Solar cultures or Tree Top dwellings need high amounts of Sun Light, day Light and bright lighting. They have no trouble sleeping with the lights on. Regardless of which type of karmic roots you have, whenever you feel a dark energy stalking your space, one of the best ways to cut their party short is to turn on the lights in the room or entire house.

If you sense a negative presence around you and you have difficulty sleeping, it is often possible to move that energy by cleansing the space with sacred smoke (smudging) or other protection techniques. You will know if you have moved that negative presence out, by how comfortable you feel and whether your energetic body is able to relax. If you feel the energy has shifted and sense that it is safe to turn the lights out or down, then do so. But if you don't feel that, then know that it is wise to keep the lights on as it makes it harder for negative energies to move about and play their games.

If children report seeing monsters, goblins, or anything scary, it is important to Respect their feelings. They are obviously seeing an ominous form and it is vital you quickly give them a protection routine that they can use whenever disturbed. It is comforting for the child to have you by their side…joining forces with them against the darkness with techniques you teach them…or they teach you! Keep in mind that whatever you share with them should be simplified enough that they can master it easily and therefore feel fully empowered in using it.

One of my young students is extremely sensitive and therefore she is constantly attacked in different ways. For a period of time her mother reported that she would literally jump out of bed in the morning, exclaiming that there were witches under the bed who would grab at her feet and bite them if she placed them on the floor. Her mother became very creative and gave her daughter a toy whip and taught her that whenever the witches tried to bother her she could crack the whip on the witches. She kept the whip by her when she slept and found it kept the mean witches away and eventually they disappeared all together.

Both this little girl, 'S', and her sister, 'P' see many things… but 'S' is affected by it all more than 'P'. Not long ago 'S' started seeing a large Aboriginal male spirit outside her window. Then she had a dream/vision of him moving about outside her house, throwing stones in an area towards the back of their property. I instructed her to make some offerings of birdseed or mustard seed in the area, calling in protection for her family and this was enough to bring Peace back to the land surrounding their home.

Another child, 'R' was brought in to see me because he was having trouble sleeping due to continual nightmares. Upon questioning his mother, she shared that he had been reporting seeing an apparition in the house that was a combination of two animals. When this four year old arrived for his appointment, he was wearing his blue cape his mother had made him to help him feel protected. He had asked her to sew gold coloured stars all over it. The blue cape was a shade I call Divine Mother Blue…electric blue. She said he refused to take it off since the nightmares began to occur. I took one look at him and knew he had been a sorcerer or magician in another Life-time…for it is written all over his face. He was also wearing a cap and when I looked at his outfit, I said to him, "This is your power outfit for protection isn't it?" Of course, he nodded "Yes" emphatically.

A three year old came by to visit me one day and we went outside to make Sacred Offerings to the land. He is an old soul whose Sacred Memory of the Ceremonial Ways is quite intact.

Due to this, I give him instructions but then attentively observe how he carries out the guidance. On this day, I asked him to take some cornmeal and birdseed to make offerings to the Fairies in our garden. He proceeded to do it in his own way and I noticed that there was one particular spot that he kept pouring large amounts of cornmeal into. I had taught him about offering to seven Cardinal Points, yet he seemed absolutely focused on that one place. His mother went to correct him reminding him that I had instructed him to feed the seven Directions, but I stopped her and encouraged him to continue what he was doing. Afterwards I reminded her that he sees things she doesn't because of his Purity. The children are wise and if you pay attention to what they sense…to what they are drawn to and what they are repelled by, they can give you an insight into the energies around them and you.

RECOGNIZING ENTITIES IN YOURSELF AND OTHERS

You can recognize the presence of an entity through the occurrence of any of the following: vile or self-destructive tendencies such as nose picking, nail biting, picking or inflicting cuts upon yourself, drawing negative or evil images on your body, steely, cold or empty gaze in the eyes, addictions, ugly qualities such as anger, attachment, greed, cruelty, lust and so on. Fear-full qualities such as insecurities, lack of Faith, jealousy, obsessions and any other weaknesses are all signs indicating the presence of psychic leeches.

What is the antidote to all gloomy, hostile, diminishing, discordant and conflictive forces and activity. Sacred ritual, Ceremonial offering to the Legions of Light and Forces of Compassion! However you do it…and whatever you choose to do…the main element is to do the work with tremendous Strength and Intention.

The rocket ship requires tremendous fuel and interaction of many factors in order to break the grip of gravity and with each opportunity to employ ritual, you are also launching a rocket ship, breaking free of previously accepted limiting energy. Ritual helps us to be bold… it is the fuel needed in order to boost us out of that classroom.

By choosing to see the energetics in play in every situation and engaging in prayer and ritual, we are able to lift-off like the rocket ship and break free of the Earth's gravity, which has convinced us we are limited, power-less beings. Sacred sound, ritual and dance shatter the layers of density that bog down our spirit.

The fire created by holy ritual, sacred sound and movement pushes us to new realities. Once we blast past old familiar realities, we rise to higher perspectives…discovering WE HAVE WINGS… AND WE CAN FLY.

This is when WE CONNECT WITH OUR Higher-Self and taste first-hand that scrumptious nectar the Seers, Mystics and Saints have promised us…the boundless Joy of knowing WE ARE Divine… PURE Light…CHERISHED AND FOREVER PROTECTED BY THE Light.

Chapter 6

HOW TO SPOT THE DARK FORCES
LIVING IN YOUR HOME

You may feel you've seen something or you may sense it on you as in the case of the psychic serpents on your feet or up your leg. The signs will be subtle and at other times very graphic, the important thing is all-ways to pay attention and not ignore the presence of these menacing forces.

As explained in the section on 'Psychic serpents' you may have already seen and sensed sinister energies in your home. You just need to tune in to your 'knowing', your inherent Wisdom, so you can acknowledge (acceptance of knowledge) what you see. The more you tune in to your innate Wisdom, the more you will realize that what you have sensed in the past was indeed real. By using your 'soft vision', you will become increasingly adept at perceiving the spirit world. When you Trust your soft vision you will be able to admit that you have often seen energetic forms or shadows zipping by you, out of the corner of your eye.

To see more, and see clearer, you will need to use this soft vision, as the other worlds are not all-ways detectable when looking at them directly. Trust what you feel…what you sense. You may feel you've seen something or you may sense it on you, as in the case of the psychic serpents crawling on your feet or up your leg. The signs will sometimes be subtle, at other times intensely graphic… the important point is to all-ways pay attention and not ignore the presence of these menacing forces. The following are ways negative energies will reveal their selves to you:

Death

If there is a string of deaths in a family or group, this indicates the presence of evil, which MUST be transformed immediately in order to change the future. Some souls try to take 4 or 5 others with them. There are many dynamics that cause this and the wisest action towards prevention would be for every person to receive a Soul Retrieval Limpia after the death of a close relation. This not only changes the Destiny for the better, but also accelerates the healing process helping the individual release grief and any other negative emotions. It opens the channel to Hope, Trust and a positive infusion, enabling the individual to move forward quickly and strongly. This can also apply to the death of close friends. There are boundless cases of beings who are ill, that remain alive by siphoning energy from those close to them. This weakens the supporting friends/family member and puts them at risk of an earlier death than was their original Destiny. Soul Retrieval Limpias change this chain of events, blocking Death…if it is God's Will. Clearing the space, all residents and those related to them is a move in the right direction.

• You should become alarmed if you have a series of deaths among pets. Since pets are Protectors, they will take the energetic hit first, absorbing the ills that head your way.

• If your pets are constantly getting ill, or one after another dies, this is a clear sign that the negative energies in your home has been allowed to build up to dangerous levels and needs to be cleaned out immediately and impeccably.

Disharmony In The Household

I have seen many cases where families who interacted harmoniously, suddenly find themselves in a downhill slide of daily discord. As disruptive forces do their evil work, the family experiences an emotional distance that sets in, creating an environment where family members no longer agree on matters. People who were once close and Harmony-usly spent time together find they suddenly cannot bear to be around each other.

• Arguments, stress and violence with household members and miscommunication are all omens of malicious visitors.

• Sometimes this happens after moving into a new residence.

The resident spirits proceed to attack everyone's mind, stirring up antagonism and making everyone irritable.

•   There are times Peace unravels as a result of someone bringing home negative energies with them. For example, a woman shared with me of a home she visited, when looking for a change of residence. The owner of the home was looking for a roommate and amiably gave this woman a tour of the home. The woman commented to the owner on feeling a presence in the hallway and the man admitted that he had also felt its presence for a long period of time. He further explained that soon after he and his girlfriend moved in, they began to battle with each other incessantly. Due to the constant arguments, they found themselves drifting apart more and more to the point where she decided to leave him. She left their home and the relationship. After she left, he found himself wallowing in depression.

The visiting woman was a student of these Teachings and she was persistent in asking pertinent questions about the history of the house. Due to her diligence, as he was speaking of the episode, Grace lifted clouds from his mind and he realized the man who lived in the house before him had died in the house. It was further re-called that the previous owner had also lived alone for many years, while suffering from depression. In that case the same scenario had taken place: a couple had moved in, they were compatible beings but after being affected by the energies of the house and perhaps also of the land/area, the relationship had crumbled and the man had been left in a mire of sadness.

Negative Attitudes

Any negative states of mind that derail you, hold you prisoner or block your soul expansion and highest expression as a Divine, Blissfull being, are sponsored by ruinous forces. These self-destructive attitudes include defeatism, pessimism, wallowing, resistance, self-pity, self-indulgence, laziness, cowardice, indecisiveness, cynicism, sarcasm, greed, resentment, cruelty, lying, distorting and exaggerating the truth, and cold-heartedness. This is only a partial list and I am sure each of you can add more to it as you ponder the widespread work of the evil ones and the way they side-track Humanity from serving Life and the Light within with Radiance…Honour…Humility…and Dignity! The many imbalances that promote suffering stem from insatiable desires for elements other than God Realization. We see the chain of suffering held in place by disorders, sexual addiction, pathological liars and cheaters…gambling, drug and alcohol enslavery…raging and ruthless hunger for power, crippling need for approval and more such pathetic behaviour. This is all due to the soul being possessed and therefore manipulated by forces that hate us and the Light/God/Goodness. It is up to each of us to do everything we can to focus our attention on our own Enlightenment and this begins with proper Spiritual Protection.

Accidents

If you find that you or anyone in your family has an accident or is suddenly besieged by a string of accidents, it is time to do an energetic inventory and pinpoint the malicious force that is setting up these situations in order to handicap you.

Accidents can result in a loss of mobility, income, and positive Life-style which then has a domino effect triggering conditions such as depression, anger, blame, regrets and so on, all of which the vicious energies revel in.

An example of this is where an accident would lead to a lack of physical activity that would then result in degenerated health. In this way, the negative forces begin chipping away at the foundation that sustains your Life, with the full intent to continue to push you down further. You must stop them before they go any further for your future is at stake!

Pets

• Like children, pets are supremely psychic and since pets are self-less caring Protectors of humans, they take the energetic blow, absorbing the harm that was intended for their owners.

• You should watch over your pets care-fully, observing their behaviour and health, for they easily sense and see the invisible worlds. Note how their eyes and ears react, noticing when they sense things you may not see or hear.

•   If your pet continues to become ill or remains sick, it is usually a sign of a strong presence in the house or on the property. One woman who came to see me for a consultation had several pets that repeatedly developed cysts all over their bodies. Another had a bird that kept acquiring serious conditions while she was going through a pain-full separation from her husband. As the child custody battle turned uglier each week, the empathetic bird developed cysts under its wings, as well as other bizarre reactions to all the negativity in the air. Pets, like children, absorb the intense waves of energy circulating in the home such as anger, impatience, sadness, frustration and other negatively laden emotions.

Illness

If you are ill it often makes it difficult to earn a living, to move forward, to have a solid material foundation for your Life or to enjoy the fruits of your relationships and Life altogether.

•   Negative forces will attempt to knock you down by constantly attacking the karmic weaknesses you brought with you into this Life-time. There are countless ways malevolent energies work towards creating illness for you. They can whisper self-destructive propaganda into your ear and hypnotize you into being careless, lazy, forget-full or resistant in other ways to that which your soul knows is beneficial for you. In this way vicious forces energies convince you to weaken your system. In order to seal off any possible entrances to menacing forces, it is vital to Strengthen your weaknesses. You can begin with the basic sacred self-defence by rattling, smudging, lighting a candle and repeating prayers/mantras in order to invoke the Light.

•   It is important to review your generational history to determine if other family members were attacked through the same symptoms and accompanying issues. Of course, apart from the spiritual solutions, it is also wise to pursue. the appropriate physical and emotional treatments.

Things Disappearing and Moving Around

In some homes, people find that there is a steady stream of items disappearing permanently. Or you may find something will disappear for a time then re-appear somewhere else. This can be a result of play-full energies, but it can also be the beginning signs of harm-full energies. One student often experienced her sacred protection and ritual items disappearing. She later had a prophetic dream where she was told the house was making her sick. I told her she should leave the house immediately if she could not determine and implement a solution to change the vibration of the place. She was resistant to this guidance...full of reasons why it was not possible to leave and months later she was diagnosed with cancer. Although the fogged over mind may view it as impossible to leave a space that is intensely inhabited by wicked forces, it is not worth losing your Life by remaining in a space that is a coven for evil.

For a period of time, another student reported that she would wake up to find that her protective amulets had been removed from her neck and placed on the pillow next to her. When I was younger, I also had several similar experiences where one of my amulets mysteriously disappeared overnight. In one episode, I went to bed with it on and woke up to find no trace of it. In days preceding this, I had already come close to losing it several times, once down the drain, as I was brushing my teeth. The clasp suddenly came undone! When it finally disappeared I never found it. These kinds of occurrences...where energies tamper with your sacred items...are clearly signs of the presence of evil forces...NOT play-full ones!

Foul Smells

•   Any kind of stench or foul smell can indicate the presence of evil. It can also be an omen of the presence of the Angel of Death, who has arrived to give you a message about your path or that of someone you are connected to. If you detect a repulsive odour in any area or emanating from you or others, this matter should be considered urgent and investigated immediately.

•   Mold is a potent poison to our physical system and is also considered a physical manifestation of the presence of negative forces. Take immediate action against it, for it is a relentless enemy to your well-being and should not be allowed to remain. Unattended, it will spread vigorously, contaminating everything on its path.

• Many people have discovered a stench that suddenly became noticeable, which could not be traced to any physical origin, nor be covered up by any means. They were not able to eradicate the foulness until they embarked on their spiritual homework and proceeded with smudging and other spiritual cleansing tools.

Aversion-Repulsion

• Any aversion to certain rooms or spots indicates the presence of sinister forces. In some cases you may feel aversion to a certain area during daytime but find that once it's dark, you will experience outright fear.

• If you or someone experience dread or fear when nearing, entering, or even thinking about a certain room, this lets you know that there is a heavy presence in the room. When fear comes up, it is your energetic field reacting to that strong presence which creates the sensation of fear or aversion. It is your body Wisdom letting you know you must be AWARE. To be AWARE is to be WARY… ALERT to that which is around you. For more clarity on this, see the section on 'Hiding Places'.

• Dark forces can take up residence in humans causing them to repel Love and Harmony. One woman, 'A' had a Harmony-us relationship with her partner until another woman set her sights on 'A's partner and sent a foul energy to attach itself to 'A'. From that day onward, 'A' began to emit a foul order. This caused her partner to be repulsed by her and he began to drift away. Soon he did not want to sleep in the same bed or be in the same room as her. He began to avoid coming home and she found that at the same time, friends began avoiding her as well. Her business, which had been previously success-full, became empty of customers.

When I revealed to her what was attached to her, she admitted she had felt a dark presence within her. She was normally an intuitive individual and her soul was well aware of what had transpired. Only after a Soul Retrieval Limpia did everything turn around for the positive. After several Limpias, the partner returned, they re-established their Harmony-us relationship, friends once again experienced her as the charming, intelligent Loving being she is and the business began to prosper once again.

VIBRATION AFFECTS EVERYTHING! CHANGE YOUR VIBRATION AND YOU CHANGE YOUR LUCK AND DESTINY. AT EVERY MOMENT OF OUR LIFE, OUR VIBRATION EITHER REPELS OR ATTRACTS THE Goodness OF THE Universe.

A Feeling of Being Watched or Accompanied

• You will know there is a presence in your home because your attention will be constantly drawn to a particular spot in your home. For example, you may find yourself repeatedly glancing at a window or doorway, with a sense of expecting to see someone standing there or watching you.

• There may be noises emanating from particular doorways or rooms, although there is no human activity in the room.

• There can be a temperature change, often a stream of cold air or a sensation on the body such as chills, goose-bumps or that of a touch or push.

• The presence around you may be positive or negative. You will need to discern this through prayer and asking your Divine Source for clarity and guidance. When I resided in a canyon area of the state of Southern California in the United States, some students shared they knew they had a Native American spirit living in their house. They had all seen him with their soft vision and they all felt he was a positive presence and were happy to live alongside him. However in Australia, due to the immense massacres of the Aboriginals, there were many areas and homes that were inhabited by hostile spirits.

Hiding Places

• The negative forces hide in dark, cluttered, messy, stinky or unused places such as closets, cupboards, attics, basements and under beds. Bathrooms and toilet rooms are also a favourite spot for them.

• The rule of thumb is that if you sense a fear-producing

presence or an aversion to any of these spaces, it is because there are menacing vibrations residing there.

• When you see shadows zipping out of the corner of your eye, if you are able to track their path of movement, you will see them go in and out of their hiding places.

• Observe how the house will make sounds at night that you do not hear during daylight hours. If certain doors squeak, it is recommended you smudge the whole house, with special emphasis on the doorway and the areas around the door, as well as any other spot emitting loud noises. After smudging, you should notice the squeak either gone or reduced.

• Never surrender your space to dark forces…never give in to apathy, laziness or resistance! The upcoming sections on 'Protection Tools and Guidelines, Cleansing Ingredients and Amulets' will give you an arsenal of weapons with which to defend and re-claim your Sacred Space.

Vents

• You have already learned that all types of sinister and mischievous energies hide in dark places. Apart from attics and basements, vents are another favourite for negative forces.

• Just as vents are breeding places for dirt, dust, mold, grime, rodents, insects and other harm-full elements, those same elements are known to represent and propagate larger foul energies that entrench themselves in that dark atmosphere.

• The challenge with vents is that unlike a basement or attic, the negative forces can appear and disappear from one part of the house to another with ease, bypassing all lights & sacred smoke in the rest of the house. If they detect cleansing ingredients, they will just run away to avoid extermination and zip over to another room. Or they will "play dead" by laying low further back in the vents, only to re-surface later.

• There are however a few things that you can do to increase the protection of the house:

*   If the vents are on the wall, when not using the vents, you could place a protection symbol or picture of your God on the vent thereby energetically sealing that channel for any negativity to flow through. If the vent is on the ground, then only a protection symbol or written declaration would be appropriate. Never use a picture of your God, as it is not considered Respect-full to walk on images of God, Saints, Angels, and other Divine Protectors. You can also cover any vent with purple or Divine Mother blue paper or cloth. One student covered wall vents with our Divine Mother bandanas. The action of covering is the first layer of transformation.

    *   Play sacred chants/prayer songs in the space day and night, to send a healing and protective vibration throughout your space, thereby uplifting the frequency of the area and all residents.

    *   Use the 'Nine Day Cleansing Kit.' It contains blessed herbs and a "locomotion" mantra that further charges those herbs, which can then be sprinkled in the vents. Be aware that if you are dealing with heat vents, it is possible the heat will toast those herbs causing fumes to be released from them and be sent back into the room. This need not be a bad thing, since it is an improvement over the musty air most vents deliver, and the aroma would cleanse the vents and the house area it reaches. How it will affect you depends on how much herb you placed in the vent, how hot the vent becomes and how strong the resultant fragrance and vapours are.

    *   When smudging the home/work place, pass the smoke through the vents as well, blowing the smoke into the vents as much as possible. You can also spray a protective scent such as lavender, basil, cedar or any of the other natural essences listed in the Cleansing Ingredients section in Chapter Seven.

    *   Repeat the "Dissolving Evil" Mantra or the Mystical Protective Shield Mantra into the vents (refer to Sacred Chants section). Of course, you can use any other mantra, prayer or sound you resonate with, including bells, rattles or any vibration that will drive out or disintegrate the malicious energies. Whatever protection command you call out or protective sound you produce, will echo deep into the vents to drive out disrupting forces.

    *   Have your vents professionally cleaned for all health hazards to remove some or all-menacing forces as well.

VORTEXES, PROPERTIES, BURIAL SITES AND HOUSE STORIES

There are countless factors that can open the door to negative energies in a home or area. There are homes that are sitting on a vortex of energy, which is an open portal through which entities can come and go as they please. This vortex can be the result of scores of factors and each portal is unique in immense ways, including the amount of energy it will require to contain it to tolerable levels, or to shut it down completely. In other cases, homes or buildings may have been built on ancient ceremonial land or burial sites without permission, resulting in a steady stream of psychic attack from spirits who are angry about the lack of Respect shown.

I have known of homes that were built on or near hospitals, morgues, prisons, torture and massacre sites, therefore inheriting lingering unhappy spirits.

As mentioned in previous Teachings, the negativity in the home can also be due to evil forces, which are brought into the home through an item or by a person.

Some homes will make it difficult to prosper while living there. In other residences you will find it challenging to sleep Peacefully, while others create bizarre behaviour changes.

The Impeccable Warrior of Light is ever on their toes as to the energetic inventory of their home. They take everything as a sign and trace it back as to when it started. They take stock of the signs the space has demonstrated, accumulating all necessary data to determine the source of the detected presence. As all-ways, once you have the data, then you can proceed to experiment with the protection tools to abolish the ominous energies and take back your space on behalf of the Light, Prosperity, Peace and Grace.

To receive Clarity and Courage, it is necessary to be still within... so you can hear the inner messages and be guided impeccably. You can reach this point of centredness through your power-packed prayers, meditation, sacred movement, music and other practices that quiet the busy, chattering mind so your spirit can experience the Serenity of Peace.

Once you receive the revealing data through your intuitive guidance, you can use the Yantras and other protective and cleansing ingredients given in the upcoming section. Combine these elements with other tools you have Faith in, to de-activate the embroiling and turbulent energetic field.

In addressing the situation through your ceremonial work, it is equivalent to taking down a neon sign above or under your home that reads, "This is the bus stop for all entities wishing to visit and create havoc!"

I once spent time in a house that contained a room which was kept closed at all times. Everyone had to pass it as it was next to the bathroom. Each time I walked by it, I felt an energy jump out at me that would make me shudder. One day, I asked the owner of the house what she kept in the room. She said she originally had thought to use it as a sewing room, but found she did not want to be in it nor go near it, so she only used it as a storeroom. Whether she was conscious of it, she kept the door closed in order to attempt to block out the menacing vibrations that had established their headquarters there. Notice how this often happens with the rooms that have undesirable energies: they become designated as the storage or clutter room. The dark forces thrive in clutter, for clutter, like darkness, is the perfect hiding and breeding place for malevolent and mischievous energies.

It is interesting how people somehow fall under the illusion that they feel better when they close the door to a room that creates discomfort to our soul. Of course, the residing negative energy is not actually contained by simply closing the door. Until we deal with it in a responsible manner, our attention will continually be drawn back to that area. Sub-consciously we never forget it is there and deep down inside we know we need to do something about it. Instead of bombarding your energetic body with the emanating vibration coming from behind 'the door', or from 'the room', you can take your space and your power back. Ways to do that are coming up in the section 'Protection Tools and Guidelines'.

The above example of shutting doors also provides an excellent analogy to the other 'doors' we close. We may be aware of unpleasant things about ourselves, but shut the door on them. In doing so, we deny their existence or re-main unwilling to work through them. In the meantime, they can eat away at our sub-conscious mind. By not confronting them, we continue to feed them through our uncertainty, fear and insecurities.

Another example of the effects of living in a possessed space, was given to me by a woman who was driven to contact Sacred Peace Center for a Soul Retrieval Limpia because of the cyst on her body and the problems she was experiencing with her children and husband. During the spiritual cleansing, Swami Durgadas was assisting me and as I have taught him, he was guided to ask questions about her home and how safe she felt in it. He shared with her that even though the cleansing would remove much psychic debris from her, if the house remained polluted she could once again become covered with layers of negative energies. She then divulged that her children, as well as her dogs had also been developing cysts. Upon further questioning, she also revealed that her children had been well behaved and easy to relate to before they began residing in their new home.

After moving in, they began to become hyperactive, insolent and violent, to the point of constantly engaging in knocking holes in the wall. They were often physically aggressive towards each other, and did not care about their surroundings. In fact, they instead took great pleasure in breaking things and living in shambles. Their mother actually became afraid of them and felt she was living in a madhouse. I then asked her about their neighbourhood, and it then dawned on her that several of the neighbours and the previous inhabitants of her home, had also experienced the same syndrome. All of them had well-behaved children who suddenly turned into 'demons'. It was then she realized that the house was sitting on some kind of energetic field, which caused these disturbances in the personalities of the residents of the area.

FENG SHUI: IS IT ENOUGH?

On one occasion I visited a family in California, U.S.A. that was in the midst of breaking up when I arrived. The energy in the house was laden with strained tension due to the increasing fears and hostility. After I gave them Teachings on Spiritual Protection they began to realize they had all felt the disturbing vibrations from a portal they had identified in their back yard. One day I went upstairs to smudge and discovered a heavy presence blocking my way. After I mentioned this to them, they shared they also felt the spirits on the second floor and often experienced trepidation at the thought of walking in the upper hallway. They sensed these were angry spirits which would rise out of the portal and travel through an upstairs window to the hallway where they chose to take up residence.

The family's house had supposedly been Balanced by a Feng Shui practitioner but the break-up in the marriage and the dis-harmony of the home reflected to me that the family was clearly still under severe psychic attack. Before I did anything to close down the portal, I recommended to them they call back the Feng Shui practitioner and give her another opportunity to finally shut down the portal. She did return and proceeded to perform various exercises, incorporating what she had learned from different traditions, as well as using a machine that was advertised to zap the negative energies instantly. Afterwards, she performed a test to make sure the forces had been evaporated and in her opinion, the test confirmed they were gone. Unfortunately, by the next day, the family was once again feeling the heavy presence of the troublesome entities.

One of my students is a sought after Feng Shui consultant, and she incorporates what she has learned from me as well as from other beings and traditions. I am not an expert on Feng Shui but I would say, as a general rule of thumb that just by following prescribed techniques such as placing mirrors or water in particular spots of the house or property, this may not be enough to close down a portal. However, it may balance the energy to a certain degree, helping somewhat.

The most revealing testament will be how the space and its residents behave afterwards. This is the only way to know if you have hit upon the perfect combination of tools and you should all-ways feel free to experiment with techniques that you have Faith in, until you see proof that whatever protection weapons you have used have been truly effective.

The telling evidence is in the outcome. By not being prejudiced or attached to the results, you will clearly see the true effects of your work. It is the results which will confirm to you that you have implemented the perfect solution for an. challenge before you. If the response shows the work is still unfinished, then you must continue to add ingredients to the remedy.

When you have formulated the absolute antidote to the symptoms of the house or the person, you and others will know you have succeeded by witnessing the positive change. Your energetic field will all-ways let you know when you have cleared out menacing vibrations through the manifestation of a feeling of being safe and finally able to relax.

Remember, you are not at all alone on each challenging adventure. I am with you...as are your many Protectors...so do not give up! Victory is possible...continue to add and do your prayer and Ceremonial Work, until you create the perfect combination that the situation is calling forth from you. When you do what your soul is asking of you...you are empowered...and you complete one more step of your SOUL DESTINY!

Chapter 7

PROTECTION TOOLS AND GUIDELINES

The Impeccable Warrior of Light is a practical being...drawing
from the past but not allowing themselves to be imprisoned by
it. Warriors of Light do not live chained to dry, rigid, intellectual
theories. Instead, through daily practice, we are all-ways learning
and growing. By adapting our practices according to what is working
NOW...at THIS moment...we constantly expand in Wisdom.

OFFERINGS

I once heard a version of the following demonstration on the
power of ignorance. This story may have come from my Most
Excellent Teacher Gurumayi, who holds oceans of Wisdom within
Her, or someone from Her organization, Siddha Yoga. Since I cannot
clearly remember the source of this excellent re-minder I ask for
forgiveness from whoever originated this story, for not crediting
them more properly. To whoever gave us this gem: merit unto you!
Great-fullness unto you!

Here is my version: Once there was a Guru who's students sat
for meditation in the Ashram at three p.m. each afternoon. Every
day, at that time, a cat would meander through the crowd, causing
a disturbance. To remedy the situation, the Guru instructed his
attendees to tie up the cat. Years later the Guru passed on, but even
after he left this world, his students blindly continued the "tradition"
of sitting for meditation at three in the afternoon and also tie-ing up
the cat. After the cat died, they acquired another cat, so they could

144

continue the "tradition" of meditating at three p.m. and tie-ing up the cat during meditation. Years later a meditation manual was written based on the Guru's instructions and as part of the instructions, the seeker was instructed to sit for meditation only at three p.m. and to acquire a cat, which should be tied up at meditation time. This was how the students interpreted the Teachers instructions and this is how "tradition" becomes absolute folly!

A wise being realizes that whatever was done yesterday was just one moment in an eternal stream of moments...whatever seemed appropriate in the past was accepted at the time, but today is the only moment that matters now...we must continually question what is appropriate at this very moment. The Impeccable Warrior of Light is a practical being...drawing from the past but not allowing themselves to be imprisoned by it. Warriors of Light do not live chained to dry, rigid, intellectual theories. Instead, through daily practice, we are all-ways learning and growing. By adapting our practices according to what is working NOW...at THIS moment... we constantly expand in Wisdom.

Offerings are a time-honoured tradition for communicating with the unseen worlds. All Indigenous cultures make offerings to Mother Earth, remembering and praising the Earth Forces that Compassionately allow us to stay alive. The Ancestors and Celestial realms, which also provide us with caring protection and guidance, are praised as well as we offer gifts of grand Appreciation.

Although there are many traditions that teach exact rituals for offerings...I feel any gift offered with Love and Respect is Joy-fully received by the Compassionate Celestial and Terrestrial Forces.

What these forces receive from you at the moment of offering, is the vibration you are emanating while making the offering. So, even if you do not say the prescribed or traditional words 'correctly' when you approach the Forces of Protection, what They sense is your Love, Respect and desire to communicate with their world. Offerings can be elaborate or they can be as simple as lighting a candle, offering an incense stick, a piece of chocolate or a flower. In the following sections you will be given many ideas on the ritual of offerings, and

I encourage you to listen to your heart…let your creativity flow as to the countless ways to offer gifts to the Universe and the innumerable ingredients you can implement in your Ceremony.

Auspicious times for Offerings:

Although there is merit to the idea of aligning with the strong wave of Positive Energy that spiritual festivals and Holy days can provide…any day and every moment is the perfect moment to offer up a prayer, song, dance, sound or any other sacred ingredient…in recognition of the Compassionate Forces that support our journey here on the Radiant Jewel. In the same way that you eat every day, so is it wise to feed the Forces that protect and defend you with at least one offering per day.

In the same way that you devote so much attention to your material world and all your material projects, it is equally important, if not more, to be cognizant of the Divine Source that created it all. You can create long rituals on days when time allows for immersing yourself in your spiritual practices, while offering short ceremony at times when your hectic schedule does not allow you to devote much time at your power base such as your altar or at a Medicine Wheel. What is important…is the consistency of communication, Devotion and reverence offered to honour the unseen Celestial and Earth Forces who Love you and support your Sacred Journey on Mother Earth.

Protect the Kingdom:

Your mind, body, spirit and home are all parts of your Holy Temple and your Life, as well as the lives of those in your home space are considered your Kingdom. You are the steward of the Temple/Kingdom and it is your duty to defend it with all your Goodness, Strength and Wisdom each day. Through your offerings, you invoke the Light and Compassion of the Universe into your Temple/Kingdom. Through your Loving actions you solidify your connection with your Spiritual Protectors, laying down a line of Spiritual Protection for your Temple/Kingdom.

Imagine that through your offerings you are calling in the Temple

Guards…that you are placing your soldiers at their posts to defend you against invasion. On the days when your schedule seems bursting at the seams, you can do quick offerings, which do not take long such as lighting an incense stick, presenting the candle or the Holy water offering described further in this chapter. If you find yourself rushing out of the house without having fed the Compassionate Forces that protect your Temple/Kingdom, you can still speedily call in the Light Forces from wherever you are. While driving or in-between engaging in other activities, you can take a few minutes to invoke the Light Forces to be present in all Cardinal Points.

By mental remembrance, visualization or verbally installing the Guardian Energies, you are honouring that Benevolent Force. In so doing, you are still establishing Spiritual Protection for your home, which should all-ways be done one way or another. Connecting to your Source is the key and the following are some ways you can activate and Strengthen that connection.

INTENTION

Just as you would introduce yourself when paying a visit to someone or making a phone call, spiritual courtesy is paramount when developing your relationship with the Grace Bestowing Powers. It is good manners to introduce yourself to the Earth and Celestial Forces whose assistance you are invoking each day. This is so, for in all offerings, it is part of the Radiant Ways to first and foremost present yourself to Spirit. It is the same principal that we follow anywhere we go, in terms of upholding Courtesy and Respect, whereby we introduce ourselves before proceeding with the purpose of our visit or appointment. A wise person will honour the being or energies they are contacting, before delving into any material matters.

To introduce yourself to the Universal and/or Earth Forces, you simply state your name, which lets all the forces know that you consider yourself fully present and ready to embark upon the sacred assignment at hand. After stating your name, you state your intention. You state what it is exactly that you are there to do. For absolute clarity on this, ask yourself "What is my purpose?"

Many traditions teach that you should state your name, the present date, the city, state and country you are in at that moment, your Lineage, who you represent and which deity, which God you are offering your prayers or other offerings to. I do agree that this is a noble way to introduce yourself, however, I also feel that God knows who you are, and as long as you are humble and Loving, however you introduce yourself is accepted Compassionately by your Divine Benefactors.

Here is an example of a simple introduction, "I, _____AM HERE, Divine Mother, I am Joy-fully present this blessed day of _____(state the day and date) to invoke the presence of all of the Angels, Archangels, Spirit Guides and Master Teachers who defend me and protect me! I call on all the Forces of Compassion to please see me, hear me and receive these humble offerings I am about to make. Please guide me perfectly so I may All Ways please you!"

Presenting yourself and praising the Compassionate forces are the two essentials for opening the doors to the hearts of those energies and beings that will be receiving your offering. It is an ancient principle to Praise the Beings you are approaching.

Praising is a universal way to foster Cooperation and Appreciation. If you want something from someone and you ask brusquely, demanding "Give me this!", you won't likely gather any support that way. However if you look for qualities that you can compliment in the other person and you go out of your way to be sweet, kind, generous, thought-full and considerate, you will melt their heart and they will feel more than happy to grant you the favour you are seeking.

On the Spiritual Path we often refer to the Teaching which states 'As above, so below'. This situation is a perfect example of what we are reviewing at this moment. This Teaching means that the rules that apply here on Earth, in the material plane, also apply in the spirit world. Excellent manners, kind ways and consideration are valued everywhere, for they are sacred qualities. However, if words do not come easily to you…remember that the most vital element is your attitude.

As you praise the Force of Goodness in your own way, as long as your offerings emanate from the heart and not the mind, your Humility and a Great-full heart will be lovingly recognized and received by the invisible world. So the first offering is your introduction, in which you are presenting your Best Self, your Shiniest Self. Through this practice, with your Devotion and Great-fullness you are presenting your heart to the Divine Ones who are your spiritual Life-line. After introducing yourself, you can then proceed with the rest of your offerings.

PRAYERS

There are innumerable existing prayers used by so many traditions to invoke Grace. No matter what your path has been so far, I encourage you to stay open by adding prayers to your Faith-full ritual and altar work that resonate with you, and feel free to change prayers as needed. The best way of knowing WHAT prayers to offer is by asking your Protectors what THEY would like to hear. It's not the tradition that matters, but instead the depth of Love with which you deliver that prayer and your intention.

If you find that your spiritual routine feels stagnant then you have two choices; you can either refresh your attitude or refresh the offerings that you make by deleting some of the old ones and adding new ones. Do not feel fear-full to make changes according to your inspiration.

You can also refresh your Gusto and enthusiasm for your spiritual practices by changing the way you deliver the same prayer. For example, singing the prayer instead of just simply verbalizing it. Or, if you are already singing a prayer and it now feels stale, change the rhythm! The rhythm with which I repeat mantras and prayers changes all the time based on the inspiration flowing through me at the time. I often use the same words and just alter the rhythm. Just as it is healthy to change your diet for greater balance, you must also keep ALL relationships fresh by introducing new ideas and activities…

and this includes your relationship with the energetic realms. It is supremely beneficial to update and maintain your spiritual practices with an infusion of fresh Zest! Zest IS POWER!

Inspiration is a BIG factor in determining the level of power within your prayer and goes hand in hand with Devotion. I encourage everyone to discard stale bread and to feast everyday on freshly baked and delivered, vibrant spiritual sustenance! So much tastier, satisfying and nourishing! Just as with any relationship, all actions and thoughts should be sincere and full of Love. So it is with your relationship with your God Source and the God Agents such as Angels, Spirit Guides and Teachers who are assigned to protect you.

It is vital we have Faith that our prayers and intentions are always heard no matter how simply we may deliver them. If you had no tongue, would you be able to deliver complicated mantras and prayers according to the dictates of strict disciplines or traditions? Of course not and with that being the case, the question is, "Would your prayers still be heard?" The answer is absolutely "Yes!" It is the language of the human heart…the primary vibration…that melts the hearts of our Spiritual Protectors. The power of a prayer is based on its SINCERITY, INTENSITY…AND Devotion.

If you ever find yourself feeling insecure about your prayers and intensions just ask for forgiveness from the Positive Forces that are receiving them. Appeal to your Divine Source to have Compassion for you and open up your Sacred Memory so you can re-member that which you have already learned in past lives. Through bestowed Grace, you will be able to re-call the prayers, songs and sacred rituals you have studied in multiple previous incarnations.

The main prayers I offer up each day originate from Mexico's Mayan Ways and India's Sanskrit tradition. The prayer I deliver as my introduction, at the beginning of the daily offerings, I usually offer. in Spanish because this is what flows from me naturally. However, there are times when I use English to voice my prayer. I normally sing my prayers, but whether I sing them or just verbalize them, I say something that translates like this:

"Beauty-full Divine Mother, I am here, I am here! You are the Queen of this Universe and All power-full! Your humble child, Peace Mother Geeta Sacred Song is present this sacred day. _____. I am here, present in this Spiritual Centre, Sacred Peace Center to full-fill Your Divine Will today. It is a pleasure and an honour to do Your work on this Radiant day!

I am Your child and humble servant. I know nothing, so please forgive me if I do not know how to make proper offerings to You! Please open up my sacred memory, so I may remember perfectly how to Honour and Respect You and all Your Compassionate Forces.

May You, my Gurus, Mayan Guides, Ancestors, Master Teachers from all traditions, Angels, Archangels and all Beings and Forces of Light that protect me and defend me, receive these offerings with Compassion. Forever thank You for the opportunity to serve and to offer.

Please accept these humble offerings on behalf of Your humble servant...as well as on behalf of all the, Sacred Peace Team, my birth family, the Peace Team's families and all souls everywhere. May this offering be accepted on behalf of all beings, that all souls be released from all suffering and reach Enlightenment immediately".

After I have made all the offerings, which I will be describing further along in this section, I continue to feed the Universal Forces and invoke protection for our Center and all our assigned projects as well as all excellent, genuine missions that uplift humanity.

SACRED CHANTS

The chanting of sacred mantras is one of my favourite practices and I highly recommend it to others because the Sacred Sounds are Divinely soothing. At SPC, every department plays sacred mantras chanting CDs all day and night. I chant out loud with the CDs off and on, in between my other activities. When it comes to mantras, even through simply listening to them, the mind and spirit are being purified, uplifted and Strengthened.

Mantras and sacred sounds heal us mentally, emotionally and physically, affecting the mind and physical body's systems. They also dissolve negative karmas and the psychic impressions those karmas have installed into our psyche which produce neuroses and imbalances.

The most Beauty-full thing about chanting is that sound bypasses the mind and carries us straight to the Heart. The focus is on the vibrational sound that we are generating through these sacred chants, not necessarily the words that our minds are addicted to feed upon.

I recommend chanting over repeating prayers in your own language because by praying with words from your own language you will still end up engaging the mind and not the Spirit. The mind can never feel Devotion, only the heart can. Through the rhythms of the music and the sacred songs/chants our heart is purified. As our mind is purified, our heart blossoms with the fragrance of Divine Love.

I especially encourage those beings with perfectionist natures and overly active minds to engage in the constant repetition of mantras and chants, to avoid becoming obsessive or bitter perfectionists. However, all personality types can improve through mantra repetition and all sought-after spiritual qualities can be birthed within you through the singing of holy chants.

You can chant at your altar, in the favourite part of your home, in your car, or outdoors. We can chant silently while working at our duties, wherever that may be. There is no reason to refrain from replacing every negative or mediocre thought with a mantra repetition.

To protect places you can write out the mantras and post them along with prayers, affirmations and power-full quotes, in any space. You can recite mantras at doorways or any place that has a negative presence to it.

If you wish to create a strong shield of protection, it is also wise to have a CD player that has a repeat function so you can play sacred chants twenty-four hours a day in your living space. When sleeping or engaging in certain activities that require a lower volume, you can simply turn the volume down, even to the subliminal level, but it is best to never stop the flow.

Every note of sacred sound is feeding the atmosphere of your living and working space. You can acquire a large selection of sacred sounds and play whatever suits your different moods or the needs of the realms around you. By remaining astute to your Divine Guidance, you will All Ways be clear as to what energies you need to nourish. The key is to remember that the invisible worlds are at all times reaching out to you…communicating their desires unto you. Heeding the messages from the invisible world, you will be inspired to play the perfect prayer/song/sound at every moment.

When the Peace Team Musicians and I record mantras in CDs such as the Mystical Protective Shield album and Peace CD, we include tracks which relax the body, others for medium level activity and high energy tracks to empower your dance movements or support you whenever you must engage in intense battle against dark forces. For all this is a science and we must have the proper tools to maintain our power at the optimum level.

As I have recorded mantras with extremely Joy-full and fresh rhythms, so have others and there is immense variety to choose from these days. So join in and SING…CHANT with full Gusto! By chanting, you ride the river of ancient science, which continually nourishes the Forces of Compassion that illuminate your path.

The formula is simple: as you offer sacred sound to the Universe, the fire of your Gusto…the enthusiasm of your actions…and the Devotion that will burst within you, will deliver to YOU waves of Happiness! The Law is that whatever emotion or intention you emanate, must return to you in a multiplied Strength. Imagine the blessings that will return to bless you as you sing out to the Universe!

Repeating prayers in normal speaking voice or in silence may fill us with serenity, chanting/singing our prayers propels us into a bliss-full state! I fully encourage you, dive into an ocean of Divine ecstasy by SINGING your prayers, mantras and affirmations whenever and wherever possible. When we sing sacred sounds with deep emotion, we are filled to the brim with the soul satisfaction of doing what our Divine Self cares most about: to radiate Love and Peace to all Creation.

PROTECTION MANTRA AND PRAYERS

1. Protection Mantra Invoking Victory For The Light

Kali Durge Namo Nama
[Kaa-lee Duur-geh Naa-mo Naa-maa]

Praise to the Warrior Goddess Kali and Durga who eternally defeat all evil. I invoke You to protect me, triumph over all obstacles, dangers and ignorance!

2. Invoking Victory Mantra

Om Jaya Chandi Jaya Jaya

This Mantra invokes Divine Mother in the form of the Goddess Chandi, *She Who Tears Apart Thought*, to dissolve and disintegrate all ignorance. Chandi eradicates all negative thought patterns that block our path to our Divine Victories. Use this for dissolution of all thoughts that separate you from your Divinity.

The word Jaya means Victory and we have recorded it on the Be Victorious Maa CD, with the chorus singing "Om Jaya Chandi Jaya Jaya, be Victorious Maa!" I am supremely pleased with the power in this track and use it often in my Shamanic Work. I recommend that whenever you feel you need an energetic boost you play it for support. . .

3. Removing Curses Mantra
For uprooting generational patterns, blocks and suffering.

Om Hreem Kleem Shreem Kraam Kreem Chaandee-Kaa
Devyeh Shaa-paa-naa-shaanu-graahaam Kuru Kuru Swaahaa

Chandika is another name for Chandi and She Who Tears Apart Thought is the Grace that bestows transformation, driving out limiting thoughts that attempt to fragment you. Using this Mantra or any to Chandi/Chandika/Kali/Durga/Tara Mantras move you into your Divine Power by eradicating false beliefs based on any type of weakness. Kuru kuru Swaha means *remove the curse, remove the curse, I am one with God!*

We must understand that a curse is the same as any limitation in our Life or limiting thought programmed within us, and therefore we all carry curses. Until we are Enlightened, we are influenced by some type of limited programming which creates obstacles, delays, confusion or dangers on our path at one time or another. Therefore, everyone can benefit from this Mantra and I also consider it an Enlightenment Mantra. For, as long as we are bound by heaps of generational programming inherited from eons of Ancestors, cultures and societies we have been related to, we can never be free.

This Mantra can be utilized to disperse any obstructions to Balance, Wisdom, Healing, Harmony, Prosperity and Happiness in your Life or that of a Loved one. It is traditionally repeated a minimum of eleven times. However, it is wise to ask for Divine Guidance as to how many times per day you can increase it to. This Mantra is also available on the SPC site on one of the CDs.

4. Mystical Protective Shield Mantra for Dissolving Evil and Clearing Spaces, 2 versions

Om aapaa sarpaantu
Tay bhutaa yay bhutaa
Bhuvi sumh* stee-ta-haa
Stay gha-chaan too
Kaali ajsh-naa-yaa
    * u in sum pronounced similar to "run" and "sun"

May all evil spirits, in all their forms, that are haunting me/ surrounding me, be sent back to the Source, to serve the Light. I command this in the name of Divine Mother Kali, the Warrior Goddess of Light.

Om aapaa sarpaantu
Tay maaraa yay maaraa
Bhuvi sum* stee-ta-haa
Stay gha-chaan-too
Kaali ajshh-naa-yaa
* u in sum pronounced similar to run & sun

May Mara/Satan/demon/ any evil force, in all its forms that are haunting me/ surrounding me, be sent back to the Source and be used for good purposes. I command this in the name of Divine Mother Kali, the Warrior Goddess of Light.

When you are feeling challenged by any negative emotion, thought and circumstance, repeat this Mantra in a loud voice if possible. While doing so, snap your fingers or clap your hands. The energy generated by sound and movement will drive away disturbing feelings, thoughts and urges.

It is best to repeat this mantra aloud, with force and conviction. When repeating this mantra people often experience goose bumps or tingling on their body. Those that are sensitive enough feel this and if you experience any physical sensations it means you are registering the presence of energetic intruders. When the sensation subsides, it means the entities have retreated temporarily, or you have vanquished them totally. Against stronger attacks you may need to repeat the mantra a large number to times.

Just as that relentless dust never stops flowing into your home, undermining forces are always at work and it is wise to utilize this Mantra in any space, to clear it from any possible build-up of hampering energies. When implementing this Mantra, walk around your home/office, fully intent to sense the invisible world. The moment you sense something, stop there and continue to repeat it aloud until any alerting sensation subsides.

By combining mantra repetition with smudging, rattling, snapping your fingers or clapping hands, you will increase its potency. When used before and during sleep time, it will help you have tranquil rest and eliminate nightmares. For this reason we have recorded this Mantra in the Mystical Protective Shield CD, in a tempo for relaxation and deep sleep. As well we felt it vital to include soothing tracks for medium level activity during the day, and "high-action" activity for high-energy work. The "high action" track was created to support you in combining this Mantra with your power-dance or power-rattling. The drumming and chorus will inspire you to liberate your full energy in commanding any infringing darkness to leave immediately!

If you wish, you may replace the word "Kali" in the mantra with any other Holy Name such as Mother Mary, Jesus, Shiva, Krishna, Tara, Buddha, or any personification of God that you connect with.

5. Mantra For Dissolving Anger and Other Intense Emotions

Om Aieem Hreem Kleem Chaa-mun-daa Yeh Vichhe

This mantra calls forth Divine Mother Chamunda (Chaa-moon-daa), who is known both as *The Grantor of Boons* and *The Slayer of Passion and Anger who Moves in the Head.* She moves in the head/mind, annihilating the demons of intense emotions and self-destructive urges.

This protection mantra is a string of power-full seed mantras and has been offered in profound fire ceremonies for thousands of years…to invoke Humanity's Freedom.

It also places a protective shield around any space, yourself or a Loved one. To add even more power, outline a power symbol in the air, in each direction. By making a sign with your hands such as a cross, snapping your fingers or clapping your hands along with this sacred sound you can place an energetic shield around anything.

In addition, you can easily produce Holy Water by repeating this mantra several times over any water and then blowing the Sacred Breath into it. The water can then be sprinkled in any space or over any object to purify and invite the Light Forces.

6. Invocation for installing Divine Mother/Goddess Protection in Four Directions

This is from 'The Chandi Path' by Swami Satyananda Saraswati. I consider the Chandi Path an essential tool in furthering your understanding of Grace and Protection from dark forces.

In the front may Victory protect me,
In back, may the Power of Conquest protect me.
On the left may the Undefeated One protect me.
On the right may the Unconquerable protect me.

7. Invocation for Divine Mother Protection In Seven Directions

Divine Mother Loves you and honours all Respect-full requests, so it is all-right to invoke Divine Mother's protection in as many directions, in whatever order, and by whichever sacred names you choose to call Her by.

Protect us in the East, dissolve all negative thoughts,
Great Goddess.
Rotate Your spear and protect me in the North,
Goddess of Victory, Kali Durge
Protect us in the West, dispel all fears,
Goddess Who Relieves All Afflictions!
Protect us in the South, Divine Mother Chandika
(She Who Destroys Thoughts).
Protect us in the Sky with the sound of Your bell,
Goddess of Bliss and Strength!
Protect us on the Earth, with the twang of Your bowstring, Grantor
of Wishes!
With Your sword of Fierce Compassion, protect the Sacred Temple
of the Heart, Divine Mother of True Wealth.

8. Divine Mother Protection Invocations

A few examples of prayers :

• *Supreme Empress, protect us...I invoke Your protection for this Radiant Jewel Planet and all souls here. I invoke Your Perfect Protection for all souls, all worlds and all realities! Uplift us all and uphold the Light everywhere! Defend us with Your Beauty-full forms as well as Your fierce forms! Please protect us All Ways...we take refuge in You Mighty and Mercy-Full Mother!*

• *Most Excellent Mother, protect us everywhere! Protect us now and All Ways! With Your weapons of Light, defeat all tormenting forces! With Your kind heart and severity in battle, drive out and vanquish all hostile energies NOW! Free us from all oppression Goddess of Light! Destroy the Great Ego wherever it exists, by slaying all negative thoughts!*

• *Praise unto You, Great Reliever of suffering! All-Mighty Destroyer of Fear and all demeaning and detrimental thoughts, protect us in every direction and on every side! Expertly utilizing all the Divine weapons You have created, defend us against every shade and grain of evil! GLORY TO THE Grace AND VICTORY TO THE Light!*

• *Heavenly Mother, wherever there is ignorance...replace it with bliss... replace it with Love and Light! JAI JAI MAAAAAAAAAAAAAAAAAAAA! VICTORY TO THE Goodness!*

PRAYER BEADS

Prayer beads are an easy way to generate great spiritual power to remove obstacles and dangers inherent in the Spiritual Path. Many global traditions such as the Buddhists, Hindus and Catholics all use prayer beads to connect with their Source. I use prayer beads from many traditions, as what is important to me is not what tradition it originates from, rather that I resonate with the colour, material and overall visual image of the beads.

The feel and visual image of the beads must be pleasing to your soul at that time. At another time, you may be moved to use another type of prayer bead. Knowing how much I Love vibrant colours, Swami Durgadas had prayer beads created to match my ceremonial clothes. That is how our webshop came to carry prayer beads in all the rainbow colours!

Prayer beads must inspire—they should attract you and fill you with a soul contentment, a Happiness to wear them, look at them and touch them. If they don't inspire, you will not be pulled use them. At times I have been drawn to using the rosewood beads from India or other wooden rosaries from Mexico and yet other times either a pink, green, yellow, purple, turquoise or electric blue 'mala'. When I began to use the electric-blue ceramic beads, everyone who saw them was dramatically drawn to them! The colour had such a tremendous impact on every man, woman and child's spirit, filling them with Happiness. Each soul was resonating with the luster of the beads and brilliant electric blue vibration, which I refer to as 'Kali Blue'…it connected each being with their regal, Divine, pure, noble nature. .

The way the beads assist you is simple yet power-full: By associating the repetition of the mantra, with the movement of passing each bead through your fingers, you are infusing your mind, body and spirit with positive programming.

Associating an action with a practice creates an alarm clock that re-minds you of the power of mantra/prayer repetition. You will then find that the mind will become accustomed to the action and you will find your hands desiring the movement, whenever you are not passing the beads through your fingers. The mind and body have recorded that the mantra is repeated every time the prayer bead is moved through the fingers, and they Love it! Any repetitive action becomes a habit…but this habit creates leaps of Joy within our spirit…so soul, mind and body all join in and crave more of this transformative practice.

By using prayer beads, mantra repetition becomes supremely easy and you will find that it instils in you a sense of refuge, connecting you to a place of Peace within you. If I recommended you do 108 repetitions of a mantra, you might feel that it would take forever to do this! However, by utilising the prayer beads you will find that 108 repetitions may only take ten or fifteen minutes to complete, depending on the speed you pray at.

Prayer beads can provide a way of offering hundreds of thousands of repetitions without straining. Before you know it, you have easily completed a previously unimaginable number of repetitions! You will discover the practice becoming natural and soothing to you, whereas without the beads, it is too easy to be sidetracked by the ever-busy 'monkey' mind that Loves to hop from one tangent to the next.

The traditional way is to hold the beads in your hand and move each bead between your thumb and middle finger moving one bead with each prayer or mantra. However, I find that personally, it works best for me to use my thumb and forefinger. I recommend you try the prescribed way, but if that doesn't flow for you after some effort, then go with what does flow for you.

You may encounter mis-guided souls who will judge you for carrying out your spiritual practices in your unique way. They want you to conform, to do it THEIR way, believing THEY know best. I do not agree with this. I believe the Purity of your heart and prayer is governs how it is received. If you find yourself feeling uncomfortable or guilty about not doing it the 'supposed' or 'right' way, simply ask for forgiveness and ask sincerely that your prayers be received with Compassion.

It has been my experience that Love is stronger than any tradition's dogmatic rules. When an action is sponsored by the heart and performed with a pure intention, it is ALL-WAYS lovingly received.

THE VIOLET LIGHT

The Impeccable Warrior must have a protective shield that is easy to transport and access. The Violet Light, which is also known as the Violet Flame of Transmutation, is an immediate transformer and uplifter.

I have called upon it for more than half this Life-time and credit it for dissolving many qualities that were out of balance within myself. My constant invocation of the Violet Flame brought forth a painting of it, which was channelled through me and is included in the 'Shamanic Healing Art Journal', along with more of my experiences with The Violet Light. I feel my years of implementing it cleared my path and opened the doorway for my Gurus and Don Jacinto to appear in my Life.

The Violet Flame is an excellent spiritual protective technique and you can train yourself to imagine the Violet Light surrounding and immersing you. This is a Universal Protection tool, which is available to everyone and does not 'belong' to any religion or group. You can visualise it as a purple-coloured flame, cloud, circle, tube or any other way that comes easily to your mind. Any shade of purple is effective. Although you can use many other hues to protect yourself, such as white or golden Light…the present age we live in, is an age that resonates most with the Violet Light and you can see proof of that in all the various products that are purposely marketed these days in shades of purple.

The same holds true with clothing. Notice how much is available now in purple. In many hospitals, the nurses are now wearing purple uniforms. Why? Because even the marketing companies know at this time of our evolution, the human psyche is pulled towards this healing colour. Although you can take refuge in any of the Universal Rays, right now all beings are longing to be in contact with the Violet Flame in order to be transformed into a strong, Balanced being who is confident of their Divine nature and healing abilities. Beings who are especially sensitive find themselves drawn to wear purple and fill their surroundings with violet and purple items galore.

To protect/heal yourself with it, simply imagine a purple flame around yourself at all times. Do not worry as to whether you are visualizing it correctly or not, for it is a supremely Compassionate force that responds to our summons immediately. It will be with you instantly, protecting you before you even finish your invocation! As you begin invoking it, you are likely to have a clear vision of it. You may see it with your eyes open or closed. So that beings can have more Faith in it, The Violet Flame Compassionately quickly appears to those who invite it. Once you have seen it in all its fantastic vibrancy, it will be easier for you to envision it. Since its nature is to uplift, purify and transform, you can surround others with it as well.

Through your petition and command, you can direct it to bring healing, balance and protection to anyone and anything through the affirmation:

> *"I am blessed, protected and perfectly healed by the Violet Light."*

Be sure to make affirmations such as this one your very own, by allowing the words to flow from you in a way that is natural to you. To assist others in their transformation you can issue a simple yet potent petition such as:

> *"You are blessed, protected and immediately healed by the Violet Light .I call forth the Violet Flame to bless you and protect you perfectly"*

If there is discord between you and another being, you can add:

> *"Let there only be Peace between us!"*

You can also direct this Divine Flame of transmutation to uplift you or any person, place, Life form and condition by stating:

> *"I blaze the Violet Light in, through and around_____!"*

WEARING POSITIVE COLOURS

Your spirit is nourished through any interaction with power colours. An Impeccable Warrior of Light knows what hues enhance their Life Force and power. You will find that when you wear certain colours, people compliment you and confirm how great you look in them. When I was a young ashramite I was on an extremely tight budget, so I bought a dress that was within my budget, but which I did not like much. It was not suitable for me, but I bought it for many "practical" reasons: it was inexpensive and met the ashram criteria of being modest. However, the energetic reality was that it was one of the worst colours for my vibration: dull, lime green. I noticed I was constantly repelled by the dress, not desiring to wear it at all. When I forced myself to wear it, because of the way that shade of green tinted my skin tone, people around me would ask if I was feeling ill!

Whenever I meet anyone, I notice what colours they are wearing and carrying. I note the hue of the clothes, bags, purses, shoes, notebooks, watchbands and jewellery, for example. Unlike the Asian, East Indian, and Middle Eastern cultures, where men and women dress in bright, Beauty-full colours…in the West. very few people dress in vibrant tones. Wherever the Western culture takes root you find people changing their traditional bright coloured clothing and accessories to dull, dark colours. In the Eastern and Asian cultures men are accustomed to wearing pink, purple and turquoise, whereas the Western cultures are only now breaking free of the ignorant attitude that pink is only for women. Pink is a "feminine" colour but this means that everyone will benefit from wearing it, as it connects us with our inner feminine energies which comprise a Divine state such as Compassion, Divine Love, Kindness and sweetness.

Many men actually need to wear more pink and feminine accessories, in order to balance out the overdose of testosterone coursing through them, which makes them overly mental, spiritually resistant and emotionally insecure. Wearing the colours considered feminine, or spiritual colours such as orange, white, gold or violet will assist in healing the imbalances in the aura and therefore the personality.

When I meet someone who shares with me the many challenges they are up against, I often recommend to them that they change their way of dressing. I instruct them to add radiant colours in their wardrobe as well as change their hairstyle, jewellery and accessories, so they emanate Strength and power.

Imagine yourself as a warrior going out to confront a battle; a wise warrior would not walk onto the battlefield in 'wimpy, lifeless' clothes. They would dress in such a way as to let their opponent perceive them to be a radiant and confident warrior. Everything about them would be symbolic and brimming with meaning. Wearing your power colours will amplify your aura and charisma. You will find that certain hues fill you with spiritual inspiration, some with emotional resilience, while others fill you with physical vitality.

Notice how today's marketing companies are producing an abundance of items in shades of purple, Kali electric-blue and vibrant rainbow colours. Children and teenagers especially gravitate to these Divine colours, due to the fact that they are old souls. Since they carry the higher vibrations, they resonate with the higher frequencies of empowering shades. If you see them wearing black it is only because either society or dark forces attached to them push the depressing hues upon them. However, very few people have strong enough energetic fields to wear black and I do not recommend it. The same applies for grey, murky or muddy colours such as dark shades of brown or burgundy.

This student's example illustrates the power of the hues we dress in or surround ourselves with.

"Many years ago I went through a stage in which I wore all black, dressing only in dark 'Gothic' clothing. This outer expression reflected my inner state of being. Furthermore, my social life consisted of being in 'dark' places with other people who also liked to express themselves in a similar manner. Within six months of this Life-style, my inner depression was taking its toll. A person in my workplace could obviously sense the negative energies brewing inside me. They suggested I needed to introduce other colours into my wardrobe.

I eventually let go of my attachment to my dark wardrobe and began accumulating coloured clothing. I almost immediately began to feel the transforming power of colours. I began to feel more positive and alive. I also began to cut myself away from the darkness of the social scene I was involved with. In time, the colours I was wearing did not continue to have the same effect and I felt the negative energies start to attack again. I approached my friend again and was given the advice that I was not wearing enough radiant colours. I took that advice and removed every dark colour from my wardrobe. I began to feel more vibrant...so much more alive than I had ever remembered feeling. I changed my 'social' scene completely and the kinds of energies I was around. I also began to learn that the colours would not do all the 'work' in eliminating the negative energies and that I would need to protect myself in many ways. For me there is no doubt that colours contain much uplifting power!"

THE POWER OF HAIR AND POSITIVE HAIRSTYLES

The way you wear your hair affects the way you feel about yourself and therefore affects your energy field tremendously. The Impeccable Warrior leads a purpose-full Life and makes conscious choices, including the statement their hair is making to the world. The choice for a hairstyle or look should not be based on the need or desire for compliments, but instead the energetic effect it has on what you is striving to accomplish.

It is important to dress for success, choosing the hair-look that will connect you with that which you wish to plug into. By selecting the perfect look for each cycle of your Life, you can choose to link up with your power-full, invincible, pure, radiant, serene, and wise self! By tuning in to your feelings, it is much easier to honestly communicate with your self, as to how you feel about each hair effect you are considering.

Whatever the choice, proceed like a scientist, considering it an experiment as to how certain styles change the dynamics within and around you. If you have ever had a 'bad' haircut you already know how much it can affect your sense of self and the flow of your power. You should be conscious and at true Peace with the statement your hair is making about you.

Hair acts like antennae and for this reason there are many traditions that do not encourage cutting the hair, since it does bring you power. However, it can also be your down-fall if you approach it egotistically, from the point of view of the petty ego, which is why certain traditions of monk hood and nun hood require the initiate to shave their head, as an act of renouncing the little personality/ego.

Surrendering the mind's attachment to hair releases them from the power of the petty ego that cares so much about what other people think. In so doing, by accepting this hairstyle, the renunciate is consciously aligning with the message they wish to send out to the visible and invisible worlds. The Impeccable Warrior understands that potent choices are those based on Wisdom, not vanity. Check in with your Energetic Self and ask what kind of hairstyle you need for that day/cycle/project you are embarking on.

Hair has the same power as blood. It carries all your data and if you were to have a hair analysis performed for feedback on your physical system, you would find the same information revealed by your hair strands as blood samples. Just as blood should not be discarded carelessly, neither should hair. When you have your hair cut, collect all the hair and treat it as a sacred part of yourself. You may wish to give it to Mother Earth, or donate it to a body of water, such as the ocean. You may choose to spread it around plants or bury it...the choices are endless. Let your creative soul guide you. Knowing how sacred and power-full your hair is, at all times, be aware to keep your hair out of the hands of evil beings. Listen to your Intuition... Never allow anyone you have doubts about to cut or touch your hair. There are people who have a "bad hand" and once they touch your hair, your hair will react and begin to demonstrate signs of imbalance. If you have any misgivings about anyone, do not give them access to your hair and take action to protect yourself.

SACRED WATER

Water is a enormously valuable offering to make each day. Water is LIQUID Light, a conductor and absorber of negative energies. The human being is made up mostly of water, so if you do not have a container of water in your home or office to attract the various negative vibrations floating around you, those forces will be absorbed by your water-rich body. This will then contribute towards the manifestation of imbalances in your mind or your physical state. We have already explained earlier in this book how negative forces attack your weak spots and there is at all times a continual flow of these energies, which will attempt to affect you. However if you set out a glass or bowl of water each day, the water will collect layers of those energies. Instead of your mind, body and spirit receiving waves of destructive energies, the water will absorb the damage intended for you.

Normally, when you set up a glass of water in any space, after only a few minutes you should be able to see many bubbles forming on the side or the bottom of the glass. These are the energies the water has collected and having been collected, they can now be removed from your home by taking them outside to nature, which will Compassionately process the collected energies. You will notice that the pattern formations and size of the bubbles varies each day.

The exception to the way water reacts is in areas where the water has been over-treated and has become Life-less. When this happens, that liquid which flows from the tap is no longer true water and therefore has lost much of its mysterious curative and protective powers. I experienced this in Hong Kong and have since experienced it in other areas I have made Pilgrimage to. In these areas the water will not register anything.

However you can place a flower or flowers inside the glass of water to help it clear the atmosphere of negative energies. The flower has Life Force and acts as an antenna to draw in low vibrations circulating around you. The Compassionate flowers perform their Self-less service by attracting those detrimental energies heading at you, INTO the glass of water instead.

When dealing with Life-less water the flower is often able to charge the water, infusing Life into it and in a short amount of time, bubbles will often begin to appear.

Normally if you are in a home that is filled with much *intrigue*, *drama* and *suffering*, or many *visitors* the glass would be filled with an abundance of bubbles. However, due to the processing which strips the water, there will be areas which will not register the presence of layers upon layers of emotions floating in the room.

Regardless of this, I still recommend that the water offering be utilized as a Protectress of your mind, body, and spirit. The

Impeccable Warrior lives by the awareness that 'The mind is the builder'…meaning that intention is what sets a reality in place.

Committed to this golden energetic rule, the Impeccable Warriors know it is their duty to initiate states and establish conditions in everything around them. They do this by programming matter and energy through their focused, determined intention. This can be done by way of positive affirmations, songs and other positive power actions, for the sky is the limit as to how we do it. The vital point is that you do take the initiative to call forth whatever qualities you desire into water, food, soil, or air that seems depleted.

Therefore, if you are in an area where the water is apparently dead, you can still empower yourself and the water by charging with your prayers. YOU have the power within YOU to program the water to collect negative energies in your space. The Holy Spirit lives within YOU and is able to work through you to imprint your intention upon the water…and infuse it with the power to protect you.

It's a very simple process to set out water offerings. First, it is best to use the same glass everyday. You should strive to provide enough water to create a sufficient force-field of protection. I therefore prefer to use a large glass versus a small one and to fill the glass three quarters full. I do not fill it too high, because it is not a good sign to spill any of this water inside your space, so you want to be able to move the glass to and from your altar without spilling any water.

I also prefer to use the local tap water so I can check out its quality, but there have been many times I have used filtered and bottled water as well. In your daily prayers, thank your God Source for this amazing gift, for water is a great mystery. The scientists are still trying to figure out the universal source of water and whenever they find water on a planet, this indicates to them the existence of some type of Life form. Water is Life and water is considered another form of the Goddess…Divine Mother. The Rivers and Oceans are considered sacred bodies and aspects of Mother God.

Whatever you consider your God-Source can be thanked every day for this tremendous boon, which we refer to as 'water'. In my daily offerings, I normally hold the glass in my hands while thanking Divine Mother for this tremendous blessing which purifies, protects and nurtures us. Water is the Sacred Blood that flows through Mother Earth's veins. All water is actually Holy Water and you can use it as such. You can amplify its powers through the prayers and invocations you do over the water.

I am very childlike so I state things in a very child-like way. I speak to Her according to what I feel in my heart, knowing She will lovingly accept my Devotion. While holding the glass of water, I say prayers over it such as this one:

"Divine Mother I thank You this blessed day for Your great gift which protects us and nurtures us. This Sacred Ha, the Holy Water, is liquid Light... it is Your Life Force, without which we cannot live. This is Your profound Compassion and All Mighty Protection. You have placed it on this Beauty-full earth to sustain us, give us Life and purify us. I give endless thanks to You on behalf of all beings for this Divinely potent boon!"

I make the sign of the cross over the water while saying my prayers. You can make any symbol over it that makes you happy and that empowers you. I continue to make the sign of the cross as I continue to program qualities into the water in ways such as:

"Divine Mother this is Your Prosperity, Abundance, mutual Respect, Love, Perfect Health, Radiance, Clarity, Cooperation, Courage, Harmony, great Devotion and Dedication to You and Your sacred laws. You have given us all this by bestowing upon us this most precious gift."

While I am doing the prayer of Appreciation and programming the Sacred Ha, I blow my breath into the water as often as I am instinctively pulled to. In this way, I am infusing it with my own unique Life Force...with the power of the Sacred Breath. This may be especially help-full for those of you in areas with water registering as possibly Life-less. Have confidence that you can instigate and awaken Life Force, and install it in previously depleted water.

In loud voice, or silently, you can also offer any prayer that is close to your heart. Any words or sounds that instil in you a sense of protection, can be uttered or radiated silently over any water. State your intention, that by doing so, you are converting this liquid into Holy Water. With any prayers/sacred sound/actions you implement, listen to your body Wisdom as to how many times you need to repeat the action to complete your Work. Do not stop your prayers until your mind and body register absolute conviction that the water is fully charged.

After I have done my daily prayers over the water to the satisfaction of my body Wisdom, I then offer it to the seven Directions, which is the way I choose to honour the Cardinal Points of the Universe. In my way of doing it *at this moment*, I honour the Cardinal Points of the Universe in this way: East, North, West, South, Sky, Earth and the Sacred Temple of the Heart. I was trained to start in the East and move counter-clockwise, but other traditions teach to move clockwise. Some begin with the South, North, or West.

I cannot stress enough that the manner in which I do The Work is forever evolving...the way I presently honour the Universal Directions is only the current way. I wish to further clarify that I don't make my offerings in a counter-clockwise direction simply because that is the way I was trained...I do it this way, because THIS is what feels in-sync with my body Wisdom. I recommend you also do what feels 'right' in your body.

The Impeccable Warrior follows the lead of the Energy, not their mind or the group mind. This is my way of relating to the Cardinal Directions and I impel you to develop your own Joy-full way and become one with it, through Faith-full practice. You can use the ideas given here as inspiration, but I pray you will feel free to birth and evolve your rituals into something that is uniquely you.

I offer the water to the seven Directions either by facing each Direction with the glass of water in my hands and saying "I offer this to the Compassionate Energies of the East." I continue and do the same with each Cardinal Point. If you cannot physically face each Direction, you can address a Cardinal Point energetically, by simply making the statement, or by making the sign of the cross on each of the four sides of the glass and one energetic cross over the top of the glass for Sky...Earth...and the Center of the Universe/ Sacred Temple of the Heart. The ways to work are endless!

If you have an altar set up, you can also then offer the water to all the Directions by sprinkling some water at each corner of the altar, then on top of something, which represents to you Sky, Earth and the Sacred Temple of the Heart. This could be flowers, stones, images, yourself, or other sacred articles. You can also sprinkle the water in the corners of the room you are standing in.

Now, after you have offered it to all the Cardinal Points, there are many ways you can use this Holy Water that you have created. If you have statues or pictures on your altar you can sprinkle the water over them or offer it to them in any ceremonial way. For example, I like to use the Holy Water to anoint the hands and feet of Divine Mother in the many pictures and statues I have of Her. You can anoint pictures of people that you are praying for, as well as your protection amulets and sacred items…or gifts you are charging for others. By sprinkling the Holy Water on them, you are blessing them each day and building up the protective power in them.

If you wish, you can take the glass of water and go to each room of your home and sprinkle some of this Holy Water everywhere including under beds, inside closets, cupboards and any dark spaces. All of which I have described can be done while chanting the Holy Names or repeating your favourite prayers and affirmations. With every step of your offerings, you are calling forth transformation and protection while emanating Appreciation and Humility.

I am often moved to tears while making my offerings, for the Compassionate Forces are so pleased with our humble efforts, that they shower us with Their Love! I feel Their Appreciation as They melt my heart…in this way, I am perpetually flooded with Love. This is why Masters do not need Love from any human as other human beings do. We are forever swimming in the Ocean of Bliss that is created by an ever-flowing circle of Mutual Respect and Love… between us, the Masters and Forces of Compassion.

Once you have finished doing your water rituals, you can place the glass on your altar and once again make the proclamation that any negative forces that try to enter your Temple will be captured and dissolved in the Holy Water. You will find that different areas of your home or property will register varying levels of energies. One room of your home may continually generate many bubbles whereas another spot may register quieter activity. This can be due to many variables: the land beneath your floor, any neighbours adjoining to that room or the surrounding energies are just some of the factors that would affect the meter.

It is vital to change the water, replacing it with fresh water every day. Before you begin your daily rituals, you can take the previous day's offering outside and deliver it back to nature, to something green. Unless you absolutely have to, it is not recommended to discard the water by pouring it down any inside sinks or to pour it onto planted flowers, fruit bearers or cacti.

The old water, which is now loaded with the accumulated psychic debris it absorbed on your behalf, is best poured at the base of trees, green bushes and plants. If none of these are available to you, you can deliver it to any patch of grass or Earth around you. Since this water is now filled with varying amounts of negativity, if you were to pour it down a drain you might find yourself with plumbing problems as others have. Therefore, if you must pour it down drains, it is wise to call upon Compassion and state that you set forth the intention that any negative quality in the water be miraculously disintegrated. Choose to believe and set up the intention that your drains will be unaffected.

As psychic transformers, trees have more power than bushes, and bushes more than plants...but they are all Protectors and have been created to absorb humanity's negativity and shower us with their Life force. They will selflessly receive the trapped darkness and then mysteriously and perfectly handle those energies. After you have discarded of the water you can then wash out the glass and start again.

It is Beauty-full to communicate with the Compassionate Forms and Forces that have heard your prayers and received your offerings with so much Kindness.

My routine consists of thanking the Master Teachers, Celestial and Earth Forces that I originally presented my offerings to, for their kind and patient acceptance of my humble offerings. I then thank all of the Cardinal Directions for also receiving my humble gift, thanking them for the protection and transformation they have bestowed upon me, once again. Then I say:

"From the Mother Earth everything comes,
and to Mother Earth it must return...
Thank you Divine Mother for everything you give to us
Please accept this offering from this humble child of Yours..
Forgiveness, Forgiveness, forever I call forth Your Kindness
and Forgiveness....
Even though I do not know how to offer and do not know how to
properly thank You,
You All Ways forgive me for any lack of attention or lack of
Respect.
I ask for Your Compassion today and all-ways take refuge in Your
Mercy, Mercy-full Mother!"

There is a simple sacred word that can be used in making any offering or with any action, which is 'Swaha'. Swaha is from the Hindu tradition and is one of the names of the Goddess. It translates to mean "I offer this at the feet of the Lord". "I surrender this to you, Divine Mother" and "I am ONE with God!" It is a fantastic sacred sound that anyone can use with great Gusto. Of course, the children Love it and it gives them something they can easily pronounce when making offerings. If you do choose to use this offering mantra, make sure you say it with great sacred enthusiasm with the accent on the second syllable: Swaa-HAA!

Now that you know all this about the energies and how they appear, I recommend you pay more attention to a glass of water before drinking it. I never leave my food plate or water uncovered while unattended. You may also find that unopened gallons and bottles of plain water may already be filled with bubbles. This is due to the fact that it is the nature of negative energies to find any space through which they can sneak in. Imbalanced energies are experts at encroaching and you now know they are drawn to water. So, since these containers are not truly airtight, depending on where they were stored and who they were handled by, the water picks up on the surrounding energies, absorbing and registering their presence.

It is your choice as to whether you drink it in that condition. I prefer not to, and choose instead to give that water back to nature whenever it is possible. However when I am in a place where there is no 'good' water available, I boil the bubble-filled water and pray over it before drinking it. Another easy technique for infusing any water with Life Force and Positive Power is to shake it robustly, while calling forth Divine Mother's miraculous power to transform it into the perfect medicine for your body and spirit.

LIQUOR OFFERINGS

If you are making water offerings and practicing all of the techniques that have been revealed in this book, yet still find your home/office is under attack, you can experiment by making an offer of liquor each day. As with drugs and alcohol, when people ingest liquor in a non-ceremonial way, it creates huge holes in their aura through which negative entities can enter. However, when you use the liquor to protect your space it creates an energetic field of protection.

In this protection practice, you offer the liquor to your Protector(s), to the guardians of the Land where you live and the spirits of your Ancestors, if you wish to include them. To do this you can use any kind of liquor you feel the spirits will appreciate.

This offering will be placed on the floor so it can collect the physic serpents that might be crawling around. It is important to place in a spot where it will not be tipped over. Once you have set out the liquor bowl and it has begun to collect negative energies, you should ensure that none of it is ever spilled.

You do not need to pour a large amount of liquor, so a small bowl that is not very tall in height will work well. My bowls are approximately 2 or 3 inches across and 2 inches high. As with the water offering, it is best you do not fill it to the top, so you do not spill any of the liquor when the time comes to discard yesterday's offering. Filling the bowl one half to three quarters full will make it easier to transport the bowl without spilling.

I use natural materials such as dugout gourds, but you can also use glass or ceramic and if you have to, even something out of plastic. I am a very big advocate of using whatever you have on hand, in order to get the job done, and then upgrading it as soon as possible. While there is always plenty of room for improvement in all actions we perform…and we can certainly strive for the 'perfect' way to do everything…the most vital ingredient in all actions is Sincerity and Love. Your intension is the key ingredient the Universe receives from you.

After you have poured the liquor into a bowl/container, say your prayers over it in a similar way done with the water offerings. You can create your own prayer whereby you address your Spirit Guides, invoking Their presence and praising Them as well as thanking Them for hearing you. You can make this offering and go through this procedure addressing all the Compassionate Forces of the Universe, offering it to all of Them. After you have praised Them and thanked Them for the great Compassion They have for you, your Loved ones and all of humanity, you can invite Them to receive your humble offering.

Speak to Them in the same way you would address any honoured guest. Welcome Them, stating how much you appreciate Their protection and the healing they provide your home and your family. When we speak from our heart, we will naturally invite them to receive our offerings with Compassion…we will naturally be flooded with the sincere desire to ask for forgiveness for any moment when we do not perform our Ceremony with the full Wisdom, Attention and Respect that is due.

Every ritual is an event and as the host/hostess, we are doing our best to please Them with our actions. It is wise to state that you are a child who is still learning… Humility keeps our offerings pure. Do not hesitate to ask Them to help you grow in Wisdom…so you can be a greater instrument with each passing day. I am forever aware of Their Patience with me…and for the immense Love They have for me that manifests in Their kind acceptance of the humble offerings I present.

So feel free to ask Their help in letting you know how They want the offering made. Tell Them that you wish very much to know how to honour and Respect Them...so They will always feel welcomed and at home. You can invite Them to enjoy this offering, to receive it fully on behalf of yourself, your family and all of humanity.

Then you can offer it up to the Four Directions, plus the Sky, the Earth and lastly the Sacred Temple of the Heart. Of course you don't have to do it this way...I am simply sharing the way I do it. If you wish, you can also chant a mantra such as Kali Durge Namo Nama, as many times as you wish...while holding the offering in your hand. In this way you are charging it through the vibration that is flowing from your hands into the container and the liquor itself. Your inner Guidance will let you know when you have chanted enough so to please the Universe. Trust your inner Wisdom...it will communicate with you and direct you as on when to present the offering. When you feel that the offering is perfectly charged, place it on the floor... in a spot that is safe from pets or feet knocking it over or any other factor that could result in the offering being spilled.

Offerings that Compassionately collect negativity from your space should never be spilled or knocked over, as that would release the negativity back into your place, so it is best to place it in such a position on the floor that it will not be disturbed. You can state a command that any negative forces that attempt to enter your Temple to bother you or your Loved ones, will be consumed in the liquor offering and dissolved immediately. You empower the offering each time you thank the Compassionate Forces for defending and protecting your Temple, bodies and spirit. We can never thank the Protectors of the Light enough for helping us do our work in Peace-full Enthusiasm. Every time you allow your affection and Appreciation to flow to your Guides/Protectors, your mind, body, spirit and surroundings Light UP!

The liquor should be taken outside the next day in order to discard of it and be poured out into something green such as a plant or a tree. However, as with the water offering or ashes from the sacred smoke, never pour the water or liquor offerings unto flowers or cacti.

Before you pour it out, state an intention...tell the Universe what you are doing, what you are planning to do and why. You can say a prayer of Great-fullness, thanking the Compassionate Forces for having received your humble gift the day before…for all of Their healing protection and transformation They provide you and your Loved ones.

I thank the Celestial and Terrestrial Forces, as well as the Master Teachers, Spirit Guides and Angels who have received my humble gift so kindly. I then state: *"From the Mother Earth everything comes and to the Mother Earth it must return."* I then pour it out onto the tree, plant, or if there is no greenery available, the ground.

When I take the liquor outside to discard of it, I always take the previous day's water offerings as well. After I have poured out the liquor, I blow on the container…uttering the sacred name of one of the Sacred Whirlwinds in between breaths.

I then pour some of the water offering into the liquor container to wash it out, and pour the solution onto the ground. I usually do this four times, one for each of the four Directions…repeating my action of blowing across the container each time. Every time I blow into the container and call on the Sacred Whirlwinds, I am clearing the container of any negative residue.

I have stated I do this four times. The reason for this, is that I am invoking one of the Sacred Whirlwinds each time. However, there have been times the Shakti/Holy Spirit has directed me to clear the bowl more than four times. Likewise, let yourself be guided by your inner Wisdom with all your practices.

At this time, I am not authorized by Spirit to share with anyone else the names of the Sacred Whirlwinds, so I cannot divulge these sacred sounds. Perhaps my instructions from Spirit will change one day, but for now, I cannot impart the Mayan sacred names to anyone who is not chosen for this particular work. At this point, the Guidance remains, as it has been for thousands of years…that certain mysteries only be revealed to that rare individual who has purified their soul to the point of being totally unavailable to any dark forces.

If someone is not committed to this specific path, then they are not recognized or accepted by these Sacred Forces. These Forces are tremendously power-full and if someone who is not known to Them calls out Their names, it could result in the body or mind being flooded by an energy that is too strong to be handled.

However, the Positive Forces are always so Compassionate that they will work with people to the extent possible. I encourage you to conduct many experiments by using various ways to call on the Cleansing Winds to help you. You can simply refer to Them as the Cleansing Winds, Sacred Winds. I feel that for now you may be able to do this phase of the work by simply invoking those energies in Their gentler forms by addressing Them either as the Cleansing Winds, Sacred Winds or any other Respect-full title that you are inspired to utter.

I am sure that Spirit will send a Compassionate Force to help you and cleanse the container of any negativity that might be present. After that, take the container back to the Temple and wash it out with water only...no soap. Soap is rarely necessary, but once again, Trust your Intuition as to when you may need soap. If you do use a tiny amount of soap for either the water or liquor container, rinse it out THOROUGHLY. You do not want your offerings to taste of soap. Now, once your container has been cleansed by the Sacred Forces of Compassion and the Sacred Healing Waters, refill it and make new offerings.

It is important to CONCENTRATE while you are doing all this... do not let yourself be distracted by others or anything else. Do not engage in material conversations or mental gyrations. FOCUS on mantras, prayers, Great-fullness...on your intention and sacred connection to The Source. If you engage in actions of limited vibration, you taint what you are doing with that frequency. When you maintain your awareness on yourself as a Divine REPRESENTATIVE... who is walking on Mother Earth with a Radiant Heart, overflowing with Devotion...then everything you touch and intend is infused with Light...AND LIGHTNING POWER TO TRANSFORM!

SACRED CANDLE WORK AND FIRE CEREMONIES

The candle is one of Spirit's most Sacred gifts. The flame represents the Great Illumination of the God Source. The candle represents the Light within each of us and this Light was and is honoured by Indigenous groups by keeping a sacred fire burning at all times. Being a keeper of that Sacred Flame is an honour and we all have that privilege available to us. You can be a Keeper of the Sacred Flame by ensuring that a candle is burning at all times. If for some reason this is not possible for you, then at leas. Light a candle when you feel yourself being harassed or assaulted by negative forces.

The forces of darkness are repelled by Light and when you Light a candle on your altar it opens up a portal for the Light/Spiritual Protection/Grace to flow into your home. There is no difference between a candle and the ceremonial fires that are utilized as prayer offerings by the global Indigenous cultures.

When you Light a candle you can call on Spiritual Protection, illumination of your mind, body, spirit and your Spiritual Path. You can dedicate this Light to all the Cardinal Points…on behalf of your family, friends and the rest of humanity…invoking Illumination into their minds, bodies, spirits, and destinies.

I offer the candle in the same way I offer the water, sacred smoke and liquor offerings. After praising Divine Mother's amazing Compassionate gift of Illumination, I offer it to all Her forms, all my Teachers and Ancestors…praying that they All-Ways be in the Great Illumination…that Their spirits forever be free of negative karma, torments or distress.

I petition that Their spirit all-ways be tranquil and serene, in Great Peace. Then I offer the Light on behalf of all the departed souls, in all realms…petitioning that their paths may be illuminated with a brilliant Light. I pray on their behalf, that they be assisted by the Light Forces to reach out to the Light…adore the Light and serve the Light Impeccably. I then proceed to present the Light on behalf of all beings on the Radiant Earth, asking the same for them, so they may all complete their Highest Destiny.

At any time, you can make these offerings on behalf of anyone and everyone you care for...you can invoke Grace for a few or on behalf of all creation. Your offerings are of great assistance to all other beings that also embrace the Light, and strive to walk the Impeccable Path...as well as those who do not yet have Faith in the Light. Grace flows where you direct it and you can send it to those who mistakenly believe they do not need to be close to their God/Spirit/Angels/Guides/Spiritual Path. Regardless of what stage of growth they are at...everyone needs more Grace and no being can ever have too much Grace. I promise you that your actions uplift all realities...your prayers/offerings do have a tremendously immeasurable impact on the evolution of all souls.

CROSSES, COCONUT AND IRON HORSESHOES

Crosses, coconuts and iron horseshoes are just a few of the articles you can bury at your front gate or outside your front door, for protection. I would recommend you repeat, chant or sing sacred mantra/prayers while digging the hole, placing the item in the ground and covering it. Afterwards you could draw a protective symbol or write a prayer on top of the ground where you have just buried the item. This will seal the energy.

Some people prefer to hang bundles of herbs above, outside or inside doorways. I am not a big fan of items that collect large amounts of dust and for this reason alone, keeping dried herbs in this way is not one of my favourite protection practices. There are endless ways to protect your space and experimentation is the only way you will realize what empowers you and your space the best.

I once closed down an intense portal with the help of the crosses I use in the Peace Ceremonies. They are made from a wood considered holy in Mexico, and they were fully charged with immense power from the considerable blessings acquired via being kept on my altar and used in a long sequence of Peace Ceremonies. I buried one in each corner of the property as well as one in the centre point of the land. I then went inside the house and placed a cross in each area that we decided represented each of the four directions and the centre point of the house.

Someone once asked me if there was a difference between utilizing a crucifix instead of a plain cross. I feel that they have the same power, which is the power that humanity has recognized in the basic form of the cross. For those who have Faith in Jesus, the combination of the image of Jesus on the crucifix, along with the primordial power of the cross can provide amplified confidence in God's protection.

In the same way that bodies are buried with a crucifix to protect the spirit of the departed on its journey to the Light, you can use the crucifix or a plain cross to protect the living. The rule of thumb is to use that which makes you feel protected…implement whatever you believe in…and resonate with. It is your Faith in the item or practice chosen, which bestows protection. There is the inherent power of the sacred element, article and practice you use…and there is further and greater power that YOU infuse it with, which arises from your Faith…from your belief in it.

ENERGETIC CIRCUIT BREAKERS: BANDS, RIBBONS AND CLOTH

The Impeccable Warrior of Light understands that in doing healing work on others, one can take on their energy as well as give energy to them. It is the nature of energy to flow and since we are all psychic instruments it is only natural that once we open a channel, energy can flow both ways.

You can block other's energy from flowing into you by wearing wristbands. I feel armbands are a choice, but wristbands are a must! They provide your body an energetic surge-protector which is invaluable. Whereas some traditions recommend the use of ribbons or string for wrist energy flow Protectors, others prescribe bracelets. I carry bracelets in my Ceremonial basket, however, I sometimes feel they either bind me too tightly or are too cold next to my skin. I find I gravitate most often to the warmth and lightweight nature of the ribbons. The main thing is to begin…do not put this practice off. Even while you contemplate this practice and meditate on what is best for you, at least begin immediately by wrapping your wrists in ribbons, string, cloth or yarn. You can always upgrade later.

One aspect of this practice is that wrapping your wrists helps you to give out energy without taking on the psychic baggage of others. Another aspect is that it protects the actions your hands and arms are performing, so that you only perform positive actions and therefore yield only good karma.

Although red is a colour utilized by many traditions, I encourage people to experiment with combinations of any radiant colour that empowers you. I have never enjoyed wearing red and so normally wrap my wrist in deep purple, turquoise or Divine Mother blue. You can mix colours and wear more than one.

In many ancient cultures men, women and children dressed stunningly, combining red, purple, pink, gold, Divine Mother electric blue, turquoise, orange and vibrant green in their clothing, shawls, jewellery, waistbands, head wear, wristbands, armbands, anklets and footwear. They wore what made them feel magnificent... incorporating that which Strengthened them and therefore assisted them in accomplishing their mission. When choosing your clothing and power accessories, keep in mind that the constant question is, "What works for you now? What is viable for you NOW?"

The healing energy that flows out through your arms and hands to others is electricity...it is lightning energy. If you are sensitive you may experience it in the same way you would the 'zing' of an electric shock. When it flows intensely, it can feel as if it is cutting to the bone and therefore be quite uncomfortable. Arm and wristbands control the flow of Universal electrical energy, protecting you from the strong wattage that is flowing through you.

Another surge protector is the colour gold and certain traditions such as the Hindu Vedic path recommend you implement it by wrapping it around your weak areas such as your hips or solar plexus. Knowing all this, I still prefer purple and Divine Mother blue and encourage you to experiment on what is best for you. Listen to your spirit...your heart...your body Wisdom...not your rationalizing mind. Trust YOUR Intuition.

THINKING HAPPY THOUGHTS

Negative forces despise Happiness, Peace, Beauty, Strength and the presence of any of the other Virtues. One way to loosen the grip of tyrannical forces is to think happy thoughts. Holding happy memories and images in your mind floods you with Power and Strength. Happy thoughts solidify you, making you a more formidable Warrior of Light. The moment you entertain a positive thought your energetic and physical body fill with Light, literally making you "lighter" as the density of this material world is replaced with luminescence. By parting company with those dark forces that spout that low-vibration storyline, the more you invite and accept the Light. The more you embrace the Light, the more you release the heaviness of this world. The more often you contemplate the Light and the power of the Light to move you into another reality, the faster you become "Enlightened".

The power of this Wisdom Teaching was demonstrated when I was contacted regarding some ancestral remains. Apparently these remains had been kept in a museum for many years and in a mysterious way they ended up in the hands of the person who contacted me. She and many others who tuned into the vibrations of these Ancestors could feel the Ancestor spirits were drowning in sadness. They were stuck due to their torment over the genocide they had witnessed.

She asked me to help them move on and I agreed. She took me, and a few others who were accompanying me, to the room where the Ancestors bones and artifacts were kept. Those present that were extremely psychically open, began to wail as they were engulfed by the waves of sadness emanating from the spirits who were still trapped in the heart-breaking sorrow experienced at the time of their death.

During their Life on Earth, their last days and moments were consumed with the indescribable horror of witnessing the massacre of their entire clan. While in the spirit world, they were still in shock…they had not moved on because they were locked into the memories of the helplessness they experienced upon being uprooted and violated. They were stuck in a void reality of re-living the image of overwhelming despair and the feelings associated with their People. The prevailing energy we sensed was of them moaning "They are all gone...gone...gone!"

I had been praying to Divine Mother as to how to help these particular souls move on. I was shown clearly how the souls were stuck and I was moved by the Holy Spirit/Shakti to twirl. Spinning is how Divine Mother often uses my physical body to create a vortex of Light. As I was twirling at high speed, I was communicating psychically with the spirits encouraging them to think happy thoughts so they could be released from the pain-filled state that was holding them here on Earth. I concentrated on mentally communicating to them that the vortex of Light was available to them. I told them they should think happy thoughts and in doing so they could break free of the gravity of this material plane and utilize the vortex I was creating, to lift them off the Earth plane.

I kept praying to Divine Mother for them to take advantage of this opportunity for Freedom and kept envisioning them in my mind's eye, lifted up into the Light...Laughing...Happy and Free. Although the others in the group may have seen me twirling, we had not spoken at all. I had not shared a word as to what I had planned to do or what I was doing. I had not given them any clues as to the message I was sending to the spirits. However, afterwards, those who had been channelling the spirits' suffering shared that they had seen a huge Eagle descend and pick them all up...lifting them to the heavens! Isn't that Magnificent! This was perfect confirmation for me that the work had been completed.

This is just one demonstration of the transformative medicine in sustaining Positive thoughts. Anytime you feel stuck, scared... or in any other negative state dark forces might be projecting onto you...I encourage you to repel them by implanting Joyous, Loving, Triumphant images in your mind, body and emotions.

HELMETS, HEADBANDS, HATS, SHAWLS, TURBANS

The saying, "put on your thinking cap", has such a deep meaning, as do many of the Ancient Teachings. Contemplation of its deepest meaning has been lost due to the Wisdom not being handed down along with the saying. When we hear the message to put on our 'thinking cap', we may not realize we are being inspired to reach for a physical piece of clothing so we can change the colour of our aura and thereby attract, receive and recognize new, Positive, creative solutions.

I see people putting on their "thinking caps" all around me... with some feeling the need to wear particular head-gear on a regular basis. These beings are drawn to do so at a deep intuitive level. 'O' is such a being. While discussing this material, my assistant was reminded of 'O', who is a young boy who consistently wears a winter hat that resembles a helmet. He won't go anywhere unless he has his 'helmet' on. In the Center, the walls are covered with an abundance of images of Divine Mother and my assistant suddenly realized that 'O's helmet is shaped exactly like the helmets worn by some of the Hindu Goddesses.

Before all this dawned on her, this same assistant, 'L' had begun wearing a purple head-wrap. She shared that she usually dislikes wearing anything on her head, but felt irresistibly drawn to buy this one. She found herself in a store with a large range of Beauty-full wraps, but heard her inner-self urging, "I want a purple one!" In that huge array of selection there was not one purple one in sight, but 'L' was insistent the shopkeeper look for one. 'L' was determined to heed her inner voice and the shopkeeper hunted around until he found a purple one for her. She now wears it quite regularly. 'L' has a busy mind and her mental state is where she needs the most protection. It is wonder-full to see people following their inner guidance and seeking out the protection items that they need to wear or have near them.

Like 'L', I am also normally too sensitive to enjoy wearing any article that creates the feeling of being bound, so throughout my younger Life, the idea of tying something around my head had never appealed to me. Yet, at one point in my Shamanic training I began waking up each day with an overwhelming desire to wrap my head. With varied cycles, I was pulled to different styles and a variety of colours, but in the end I got the clear message that for my work I should wear a headband of vibrant colours, or a crown of bright short feathers. From time to time, I receive other instructions and I heed those messages, creating and implementing the images I receive. I have since then followed my Guides' instructions and wear some type of the head-wear during all Ceremonial work, concerts, programs, meetings and consultations. If I need to wear it at other times, my Spirit Guides will alert me with a clear message and I quickly move into action.

Head-gear is a seal of protection for two of our inner Temple doors...the Crown Chakra and Third Eye Chakra. Some cultures realized the spiritual significance of this, while others continued the tradition of head-gear, justifying it as work or fashion-related. Nonetheless, whether or not societies have been conscious of the highest purpose of head wear, throughout history both men and women have embraced the idea of covering the spiritual energy centres at the crown of our head and in-between our eyebrows.

This is especially important for women, who tend to be more psychic, for the more intuitive you are the more open your energy centres are. Yet it goes without saying that there is a wise reason men have also consistently worn hats, helmets, caps, bandanas, turbans, shawls and a myriad of other types of head coverings.

When I was a young girl I rebelled against the idea of women having to cover their heads as they do in many traditions, but time and experience showed me the Wisdom of this ancient practice, as I encountered one person after another in the Soul Retrieval sessions who had entities attached to different parts of their head.

As mentioned in another section, this sometimes shows up in the conditions, such as:

* itching
* headaches
* obsessive anxiety
* confusion
* hearing problems
* bi-polarity
* pessimism
* fears
* cruelty
* schizophrenia
* self-aggrandizing patterns
* any other self destructive actions you can name

* memory power decrease
* dull mind syndrome
* loud voices in the head
* excessive perfectionism
* self-degrading behaviour
* hyperactive mind
* anger flashes
* sarcasm
* addictions

'SK's experience is a perfect illustration of the truth in this Wisdom Teaching. 'SK' was constantly under intense psychic attack, as she was a tender-hearted, sensitive, psychic, artistic, child-like person. She strove to embody Pure Love and had learned few defences against the disruptive forces that attacked her relentlessly. Punishing forces would have a field day with her emotions and she was constantly bursting into tears, as endless horrible thoughts would impose themselves unto her mind screen. After attending the Impeccable Warrior of Light Intensive, she understood clearly what she could do to protect herself. She prayed to find the right items for her sacred defence and she miraculously was led to a purple shawl, which she purchased immediately. She KNEW INTUITIVELY how desperately she needed its protection. She walked out of the store wearing it on her head, draped around her shoulders, immediately feeling the power of the protective shield. The next time she saw me, she was wearing it and shared that as soon as she placed it on her head, she could actually see the little malevolent arrows that the forces of suffering had shot at her, bouncing off the shawl!

SYMBOLS

Symbols have tremendous power, both positive and negative, depending on what they are associated with. Here are several

instances of this:
- The Hindu Vedic tradition has always used the swastika to denote the four directions and they show it flowing clockwise. The North Native American tradition also has a version of the swastika to symbolize the four directions. Hitler, who was an obsessed collector of spiritual artifacts that held great power, chose to use the swastika as a symbol of the Nazi movement, but he turned it around so it represented an energy moving counter clock-wise.
- The cross is venerated by Catholics, but long before they and the Christians adopted it, it was being used by the Mayan Indians and other ancient cultures to symbolize the Cosmic Tree/World Tree/ Universal Tree.

So symbols have their roots and if a symbol helps you to feel close to God/Higher-Self/Angels/Spiritual Protectors, then it will bestow its blessing upon you. You can put these symbols on your door front, windows, walls, automobile, equipment or any other place you wish to set up an energetic barrier of protection.

As an Impeccable Warrior, it is astute to notice what symbols are being used by your friends, co-workers and Loved ones. This will always tell you a lot about what is going on in their lives and alert you if someone is being pulled towards the dark side. Baba Muktananda imprinted upon me that 'carelessness and error lead to endless suffering and pain.' The Impeccable Warrior is fully aware that it is their Sacred Duty to be ALERT. Wise Warriors are EVER AWAKE to which way the wind is blowing…in what direction their boat is heading…and the directional flow of vessels all around them as well.

PICTURES, STATUES AND IMAGES

A mother once brought her son to me for a Soul Retrieval Limpia after becoming alarmed that the boy, who was normally a gentle being, had begun drawing images of Satan on himself. During his consultation, he revealed that he had an irresistible urge to write the different names of the devil on himself as well as to draw pictures of demons all over his body and his notebook.

When your Loved ones start associating with ghoulish attire, friends, images and ways, it is important to do everything you can to free them from the spell of that hideous entity that is trying to drag them down a terrible path. Negative images bring enslavement to pain-inducing activities, whereas Positive symbols and images align us with Freedom. At times you may resonate more with one soul-enriching path than another and it is natural that you may find your self more attracted to certain symbols or images than others.

IF there is someone around you that does not resonate to ANYTHING positive, this is a case for alarm. For symbols and images do bestow their blessings of protection upon us…and when someone is not using any of them, they are a sitting target for the force of Evil.

You can use the power of images to help you do your work in the following easy way: when you are concerned about someone or something, write a prayer request and place it under a sacred or positive image…or in a box that has sacred images on it or in it. This is symbolic of surrendering the situation or the person over to the hands of the Grace-bestowing Forces.

One of the best ways for re-claiming a space that has been inhabited by sinister energies is to fill it with sacred symbols, pictures, statues, prayers and mantras. Our mind and imagination are windows through which energies travel, so when we focus on a positive image we invoke that vibration…inviting that world and that source into our space. The Impeccable Warrior of Light is totally discerning as to what images they surround themselves with.

Statues and images should be treated as being alive. There is a Teaching in the Buddhist tradition stating that when you think of your Teacher or Guru as an ordinary human being…you will only receive ordinary blessings. On the other hand, if you relate to your Teacher/Guru as the Buddha himself…then you will receive the Buddha's' blessing through your Teacher. In the same way when you put up images, they need to be cared for as the living energy of that Protector.

If you wish to have blessings that are full of Life Force, then you then you need to care for the Protectors and feed them as if they are indeed alive. I was taught that you never put a holy image on the floor and of course you would not throw them around or sit on them. I like to offer incense everyday to all of the images in the Centre and on my altar. I also take a glass of water and put it up against the image's lips and hold the glass there asking them to sip some water and I remove the glass when I feel in my Body Wisdom that they have finished drinking. In Hindu Temples, Mayan Ceremonies and Buddhist pujas, we see the ancient tradition of offering hot food to the Forces and Beings of Light. The Grace of the Universe is invoked to receive the essence...the aromatic and nourishing steam emanating from the offering...and sustained through this act of Loving Appreciation.

Another Devotional action that I practice, is to apply Holy Water and special oils on the images forehead, hands, feet and heart. As world Temples do with their deities, we also shower our statues and images of the Divine Ones with flower petals. If I put flowers in front of them I am vigilant of when the flowers begin to lose their Life Force and when the water needs to be changed.

I am awake as to what the Positive Forces enjoy and may not wish around them. In this way the Compassionate Forces and I are interacting at all times. I experience Them and communicate with Them as Living Grace-full Energies who are all-ways with me. In this Beauty-full way, the door is wide open to Their presence in my Life and They are forever bathing my daily activities with one miracle after another.

AMULETS AND TALISMANS

Throughout history, the Wise Ones have recognized that certain medals, stones, symbols and materials boost our immune system and aura. In Hindu Vedic astrology as well as other mystical paths, there is a whole science as to what metals, stones and symbols to wear during the different Life cycles, and where on the body to wear them. If you do not have access to someone who can impart this Wisdom to you, you can pray for clarity and higher knowledge, asking to be guided on how to proceed in acquiring and wearing or talismans. In order to provide people with instant protection, Sacred Peace Centers provide blessed amulets that are charged with Divine Mother's blessings.

Certain amulets will influence your material wealth, or projects… others protect against dangers and some are blessed to protect and increase Harmony in relationships.

In case you wish to make your own, I will now share some basic guidelines. For jewellery, silver is normally recommended over gold, as is copper. In ancient solar cultures such as the Egyptians, Incas, Aztecs and others such as the Tibetans, gold was prized. Today, many people still wear gold, but this is only because of the current society's preference. For example, in Yucatán, Mexico, all of the Mayan women judge each other's prosperity by how much gold jewellery they wear.

I have seen this obsession with showing off one's gold in other cultures as well such as India and America. However, we should not wear gold because we crave to be like everyone else in our community. Some people are ignorant of the fact that gold may not even resonate with their energetic field. Others have been told which metals would assist them energetically, but insist on wearing gold out of attachment to its shiny colour or the 'prestige' they believe it brings to them in their material society.

Due to the demons of insecurity, unwilling to break free of the herd, they continue to be the pawns of those very demons instead of wearing the metals necessary in order to shield themselves from ignorance producing forces. In many 'modern' current material societies, gold is considered more valuable and fashion prevails… although protection-wise, silver is a better instrument to defend and therefore augment our Light.

Copper jewellery, is known to alleviate arthritis and rheumatism. If you do not wish to wear it as jewellery you can carry a small amount of copper in a medicine bag or on you in some other way. If you choose to place some in your medicine bag, you can also add other items from the following section on 'Cleansing Ingredients' and/or from the Protection Items listed at the back of this book.

Iron is also used by many cultures as a protective device and is used in the Yucatecan Mayan amulets. In this case, they wrap mini iron horseshoes in vibrant colour paper or ribbons...adding other ingredients such as garlic, rosemary, iron fillings and sacred images for protection of the home or a change in luck.

In some cultures, people consider iron to be a deterrent against Fairies. Obviously they are concerned about mischievous or mean fairies. If your fairies are kind and help-full, you don't need protection against them. However, if the Fairies in your space are creating chaos or disrupting your home negatively, then you may wish to try placing iron horseshoes outside your front door, or different ones in various key energetic point. To know exactly what you need to do for the most complete solution, pray, tune in and follow your instinct.

If you are extremely sensitive, wear grounding stones such as turquoise, jade, amber, or protection stones such as amethyst. You can buy talismans already prepared, or prepare one yourself. If you plan to make your own, there is a long list of ancient symbols that can be used in the creation of amulets and talismans. The cross, which is an ancient symbol of wholeness, Jewish Mezuzah, Hindu Swastika, (which was later borrowed and reversed by the Nazis) Om symbol, pentacles, circles, and Yantras are just a few power-exuding symbols.

YANTRAS

Yantras are ancient power designs that invoke and establish the protective presence of Divine Mother for healing, protection and Prosperity. The Yantras in the Sacred Peace Center catalogue are etched in copper. Yantras are made in various sizes and I utilize all the sizes in the Ceremonies. They can be placed at door fronts, in the four cardinal points, in portal or vortex areas, on your altar, on your body, or carried in your wallet, bag or briefcase for protection and blessings.

Yantra enthusiasts also rave about the power of Yantras to transform the quality of drinking water and other items, by placing the Yantras under the item or in the case of water, under the water container. Some people place it in the water itself. Some people may have too much copper in their physical system and should therefore not place it in the water, but I feel everyone can benefit from placing them under items, on the altar or on doorways.

It is vital to be aware of the attitude of the beings handling amulets you purchase. It is one thing when you purchase a talisman from a Sacred Center like ours or Siddha Yoga, where blessings have been infused into all amulets. It is another story when you are making your own talisman or you purchase one from a shop that relates to it as simply part of their inventory stock. In the case of store bought amulets, be aware they have not been charged for you and you will need to charge them with protective Life force before putting the amulets to work for you.

You can do so by holding it in your hand while repeating a mantra or protection prayer or song, nine times or more. If possible, do this at least once per day, for nine days. After anyone begins wearing or implementing the amulet, it is best to re-charge it every nine days. This is done to re-Strengthen the talisman, for it is similar to a battery. It has been radiating its power into you and around you and will at some point become drained and need re-boosting.

This can be done by holding it in your hand while praying, singing or chanting sacred sounds or by placing it on your altar next to a candle. State your intention and summon the Light into the amulet, to nourish it and emblazon it.

Don Jacinto believed in covering the protection article with a white cloth and I feel you could shroud it with paper or cloth of any vibrant colours, such as red, purple, rose, gold, green or turquoise.

If you are wearing amulets that you never remove, you can feed them through your constant prayers and mantra. This will only be effective if you are able to be vigilant as to the state of your mind and attention while repeating the prayers. Otherwise you are simply radiating a fragmented frequency into your protection items. To determine if you need to remove the item to recharge it, you have to be honest with yourself. During your self-inquiry, you must ask yourself if you are charging the amulet more than draining it, while wearing it.

I do have talismans that I wear day and night and I do not feel they need to ever be removed or to be recharged because my mind is constantly praying and repeating mantras. When I am in the Sacred Peace Center, there are mantras playing twenty-four hours a day and my mind is chanting along, twenty-four hours a day, charging me along with everyone and everything there.

When I am not at the Center, I have my prayer beads in my hands, which re-mind me to turn the wheel of Dharma continually...with constant mantra repetition. Due to the vibration of the ever present mantra within me, wherever I am, the Positive Universal Energies are being nourished. My talismans are being charged constantly while all Goodness and Greatness are being upheld through my focus on Compassion and Love for the Universe. This ultimate state sustains any area I travel through and an endless circle of blessings unfolds continually; I am radiating blessings into the Cosmos by praising it and the Cosmos is emanating Grace into me...protecting me endlessly and Compassionately.

CLEANSING INGREDIENTS

Each global traditions has their favourite ingredients and although each person you meet may have their own recipe for protection, you are certainly encouraged to tune into the storehouse of All-Knowledge, which is Spirit. Your Higher-Self will tell you which substances to combine...in what measures...and in which ways. All healing essences can be used in a variety of ways, so let Spirit guide you.

These ingredients can be used for the creation of sacred smoke... for cleansing baths or inside medicine bags and protection amulets. As well, you can use them for wiping down furniture, floors and counters to remove any residue of psychic intrusion. In some cases you may want to use ingredients such as salt, for the laying down of protection lines. Below is a list of ingredients, and you are sure to discover others as you build up your arsenal of protection tools.

* Basil	* Cloves	* Burdock
* Bay	* Rosemary	* Thyme
* Garlic	* Parsley	* Peppers
* Cayenne	* Cinnamon	* Rue

Many people believe in setting up a line or circle of protection by planting herbs such as rosemary, basil and rue around their home. In Mexico the open markets sell fresh rue and basil, as it is the Indigenous custom for homes to keep a bunch of protective herbs in the home...both in the kitchen or on the altar. Rue has been praised as the 'The Herb of Grace' throughout history. This strong-smelling, bitter herb plant is known in many traditions for its protective powers to ward off evil spirits.

The Mayan Shamans use rue or basil for sweeping the body... as a ceremonial offering...and for bestowing blessings. In past cycles, such as during the Middle Ages, rue was used to ward off pests and diseases. It is one of the traditionally used 'bitter tonics' for sore throats and headaches, while others use rue herbal tea to relieve cramps. Rue ointment is also said to relieve joint pains as well as repel fleas, flies and stinging insects.

Copal, frankincense, myrrh, sage, eucalyptus, sweet grass

All of these ingredients create a sacred smoke that cleanses negative energies from our auric fields, homes, offices, buildings and articles. I personally Love to use Copal, which is the main resin used throughout history by the Mayan culture. It opens up the Celestial realms for you, making it easier to access ancient Wisdom and understand higher knowledge. It creates a vast field of protection that extends beyond your living area by quite a distance.

Sometimes I will burn myrrh or sage simply because I hear the Spirit Guides asking for a different scent that day, as this is how I always determine which ingredient to offer. The various traditions have their own preferences, as we see with the Catholic church utilizing frankincense as an offering during there Mass service... the Aboriginal tradition burning eucalyptus leaves...and the North

Native American path reveres herbs such as sage for cleansing.

Sweet grass is a traditional incense of the Plains Indians, often used after a cleansing smoke of sage or cedar. It is a long sweet smelling grass, typically sold in braids. Suggested use is to cut off the tip and offer it back to the land, then Light the braid tip until smouldering. Or you can break off small pieces and burn them over charcoal. This smoke offers a gentle sweetening of the atmosphere, bringing Peace, Harmony and Healing.

Cedar, lavender, camphor, ghee

All of these agents have a cleansing power. In the Native American tradition, sage is often blended with cedar and lavender for a powerful protection smoke. Camphor is used by the Hindu tradition in daily cleansing rituals as well as the ceremonial fires, along with ghee, which is clarified butter.

Camphor can be purchased through the Sacred Peace Center, or possibly in outlets in your area. It comes in a package of 3 or 4 squares and is often found in the section of cold remedies. To create a cleansing smoke, you would break off pieces of one of the squares and drop it on top of lit charcoal rounds.

Be aware that in these modern times, some companies offer "smokeless" camphor, which smells like camphor, but is treated chemically to not burn. Natural camphor is actually an excellent antibacterial cleanser of the atmosphere, as well as a repellant of dark forces. I do not care for burning chemicals, so the synthetic camphor is not preferable to me, but I feel there may be times when vendors may not even know if the camphor is natural or synthetic. It may not be marked either way. I also wish to warn you that I found the synthetic camphor difficult to extinguish, so only use a small amount until you learn to gauge its patterns of behaviour.

Ghee gives off that wonder-full butter aroma and traditions from the Hindu and Buddhist paths offer up butter lamps to the Gods and Masters. If you cannot tolerate chemical laced candles, you may wish to try making ghee lamps. Ghee is utilized in homes and Temples to make the sacred fire/candle offering. By soaking wood or cotton in the melted, clarified butter and then sprinkling some camphor on top of the fire offering, a strong blaze is created. Not only do negative forces intensely despise the smell of both of these ingredients but their mystical properties cleanse the atmosphere of both physical bacteria and psychic intruders.

Holy Water, ash, ammonia, Florida Water, Rose Water

You can create your own Holy Water or you can obtain some from any Catholic church in your area. Normally, the Catholic churches allow you to bring your own container and fill it on a donation basis. Holy water, sacred ash from a fire offering and Florida Water can all be used to bless or cleanse people, places or items. They can be sprinkled upon a person, place or item, and utilised for laying down protection lines.

In some traditions sacred ash is used to place ritualistic marks on the face or body or to mark doors and windows for protection. Ash is also sometimes blown into corners of rooms or in any direction where trickster or vicious energies are felt.

Diluted ammonia can be used for spraying on furniture and equipment to clear other people's energies, but be aware that even while diluted, it is very strong and it does weaken your immune system. So if you use it, I recommend you open the windows, leave the room afterwards and do a 'thymus thump' on your self afterwards. Your thymus regulates your immune system and you can boost it by doing a Tarzan-like thump on your chest (your closed fist should land on the flat part of your chest, in the area below your throat). You can also stimulate the thymus by simply tapping your finger on that area. Either way, the exercise is similar to jump-starting a battery…it boosts your immune system defences.

Florida Water is perfumed water that has protective powers. It has a subtle, pleasing scent and can be used in place of Holy water on people, items and places. Some people have great Faith in rose and lilac water as well. There are some individuals who believe in placing crystals and certain stones in various combinations of healing waters in order to clear and charge them before implementing them for blessing and protecting others.

Once again, different moments may call for different actions and different formulas. Although many situations may seem similar to others you have crossed paths with…The Impeccable Warrior remains aware that each moment is supremely unique. I recommend that you take everything that you have seen or read in this book or in other sources, as guidelines or inspiration towards the possibilities.

The Primordial Teaching is:
TUNE IN…
TUNE IN…
TUNE IN TO THE PURE Wisdom IN YOU!

Salt

Salt can be used in a variety of ways…some people throw it over their left shoulder. Others drop it along the doorway to ward off negativity and yet others use it to cleanse crystals and other items of any negative energies. To cleanse items, simply place them in a box or container of salt.

Some beings teach that salt is too harsh for crystals, yet I know the Ocean water is a fantastic purifier and healer. Therefore I feel that if you are lucky enough to be able to go to the Ocean, any crystals and sacred items would Love to be in the salt water as much as our physical spirit does. As with all other actions, I choose to act out of guidance, not on what someone else believes…I flow with what I feel Is wise and right at the moment.

I highly recommended clearing items by immersing them in the ocean water. A protection practice is to go to the ocean and to dunk your whole body underwater either three times or nine times. The air surrounding an Ocean is charged with the healing sea salt and your whole aura can be cleansed simply by sitting on the sand in front of the ocean. If you feel you resonate with the concept of using salt water to cleanse articles and it is not possible to use Ocean water, you can mix packaged sea salt with water instead.

You can also use any type of salt to lay down protection lines. In some traditions it is taught that if you put a circle of salt around you, negative forces cannot reach you. It is possible to use it by itself or with other ingredients for laying down protection lines along your property line to keep the neighbours' energies from spilling into your space. This can be help-full in apartment buildings where very little separates you from your neighbour. The close proximity to another's abode creates constant leakage of energies from apartment to apartment.

If you feel it is necessary, lay down the protection line along the adjoining walls and the whole parameter of the apartment or condominium. I once stayed at a property that was a huge vortex due to a combination of negative factors. In that case, I took some of the spiritual bath powder that our Center creates and established a vibrational line of defence by sprinkling it as I walked the parameters of the property. I began with the Eastern-most corner and proceeding counter clock-wise. This is the directional flow that I normally move in, but I Respect those that might be pulled to go clock-wise. If you choose to create a line or lines of protection, I recommend you first pray…invoking Spirit's Will on how to close that doorway, threshold or portal of disruptive energy.

Spiritual baths

The Sacred Peace Center offers bath powders for spiritual cleansing, which provide healing for your spirit from a precise blend of vibrant herbs and other protective elements. I encourage you to create your own formulas and rituals but I also teach it is wise to first meditate on what your spirit needs at this point of your path. Secondly, it is prudent to do research on the properties of the ingredients so as to not wander off into destructive actions. Through meditation and focused contemplation of the knowledge you have gathered on cleansing elements, you will be able to experiment with various combinations to discover which herbs resonate with your frequency at the time.

Wisdom must prevail, not foolish disregard for your body or spirit. One woman shared with me that some phony healers directed her to take baths in bleach! It is amazing she endured something so utterly toxic! So remember, whether ingesting herbs or applying them to your outer body, they are potent, so acquire knowledge and adhere to Wisdom. Too much of a good ingredient can still end up being "too much" if you over-do it and go over-board.

Balance...Balance...Balance is the key. If we honour Balance and strive for Balance, Spirit will help us succeed in our quest. Pay attention to your body's reaction...notice how your skin reacts and how you feel mentally, emotionally and physically after any treatment. We must be willing to hear our inner voice as to the success of what we are undertaking. What is perfectly suited for one person may not be appropriate for someone else.

Nine is a potent number adhered to in many traditions for casting out harm-full spirits. You could start out with a series of nine, taking a bath each night before you go to bed. In the case of the bath powders that we carry, it is recommended that you pour the solution over your head as well as the rest of your body, and accompany that action with prayers or mantras, such as the protection mantra 'Kali Durge Namo Nama.'

In some cases, depending on the contents of the bath, it is recommended you not rub off the ingredients while drying yourself but instead to just pat yourself dry, to leave as much of the cleansing ingredients intact on your body.

You will find it easier to put more Gusto into your mantra repetitions if you play the CD and chant along with it. The music will empower you, and your increased Zest will augment the power of the healing herbs...flooding your being with the vibration of transformation.

I also recommend that after any cleansing, you continuing to play a soothing protection mantra on low volume while you sleep.

Rocket Strength Mantra 9 Day Clearing kit for self or remote healing for others:-

This is another nine-day program we implement often, which we also make available to you through our website. This kit is to be utilized for dissolving negative energies in your home, family, friends and others. It comes with what is known as a 'rocket' Strength mantra that sweeps out malevolent energies. The whole procedure takes only fifteen to twenty minutes per day and can be done anytime, during day or night. It can be done without other household members knowing you are doing it, which enables you to move out those negative forces that are creating discord or any type of unhappiness, without any interference from others' judgments or misconceptions. The same mantra can be used on behalf of others to clear them and their lives of any type of negative forces.

The White Tornado: A Tornado Strength Cleansing Kit for clearing home/office/space from All kinds of Negative Forces

This kit is a Tornado Strength defender and comes with all the necessary materials for dissolving harm-full energies from any home or space. It constitutes of three treatments, to ensure you move out every particle of sinister energy. It involves a one to two hour process for each treatment, which creates a thick Compassionate sacred smoke-out that dissolves and sweeps out hostile influences.

With this treatment every household member, including pets, must leave the house for the one to two hour period during which the sacred smoke elements are battling against antagonistic forces. The smoke produced needs to reach every single particle of space, so you open all the cupboards and closets for the smoke to go into every corner of the space. All Windows and exit doors are closed so the smoke will stay inside the house to thoroughly clear out any darkness.

Since all family members and pets must leave the premises for the one to two hours period, if you are living with others who do not wish to co-operate with you, you would need to do this procedure while they are gone. If this is not possible, then I recommend the Rocket Strength Mantra Nine Day Clearing Kit, which allows you to do the transformative work without much interruption in your schedule or the schedule of others.

For years now, I have observed people continually utilizing the exact same protection ingredients, with the exact rituals they have been using for years, even though it was clear the formula they were utilising was no longer effective enough against their current attackers. The Teaching is simple: what might have worked years ago...or even one year ago...may not budge the current strain of evil.

This should not be that difficult for us to understand. In the physical world the medical community is constantly finding new strains of viruses that previous antidotes no longer cure. If a healer or a physician is paying attention, they will release any fixed ideas in order to open up to the current solution. A true scientist is not attached to their theories...their commitment is to the obtaining of effective results through steady research and a receptive outlook. By discarding prejudice, they are able to clearly identify the root block, its cause and the perfect remedy called for. This detached way of proceeding allows them to birth new realities.

Why is this modern strain of evil tougher to eradicate? I realised years ago that since the battle for our soul is escalating, the negative forces are indeed flying at us with greater Strength and Determination. With this knowledge, I whole-heartedly encourage everyone to be receptive towards constantly adding new protection tools to their spiritual practices.

You may need to use many things to move out psychic attacks, so it is very important to not marry just one idea. Be open to new ways and better ways. Feel free to experiment! If you cannot move out energy by yourself, be humble enough and wise enough to ask for help. If you need to move a small box across the room, it would only take a small amount of energy but to move a huge heavy desk takes more. You may be able to move the box easily without asking anyone for help. To move the desk you would need the assistance of others, so you would ask your friends to join you in the effort.

If I ask you to move a house, you would definitely need to use heavy-duty equipment, iron strong tools, as well as help from others. For those occasions where you are required to move a mountain, you will need to use much more equipment, of a superior Strength... and a huge assortment of tools...along with Spiritual support...and help from friends and supporters of your mission.

This is how it is with the endless stream of challenges Spirit sends us, in order to give us the opportunity to learn...grow in power, expand in knowledge and rise in Wisdom. Again and again I en-courage you...Be the Impeccable Warrior...never give up, keep going, keep experimenting...

Keep praying, singing, dancing, and drumming to call in the Light Forces! Interact with your Spiritual Protectors, offering up your Goodness! Allowing your Light to blaze, saturating All beings, All Worlds, All Realities...All Creation with your Golden Energy!

Even if you live to reach one hundred years old, at the end of your Life, you will feel your time here zipped by you. Once your soul leaves this plane, once you are on the other side, you will celebrate your challenges and brim over with soul satisfaction that you mastered the lessons and learned how to walk in Balance...in Wisdom...in Pure Strength and in Love.

You can do it! I have Faith in you!
The Masters of Light and I are with you...
Your Protectors are with you...The Light lives in you!
May you forever remember this and in this way...
Walk on this Beauty-full Flowering Jewel
As The Impeccable Warrior of Light!

Chapter 8

QUESTIONS AND ANSWERS

- *How often do we need to go back to our prayer requests once they are written and sent out to the Universe?*

As often as you FEEL pulled to address them. There is no exact formula. You must discern what must be done and when it is to be done. Listen to your spirit not your mind. Do not let the busy mind over ride what Spirit is asking you to attend to.

- *Should we keep them until they are manifested?*

Yes, but you can continue to update the petition and therefore infuse it with fresh energy. You can replace the previous prayer requests with new ones addressing that particular situation. You may re-write them as often as you feel drawn to. This will give you an opportunity to re-create them by changing the mantras, symbols or essences you are putting on or around each prayer request. In other words, keep the energy fresh one way or another. By taking action, instead of just mentalising about an issue, you become filled with a sense of power, Hope and new Determination.

- *Where do we keep them?*

Keep them where you feel they will be charged with positive force, such as on your altar, in a holy book, or under the image of a Divine Protector. It is also wise to keep them private, so no one casts their doubts on your prayers. The human mind tends to hold negative perceptions, so even our Loved ones can throw negative energy on our positive visions due to their own lack of Faith or attitudes such as envy, pessimism or fear.

- **Do we create new ones if they are not manifested within a space of time?**

Yes...you will often find that with the passage of time, changes have occurred in your viewpoint towards your desires. Re-stating your prayer request will allow you to reflect on what your current desire is. You may have new feelings or insights into your goal/wish/ dream/focus, and so it is good to write from that new perspective. You can never go wrong in re-writing any request, as it gives you a chance to connect with the Creative Force in a firmer way and implement the Wisdom tools you have acquired since the last petition.

- **It seems we would obviously give more attention to the most urgent requests. It feels overwhelming for me to give a lot of energy to each petition every day, as the number of prayer requests on my altar for my Life, family, friends and our Planet keeps growing!**

You should not let your Prayer Work overwhelm you. Find a way to do what your spirit is reminding you to do. There are a million ways to do any one thing, so find a way to make it work. Become efficient and work wisely.

- **What is a quick way to do this work?**

A quick way to pray for all your Loved ones is to donate one prayer for everybody. Grace is often misunderstood...it is unlimited! The Grace your prayers generates will not have to be divided into tiny little scraps. Everyone you pray for will receive the full amount of Grace your petition draws for them. Just as the Bible states that Jesus Christ took a few loaves of bread and fish and miraculously fed thousands, you too have the same miraculous power to multiply the Goodness so everyone on your prayer list is nourished. Trust that you can donate Grace to everyone who needs it. One prayer can benefit all beings.

One action sends out an ocean of Grace to everyone. You can donate prayers like the Dissolving Curses or the Peace Invocation for uplifting all beings.

As mentioned in your question, sometimes there are high priority situations, such as serious illness...beings involved with intense self-destruction...drastic violence...or impending vital changes in any situation. Of course, these kind of situations will pull you to dedicate more time and energy to assisting them.

Listen to the inner voice guiding you on how to make the highest contribution to Planet Earth and to all planes of existence. You will be able to hear the Divine Guidance if you spend less time with television...if you cut down on unimportant talking...and less time listening to others speak endlessly about the material world. We can hear the voice of Spirit when we quiet our mind. We can clear our mind of clutter by devoting more time to quiet reflection. By choosing to set aside more time for prayer and ritual for the protection of all those beings, conditions and places that have reached out to you instead of activities that bring fleeting satisfaction...your soul will earn more merit, garner more Strength and move closer to existing as a Pure Light Being.

It is supremely satisfying to listen to the Will of Spirit. We can feel the infusion of Light,.. we can feel the Ocean of Contentment and Serenity moving within us when we do what our spirit is directing us to address. At the end of your Life, knowing you chose to invest your Golden Energy in the wisest priorities will bestow the supreme Peace.

• *I was wondering how important it is to pray out loud. From Teachings I have been given at various times in my Life, I understand it is important to pray out loud, but sometimes I feel much more connected to Divine Mother when I pray in silence! Should we have a balance of the two? I was thinking that if I had been born dumb, I would have to pray in silence and I don't believe the Goddess would hear me any less!! Do you?*

Mother God/Father God and the Holy Spirit will hear you whether you speak your prayers, shout your prayers or pray in silence. It is the earnestness...your Faith...the intensity, Sweetness and Purity of the prayer that counts. Let us all-ways listen to our inner Wisdom as to how Spirit wants those prayers offered.

In my favourite Divine Mother scriptures such as India's Chandi Path, Divine Mother describes the perfect Wisdom, making it clear that the greatest initiates are the ones who give themselves to absolute Devotion. She specifies that when prayers are spoken, the petitioner receives merit, but if the prayers are sung loudly and better yet, if the devotee dives even further into Joy-full worship by dancing their Devotion, this is the best. This kind of offering is received with the greatest Appreciation by the Celestial Forces. For it demonstrates the seeker has gone beyond egotism and rejected the 'Demon of Self Deprecation' that keeps the majority of humanity in a state of smallness.

So, although there are times when quiet prayer is the perfect action, we must ask ourselves WHY we are praying quietly and be willing to hear the truth. What is our true motive? Is it really that the Holy Spirit is directing us thus…OR is it that we are being ruled by self-consciousness. For most people the latter is the case and for them, the antidote IS to practice being Courageous, singing out loud and dancing up a storm! The seeker, who is moved by overflowing Devotion to break free of self-imposed limitations, pleases the Light Forces tremendously, bringing the Light immense Joy. Make sure it is Spirit that is speaking to you and not a negative force that wishes for you to stay in low gear when you should be driving in full throttle!

Chapter 9

THE ANCIENT SCIENCE OF MAYAN SOUL RETRIEVAL:

MAYAN SHAMANIC LIMPIAS SESSION.

QUESTIONS AND ANSWERS
BY SWAMI DURGADAS

"Soul Retrieval Limpias alleviate suffering by clearing spiritual, physical, mental emotional and material blockages (karmic or otherwise) that torment the soul. Just as a whirlwind lifts and carries away debris, these Compassionate Forces clear obstacles that sabotage Peace, Balance, Vitality, Faith, Clarity, Enthusiasm, Determination, Happiness, Intuition, and other qualities elemental to our Highest Destiny. By removing negative energies, limiting patterns are diffused, pain-full experiences are dissolved and the tattered, weakened aura is Strengthened." Peace Mother Geeta Sacred Song.

Many blessings to all of you! It is my pleasure to contribute to the Holy Mother's profound work by sharing with you my experiences with the Holy Mother's healing power. She has written on the subject of Soul Retrieval and Sacred Sound often and I shall attempt to do justice to Her Work with my humble additional notes. First of all, Sacred Peace Center offers many Sacred Therapies based in ancient Wisdom and traditions. The Holy Mother is the Living Sound of Light. I have experienced that every word she utters is actually, amazingly, the Universe speaking! It is beyond proper description and is possible due to Purity that lives within Her.

She bestows immense blessings upon us through Her Teachers, the chanting CDs and the Mayan Soul Retrieval Limpias. The word 'Limpia' refers to a spiritual cleansing, and each Indigenous Tradition and individual Medicine Person has their own way of carrying out a Limpia.

In this manual, Peace Mother has given you many ways to perform a cleansing over yourself and others. However, due to Her Purity and Power, the Soul Retrieval Limpia administered by Her Holiness is the science of Soul Retrieval at the most miraculous level. I have had the honour to receive one-on-one Soul Retrieval Limpias from the Holy Mother and assist in the healing sessions of other devotees around the world, as well as document the immediate and profound transformation in the fortunate beings receiving Peace Mother's prayers. I know God has bestowed a grand privilege in allowing me to be a part of Divine Mothers mission and the Holy Mother's Soul Retrieval Work is absolutely indescribable. The following is simply a humble attempt to share its deep, transcendental, cosmic nature with you.

Soul Retrieval is an ancient science used to identify, diminish and remove negative forces creating imbalance in the aura, mind, body and personality. These imbalances fragment the soul, and thereby show up in your Life in the form of mental, emotional, physical, spiritual or material problems.

Peace Mother was trained in the Ancient Science of Mayan Soul Retrieval by the Great Mayan Peace Shaman Don Jacinto Tzab. Don Jacinto was initiated into the role of Peace Shaman at age 14, by his Teacher, Don Feliciano. The Holy Mother's Lineage consists of Beneficent Beings who dedicated their lives to the protection, Strengthening and upliftment of humanity. The Soul Retrieval Limpia Prayer which the Holy Mother offers the Universe during Soul Retrieval sessions has ancient roots, having been bequeathed by each generation of Impeccable Shamans to the upcoming Chosen One. Peace Mother Geeta Sacred Song is the Chosen One of this Lineage. She is the Peace Shaman of our times, who is the embodiment of the Grace cultivated by a long lineage of Peace Shamans.

During the Soul Retrieval Limpia, a petition in the Ancient Mayan Holy language is delivered on behalf of the recipient for a shower of Grace to flood the individual, to wash away whatever is obstructing the Purest, Brightest Light.

With the Soul Retrieval Invocation, the Holy Mother calls on Divine Mother Grace, naming the specific Divine Mother aspects that work through Her, as well as the Mayan Lineage of Master Healers, the Legions of Light and Compassionate Earth Forces that assist this miraculous Work.

The Compassionate Celestial and Earth Forces each have a sacred name and as the Holy Mother calls out Their name, each one is summoned to be present and bless the seeker. These Forces respond in a supremely powerful way, like a whirlwind, lifting negativities from the mental, emotional, physical and spiritual bodies. The Holy Mother describes the Mayan Soul Retrieval this way, "Just as a whirlwind lifts up and carries away debris, these Compassionate Forces clear the obstacles that sabotage Peace, Balance, Vitality, Faith, Clarity, Enthusiasm, Determination, Happiness, Wisdom-Intuition, and other Divine qualities elemental to our Highest Destiny. By removing negative energies, negative patterns are diffused, pain full experiences are dissolved and the tattered, weakened aura is Strengthened."

The Divine Grace petitioned is quickly gifted to the recipient. Everyone who experiences Soul Retrieval Work with the Holy Mother feels the effects immediately and emerges looking radically different; they absolutely glow! Once free of the layers of limiting energies acquired over a Life-time, they are able to feel an intense connection to Spirit. They look younger, feel lighter, stronger and clearer about their Life, as Trust and Peace are heightened in them.

The Soul Retrieval Limpias open the door to unlimited blessings. Some of these blessings are easy to spot immediately while others will reveal themselves later on, as the movement of the Kundalini is Balanced, and Wisdom is activated within the individual.

Messages regarding one's Life condition often surface within the seeker, as well as clarity as to which spiritual practices will benefit them the most. All knowledge that arises in the individual from each Soul Retrieval is a direct communication from Spirit in order to help the seeker reach their Highest Destiny.

Although Her Holiness no longer performs individual Soul Retrieval Limpias in person, we are blessed She continues to shower this Soul Remedy via the internet recording for individuals and at times, through conference calls with large groups. As some beings have shared in the Soul Retrieval Experiences section, whether a Pure Being such as the Holy Mother performs Soul Retrieval prayers over someone via phone or remote means, individually or in a group setting, the power of those prayers is tangibly seen and felt, for Grace knows no limitations. As is the case with other Saints, the Grace residing within the Holy Mother transcends walls, time or distance.

Whenever I have a challenge block my path, I listen to the recording of the Soul Retrieval Limpia and find the problem is quickly moved from my path, as solutions miraculously appear! In the time I have known the Holy Mother, I have witnessed the Soul Retrieval Limpias assist me with spiritual—emotional—mental—and physical challenges. When I first began to support the Holy Mother's Work, I walked hunched over. One day Her Holiness told me to straighten up my posture and I confessed I could not. To attempt it would put me in intense pain. The Soul Retrieval Limpias healed my back and now I am able to stand up straight! I have encountered constant challenges as other do in Life and there is no area of my Path that has not been improved due to the Holy Mother's Grace. I believe I could not have grown spiritually as fast as I have, without the Soul Retrieval Limpias and the constant implementation of the Holy Mother's Teachings.

One day I will write a book on how the Holy Mother and the Grace She emanates revolutionized my Life! For now, I will attempt the impossible in trying to do justice to this awesome Sacred Work. I have taken some material She has written on the subject and added to it.

My prayer is that it will be of service to all of you and I look forward to meeting you one day in person!

THE SHAMAN'S ROLE IN SOUL RETRIEVAL LIMPIAS

Describing the Work of a Master Peace Shaman, The Holy Mother once wrote, "A Shaman is one who understands energy, perceives energy and can transform energy. They understand the laws of the Universe and have full Faith that their thoughts and spoken invocations are heard throughout the Universe.

It is imperative to understand that there are many levels of beings that call themselves a 'Shaman'. Especially these days, there are abundant half-baked men and women who mislead unsuspecting, trusting souls by promoting themselves as a fully knowledgeable and empowered Shaman, although they possess only limited knowledge and powers. It is not honourable to claim to be that which one has not yet earned! Therefore I encourage these beings to avert negative karma by being honest. I challenge them to disclose they are a Shamanic practitioner, trainee, apprentice or Shamanism student...but NOT a Master. Be aware dear ones that the problem here is that since these individuals are themselves possessed by dark forces...they actually believe themselves to be a Master. It is up to each of us to discern who is real and who has not yet graduated. Humility is essential in being a Peace Shaman.

It is also vital to realize that among the accomplished Shamans in the various traditions, there are many who are dark sorcerers, beings who still work for the dark side on some level, in one way or another. Unlike a Peace Shaman, they are not wholly committed to the Light... they do not Love the Light."

The Holy Mother teaches, "A real Peace Shaman is someone who ADORES the Light. They contemplate and invoke the Light constantly, day and night. There is no break in the focus of a genuine Peace Shaman...they are dedicated to working ONLY for the Good...ONLY for the victory of the Light Forces in every situation.

Their Faith in the Light is iron-strong, their commitment to the upliftment of all souls and all creation is unwavering...Their connection to God and a constant spiritual discipline is unbreakable!

They are recognized by ALL Creation as a Heroic Being and are accepted by the Legions of Light and Compassionate Earth Forces as a Perfect instrument for Good.

Therefore, when a Peace Shaman makes a petition on behalf of someone, the prayers are heard clearly and immediately by the Forces of Light. While evil sorcerers invoke the Dark Forces to disrupt the sacred balance in All Creation, the Wise Shaman works in Harmony with Mother/Father God's Laws of Compassion and Purity, to constantly release us from bondage. A Peace Shaman protects us from further enslavement to negativity in any form."

Having travelled with the Holy Mother I have seen for myself, over and over again, that a Master Peace Shaman, such as Peace Mother Geeta Sacred Song, is a rare being, even amongst Shamans. For She is an Enlightened Master and Impeccable Warrior of the Light. She is Divine Mother Grace in action, The Highest degree of Peace Shaman, a Divine Instrument for removing obstacles from our path and bestowing blessings. With such a Being, every single thing They do provides ongoing refuge for humanity.

Speaking of the Masters, the Holy Mother has said, "The prayer songs, rituals, sacred dance and petitions the Masters deliver to the Universe…every word, every action…is ALL laden with the liberating vibration that delivers us from destructive forces."

As the Holy Mother's assistant and student, I can add that when we have excellent karma, we are able to connect more intensely with the Grace of a Master Peace Shaman through a remote or phone Soul Retrieval invocation. Such a direct encounter with the Grace of the Universe is the most auspicious occurrence!

As a Master Peace Shaman, Enlightened Master and Divine Mother incarnation, *the Holy Mother is a Champion -- a fierce Warrior of the Light*, working Joy-fully and tire-lessly to shield us from attack and en-rich us with Self Love. The dark forces fear Her, for they recognize the liberating power of the immense Love and Brilliant Light that reside within Her. The forces of evil that delight in our distress, cringe when someone aligns with the Divine Mother Grace that lives within our beloved Peace Mother. The dark forces know that any individual will be empowered to live happily, once they cross paths with a pure instrument for The Grace. The Legions of Light rejoice in the work of a Master Peace Shaman and count on Beings such as Peace Mother Geeta Sacred Song to fortify them through Soul Retrieval Prayer Songs and Offerings.

Her Holiness believes we can ALL reach our Highest Destiny and it is Her Life Work to continually unlock the floodgates to humanity's greatest Good. Know that She is already constantly praying for you, for me and for the Enlightenment of all beings. In order for each of us to accelerate our growth and reach the state of permanent Peace we can practice the protection techniques the Holy Mother so clearly shares, as well as committing to ongoing remote or conference call Soul Retrieval sessions.

With the assistance provided by Soul Retrieval Limpias, your spirit becomes stronger and will motivate you to utilizing this book as a daily guide. Every layer that is cleared allows the voice of Self Love to influence us to chant along with the mantra CDs. As our inner Light Force becomes brighter, we become inspired to rattle and implement the many other protection tools the Holy Mother has established for us. With each Soul Retrieval Limpia the door is opened for more Good to flow unto us…enabling us to live Life in the most magnificent way!

Q: How do Soul Retrieval Limpias dissolve my Karma – past Life and current?

As the Holy Mother teaches, "Karma locks you into certain patterns of behaviour, experiencing repetitive Life lessons and a feeling of lack of choice. Yet, the truth is you all ways have choice! With the help of Divine Grace, you can travel the direct path to Happiness and full-fillment, instead of remaining stuck on the much longer route full of pain-laden adventures."

Peace Mother Geeta Sacred Song has been 'donated' to humanity by The Divine Mother of the Universe, as Her Grace bestowing instrument. During the Soul Retrieval Limpias, all of Peace Mother's Spirit Guides, as well as your Angels and Spiritual Protectors, are called forth to scan your past and present karma as well as your Highest Destiny. The Divine Forces are petitioned to dissolve any negative, limited karmic impressions – past Life, childhood or current. Through Divine assistance, the healing process of any condition or issue, past or present, is sped up. Karma can be burned up quickly, allowing you to experience Freedom and an exciting new future. The ultimate purpose of each Soul Retrieval Limpia is to help you reach your Highest Destiny in this Life-time by dissolving karmic self-destructive patterns. By liberating you from these chains, an opening is created for you so that:

a) All the possible good can be BESTOWED by the Compassionate Divine Forces;

b) All the possible good can be RECEIVED by you.

Q: What kind of conditions can be dissolved or improved through Soul Retrieval Limpias?

For thousands of years, this Shamanic Sacred Therapy has been used to disperse emotional, physical, mental and spiritual torment. Soul retrieval Limpias have been utilized to assist in the treatment of dissolving both short-term and long-standing physical conditions involving all the major systems and functions such as: muscular, skeletal, skin, lymphatic, respiratory, reproductive, blood and circulatory systems, digestive, etc.

They can help ease: muscle pain, joint problems, any lack of mobility, migraines, insomnia, obesity, heart problems, cancer, tumours, arthritis, dysfunctional organs, fibromyalgia syndrome, fatigue syndromes, sexual dysfunction, diabetes and much more.

Soul Retrieval Limpias may be of assistance in releasing emotional issues such as: loss, grief, hurt, anger, resentment, bitterness, jealousy, obsession, depression, painful memories, emotional/physical abuse, insecurity, lack of self-esteem/confidence, phobias, neurosis, perfectionism, anxiety, fears, struggle, confusion, guilt, anguish, withholding Love, frustration, resistance, victimization, blame, fear of intimacy, negative beliefs and patterns, etc. If an issue is holding you back or blocking your Happiness, prosperity or balance, then you could benefit from LIBERATING Soul Retrieval Limpias!

Q: How do Soul Retrieval Limpias help in dissolving the discomfort that I am experiencing in my Life?

First let us review the Holy Mother's excellent, clear Teachings on the dynamics of the discomfort and its causes: "Mayan Soul Retrieval Wisdom, which teaches us that all discomfort in Life is caused by some degree of psychic attack…by one type of negative energy or another. Like most people, you may not realize how sensitive you truly are. However, whether you are conscious of it or not, you are picking up vibrations from both positive and negative forces that although unseen, are definitely around you.

Negative forces ARE a fact of Life and no one can escape interaction with them! For example: if you were to leave all your doors open to your home, you would naturally attract some positive guests as well as experience some negative intruders. This is 'natural'…it is to be expected…it is part of the package that goes along with leaving the doors open. In the same way, all your psychic doors ARE OPEN to unwanted negative forces. Unless you have learned to consistently – and fully – protect yourself…you WILL pick up negative forces or energies throughout your daily travels and activities. Day after day, these sneaky negative energies keep accumulating, and as they add up, they form a dark cloud around you, obstructing your good luck, health and blessings. The experience of negative forces in your Life can range from slight dis-comfort to the feelings of being persecuted by absolute evil. Any shade of the above can be considered 'spiritual torment'."

No evil exists that is greater than Grace and Peace Mother is ONE with the Source of Grace. Crossing paths with a Pure Instrument, through which Divine Grace flows in an unimpeded way, such as Her Holiness, is a moment of Great Fortune. To actually have Her concentrate that flow of Grace on your aura and Life force is the most marvellous boon to your soul. A Soul Retrieval Limpia administered by a Master Soul Physician such as the Holy Mother, is a Life-altering, immense phenomenon.

Through contact with Her concentrated Sacred Flame, our own inner Light is intensified, driving out layers of inner darkness. The

Holy Mother is able to see with the utmost clarity what we need to change in our Path, what spiritual practices we should do at each level of our spiritual unfoldment. The combination of Wisdom Teachings and healing power of the Holy Mother's Prayers renew us, refresh our point of view and re-direct us on our path. The busy, cluttered mind becomes aware of its Divine Nature, enabling us to tune in to our inner guidance. The transmission of Grace that occurs in a Soul Retrieval Limpia fills us with Self Love, helping us live in Harmony with the Universal Spiritual Laws by making positive choices.

Soul Retrieval Limpias help dissolve blockages and accelerates our karmic path. They help the aura Strengthen and expand, which then opens the door to your highest Good. With the help of Soul Retrieval Limpias, it becomes possible for you to receive spiritual gifts such as increased Vitality, Clarity, Prosperity, Love, Co-operation, Support, Success, Enthusiasm, Recognition, Balance, Strength, Courage, Patience, Wisdom, Enlightenment and Peace in your Life!

Q: What are some of the signs that negative energies are present in my home or office?

The Holy Mother reminds us, "Negative forces do often torment individuals by taking up residence in the living or working space. This then affects all aspects of your Life and Tranquillity. Evidence of negative or evil forces can include: nightmares, insomnia, discomfort or feeling of fear within the home or workplace, dis-harmony, relationship difficulties, arguments, illness, consistent bad luck, losses of any type, and lack of progress.

You may feel like you are being watched, or you sense a malevolent or harmful presence. Sometimes you may see, out of the corner of your eyes, shadows or figures darting. If you have a child that is fearful of the dark or reports seeing a ghost, a 'monster' in their closet, in or under their bed and will only sleep with a Light on, you can be assured that you have negative forces lurking in your home. It is quite amazing how our 'rational' mind will explain or discount these types of events and activities. Yet these forces are

REAL, and definitely need to be dealt with, in order to be removed or transformed."

Q: Can Soul Retrieval Limpias be used for Shamanic Journeys, Spiritual Initiation or past-Life insight?

Yes. The type of Soul Retrieval Limpias Peace Mother bestows has been used in many spiritual cultures to activate the Third Eye, opening a portal to higher Wisdom, sacred intelligence and sacred memory. Very importantly, the Mayan Spiritual Protectors are called forth to protect you and the necessary portals opened. This way, you can trance-journey in safety to the Higher Mysteries awaiting you. Since the mind, body and spirit have been swept clean of imbalance and burdens; you can truly relax and go into a deep spiritual state where the higher mysteries can be revealed.

During Soul Retrieval Limpias, some people see or hear messages from their Spirit Guides or Animal Totems. Some see colours while others receive messages from their Loved ones on the Other Side. At times flashes of past lives are shown or one may travel to mystical sites or Celestial Realms. I have had many Soul Retrieval Limpias and have known others who also signed up for series of Soul Retrieval sessions and I can definitely assert that no two Soul Retrieval Limpias are ever the same.

Q: How often should I have a Soul Retrieval Limpia?

We once asked the Oracle of the Light this question, since She has also been blessed to experience Soul Retrieval Limpias with the Holy Mother and Shree Dayananda replied, "How often do you have a meltdown? Every time we experience a crisis we lose some of our inner power, therefore we must seek help in quickly rebuilding."

Whereas in certain cases, some conditions are miraculously healed with only one Soul Retrieval Limpia, there are conditions that require continuous attention. Just as some physical wounds heal faster, the severity of a psychic weakness will determine how much healing work must be performed on it to bring about transformation. How many Soul Retrieval sessions are required will depend on many factors such as:

- How long has the condition pre-existed?
- How deep is the thought or belief pattern holding the condition in place?
- How ready are you to let go of your suffering, pain and struggle?
- And very importantly, how much Faith do you have?

Whether conditions are assisted in healing with one session or more, recipients emerge feeling encouraged, enthusiastic, relieved of worries, full of Hope and Serenity!

Q: What are the benefits of frequent Soul Retrieval sessions?

In each session, you are flooded with Divine Grace. With each additional session, you are able to retain more and more of this Grace for longer periods of time. As layers of karmic patterns drop away, you are further catapulted towards your highest destiny, at a faster rate. Confidence, Creativity, Intelligence, Boldness, and Clarity, along with renewed ecstasy and Appreciation for Life is magnified, so that you can travel through Life with full spiritual understanding, enabling you to enjoy it to the fullest! Thus, you are able to easily and powerfully materialize your positive wishes, dreams and visions.

Q: Who can benefit from Soul Retrieval Limpias?

Anyone that has a challenge, problem or unfulfilled desires in his/her Life, **especially children and individuals who are sensitive** can benefit. All beings that choose to remain aligned in their spirituality and strive for Strength, success and total balance, benefit from these Soul Retrieval Limpias. All those who wish to amplify the Prosperity, Love and strong foundation in their Life can benefit from a shower of Grace. Our ability to attract Good, sustain Goodness, enjoy a Great, Wholesome, and a Vibrant Life is enhanced by Mayan Soul Retrieval sessions.

Q: How does one prepare for a Soul Retrieval session?

This is a very easy process. Just present yourself with an open mind and "the Faith of a mustard seed'. It is help-full, although not mandatory; to get as clear as possible on what areas you want help with. This can be done by preparing two lists which detail:

- All that you wish lifted, released, healed or transformed
- All that you desire to be gifted with.

Q: What happens after the session?

Your prayer request is placed on Peace Mother's altar and She will continue to petition the Divine Forces on your behalf. A spiritual connection has taken place during the session and continues even after the Soul Retrieval Limpia is completed. Through that connection, spiritual assistance continues to be given to you.

Q: What results have been seen from Soul Retrieval Limpias?

All the Divine Forces work together to cleanse you psychically, physically, emotionally and spiritually. They help remove obstacles and karmic chains causing the problems, often with miraculous results. There have been cases of people who could not speak, eat or move due to dark forces pushing them towards death. They quickly regained Life Force and began to lead a healthy Life once again. In other instances, through the Holy Mother's prayers, there have been those who were suddenly able to walk, even though minutes before they could not even stand up! She has done healing work over individuals with multiple large tumours, and has seen their tumours shrink to small ones, sometimes immediately, and in other cases, within a few months.

Addictions of years upon years have been dissolved, allowing the person to go forth and blossom. Personality disorders have been replaced with Balanced, self-honouring behaviour. Couples who were entangled in hostility were able to discover harmonious ways to proceed and interact with each other. Some divorces were avoided as the couples re-conciled with new understanding and Appreciation of each other; other's whose souls had completed the time they were meant to be married, were able to move on to a different way of relating to each other, in Peace and Respect.

Mayan Soul Retrieval Limpias have changed family dynamics, helped children, men and women through their karmic challenges and empowered many to emerge triumphant! Each time the Holy Mother lifts negative influences from the soul, Divine Mother gifts the being a thicker protective shield against psychic attack. Each Soul Retrieval Limpia dissolves layers of fear and bestows greater knowledge on how to disintegrate evil forces. Grace breaks down inner and outer barriers and the individual is able to experience a sense of Spiritual Protection and safety.

Most definitely the list of transformations and salvations is too long to cover here, so I just share with you a few examples. It is utterly amazing to watch the soul healing occur! Many cry during their sessions or afterwards at the miracle they saw and felt. Many share that Soul Retrieval Limpias opened up their Third Eye enabling them to actually feel or see the indescribable presence of their Angels or Guides, infusing them with a lightness and closeness to God not known before. Soul Retrieval Limpias by the Holy Mother are known to bestow a new Life brimming with fresh enthusiasm for the Path and a bright outlook on Life! They help us be the Divine beings we truly are! As the Holy Mother often says, "Glory to the Grace!"

MAYAN SHAMANIC SOUL RETRIEVAL EXPERIENCES

Dear Peace Mother and Swamiji,

Deep thanks and much Appreciation for the Soul Retrieval Limpia. My body began vibrating when Peace Mother's voice was heard. Much vibration and release of negative energy transpired during the entire chanting. It was as if dark mud was being hurled out of my auric and other fields. My brain and spinal cord are now out of pain, tension and tightness. There is a wonderful lightness of being and Love surrounding my body as I walk through the day. I am sure the digestive system and nervous system are in balance now and with each breath I feel a sense of Peace and Balance which I haven't felt for a long, long time. Especially my right side, from head to toe feels released of negativity and filled with Love.

I will increase Spiritual Practices, cleanse my home frequently, as well as increase fun and play in my Life, as I was instructed to do.

Please send me the special Mantra CD to dissolve negative thoughts. Thank you so much for all the guidance and the wonderful Limpia. Blessings to you both and safe journey to the Yucatán!

Dear Peace Mother and Swami Durgadas,

Thank you, thank you, thank you. I am so very grateful to have had the honour of receiving Soul Retrieval Limpia prayers from the Holy Mother. I understand now what it means to be Loved and that I am truly Loved. Since the Limpia I've been healing a little more every day.

At first I saw a lot of movement even though my eyes were closed. I opened my eyes and saw nothing, but once I closed my eyes again, I saw all these shadows leaving me. I then experienced an internal wave come up from deep inside and I started shaking. Tears started to flow…it wasn't a steady flow but rather a choppy, choked up kind of crying. I cried on and off and all the while, I felt my whole body and inner being worked on. I stopped seeing all those shadows after a time and saw a flickering Light somewhat similar to a dimmed strobe Light. This flickering only lasted a few moments.

At one point when Peace Mother said "Adios" my shoulder moved in reflex as if someone had grabbed it and squeezed it. I slowly fell into a deep, Peaceful, meditative state. After I hung up from the call, I sat for a moment in stillness…a stillness I had never felt before. I was exhausted and heavy after that. I could barely go back to what I was doing. I had to just rest and receive care as it took me a couple of hours to regain Strength.

I am so grateful, so amazed at what I felt. I didn't know what to expect. I wasn't sure I would believe, BUT I DO NOW. There is no doubt that something very profound and absolutely Life-altering occurred. I'm letting emotions come up for me as they may. I'm letting myself give Love and receive Love. I feel so free. I had been bound for so long.

I now have the knowledge to move forward and protect myself. What an amazing gift! I am more in touch with this part of myself that is beyond this physical plane. I feel so much Love. I've told my boyfriend about all of this and he wants to experience a Soul Retrieval Limpia as well. He sees how different I am and how my anger has been transformed into Peace and Joy. He feels how much I Love him - unobstructed.

I will purchase the items I need in order to protect myself. I must ask about a prayer called 'The Armour of the Goddess.. I was told I needed it. I believe there is a book, 'The Chandi Path,' that contains the Armour prayer. I need to buy that and I definitely need to cleanse my space at work. How can I do this.

I have been humbled by Divine Grace, and am ever so grateful, Love and Light!

I received the blessing of a Soul Retrieval Limpia from Peace Mother and immediately afterwards I experienced Graceful Peace in the deepest places of my heart where doubts and fear had previously existed. I felt new pathways and connections to healing and guiding powers. I also felt an increased connection to my own Strength and knowingness.

Those experiences continue to this day and the intention I stated before the Limpia - to accelerate the highest good for my relationship with my partner - was manifested in only three weeks. I now have a deep understanding, Peace, and resolution for that relationship and also I feel aligned and on-track with my Life's purpose. Many, many 'synchronistic' events happen each day since the Soul Retrieval Limpia. Thank you, thank you, Peace Mother and Swami Durgadas for your gifts.

<<<<<<<<<<<<<<<>>>>>>>>>>>>>

Good morning Swami Durgadas,

Thank you so much. Yes, my Soul Retrieval Limpia with Peace Mother was WONDERFUL. She is truly a force of Light and brilliant, Positive Energy. I am grateful for having had the opportunity to receive Her Grace. Her Wisdom Teachings have helped me learn strategies for bringing more Light into my Life, my children's lives, my home and to all those with whom I connect. The Limpia was an experience I will not forget, and I am so thankful to the Holy Mother for the blessings and prayers She made and continues to make on my and my family's behalf. Blessings, Light and Love!

<<<<<<<<<<<<<<<>>>>>>>>>>>>>

Dear Peace Mother, Swamiji and Peace Team,

I just want to say that I am truly thankful I found you. My grandmother is feeling better and more positive than I have heard her in a long time. She slept in today, which she never does, so I am glad that whatever was released in the phone Soul Retrieval Limpia has left her in Peace to feel better.

As far as the group session, my grandmother will be present for the next session as well. I am hoping that if there is anything left or lingering on her, it can be resolved at that time.

I do want to mention that my cousin is still the one most in need. We've had much trouble with him because he is isolating himself from our family and instead keeping company with people who are possessed by sinister energies. If he does not attend the conference call session, I will be sending you a picture and we can take the route of a remote Limpia for him instead. I appreciate everything that you are doing. With much gratitude!

Dear Swami Durgadas and Peace Mother,

Thank you for the Soul Retrieval Limpia! I especially felt the energy powerfully clearing my solar plexus. Since the Soul Retrieval Limpia things have been very good and opportunities have opened up for me. I have started painting lessons after months of meaning to do this and it is good to get into creative things again. I have also felt very grounded and connected to Mother Earth. Angels bless!

Thank you Swami Durgadas, I had a wonderful Soul Retrieval session, thanks to Peace Mother! I am feeling stronger and calmer since my session, and as the day and evening have progressed, I am finding that Her guidance is right on track. I am very grateful and happy, thank you for all your efforts.

I would like to order a set of rattles to use and would also appreciate if I could pay for an additional set to be given to Peace Mother, to take the place of the one that broke during Her prayers over my soul. Yes, I do understand that the rattle breaking is a very good sign...and my gifting her replacement rattles is my way of saying "thank you" for Her help.

I would also like to purchase Peace Mother's CDs and a sacred smoke cleansing kit from the website. Thank you again for all your efforts and Love, and thanks to Peace Mother. Her singing is amazing, and Her work is so appreciated.

Dear Swami Durgadas,

Regarding the Soul Retrieval Limpia: when the Limpia was first scheduled, one of my main prayer requests was to dissolve my difficulties with relationships. My partner and I had broken up and now I want to report that we are back together now and engaged to be married. So thank you for your help!

Dear Peace Team and Swami Durgadas,

I was able to do the online Soul Retrieval Limpia last night, unexpectedly! I am writing to report my experience. During the third section of the Prayer, I was in tune to my husband's and step-daughter's spirit. I saw them as though their energy was that of Siamese twins, joined between the torso areas. I told them both that I could no longer have them in my Life if they continued to be joined as they were now. I told my step-daughter her violence was not welcome in my Life and she needed to move on from me. I told my husband for me to remain married; he needed to be with me as a full and separate soul from his daughter and the rest of his family. As you know he is constantly putting his violent daughter and rest of his family before me. I told his spirit that we couldn't have much of a marriage if he continued to bring in other souls who create constant disruption.

They did not seem willing or comfortable with that request/expectation of mine. My husband's daughter definitely was not and did not seem to care about what I was saying. My husband was not happy. I told him he needed to think about what he wanted in a marriage and if he wanted to be married to me, he needed his soul free from all others. I explained to him that perhaps he wasn't ready in this Life-time to be married to me, that he had too many unresolved issues with his daughter to embrace a marriage.

I explained to him that each soul has its journey and lessons to learn. He needed to decide if he could separate from his violent daughter and if not, he needed to move on. I then went on to another spot, and my husband's soul image came back to me and he asked if I would reconsider my request. I told him he would at sometime, sooner rather than later, be faced with his own soul's decision of whether to separate from his daughter or not. And that it was his choice, not mine, for him to be a separate soul.

I let him know that if he could not, he needed to let go of me and we would meet again in another Life, that I could not be married to someone who was not a full soul because our marriage would not be good for either of us. My choice was to be married, yet only to a soul who was independent from others. His choice was to separate from his daughter if he wanted to remain married to me. I felt okay with all of this, and the rest of the Soul Retrieval Limpia was pleasant. While listening to the music and Mother singing and chanting, I was letting go of what I needed to and opening to the Light. I felt very relaxed and Peaceful afterward and slept fairly well all night.

As I write this now, I am trying to be a logical human being and figure out how this all can be. I know that letting go of the outcome is needed. I wish to be a warrior of Light and let go of how this happens.

Thank you dear Mother for your Limpia and the continued prayers on your altar. Thank you Peace Team and Swami Durgadas for your prayers…for helping me let go and be strong in the Light all ways! Many blessings to all of you for all you have done for all the world. Peace, Peace, Jai Kali Ma!

Many Blessings! About the most recent Soul Retrieval Limpia: I have been very busy with new business since the Limpia so it must have cleared a lot of stuff. The interesting thing that has happened is that everything worked out perfectly about my stolen bag. I had asked Peace Mother about it and She instructed me to use the affirmation "Everything works out for the best." The insurance claim was settled surprisingly well and replaced everything that was stolen. We can even update the camera that was stolen and get a digital one instead, and I got a far better cell phone.

Dear Swamiji,

During one of the Soul Retrieval Limpias, The Holy Mother suggested I say "Let there be Peace between us", when thinking about my neighbours. I Love that lesson. What a beautiful prayer and affirmation!

As directed, I have affirmed "Let there be Peace between us", many times. A few times since then, I had two friendly encounters with the neighbour and yesterday, I had another twenty minute conversation with her and it was friendly. It then occurred to me -- there is Peace between us! Isn't that wonderful!

Regards and gratitude for all the assistance you and the Holy Mother provide to humanity!

Dearest Peace Mother,

It's a few days since you left Hong Kong for Sri Lanka. I am very grateful to you for recording a Soul Retrieval Limpia prayer that is available to humanity online. Thank you for taking the time and effort to offer prayers for me.

I have been suffering from foot and ankle edema for a long time now. Subsequent to your two prayer sessions, after you left for

Lanka, I noticed distinct reduction in the foot swellings. Previously the swellings used to build up through the day and subside at night when the body rested in a horizontal position. For the last few days, I notice that the swellings completely subside by morning, and remain the same through the day with very little buildup of swelling through the day. This is a very good sign of recovery of the edema. I Trust it will continue to stay that way. Do pray, Peace Mother, Your prayers have already given me one positive indication of the efficacy of Your spiritual healing.

As my condition improves, I will seek your guidance as to the Teachings You gave me on devoting my efforts towards alleviating the suffering of humanity in whatever way I can. Let us see what we can do together. Do please give me the continuing benefit of your efficacious prayers. I look forward to your return to Hong Kong someday. Meanwhile, please pray for me. God bless you.

In all sincerity, Love and all best wishes.

Following my Soul Retrieval Limpia I am feeling more intuitive and `myself`. Yesterday both my six-year old son and I felt unwell, like a `healing crisis` or detoxification process was taking place, but today there is a vast improvement. I am very grateful to God and the Divine forces for providing me this wonderful experience, thanks to you all and especially Peace Mother for all the Love and prayers on my behalf.

Amazingly this morning, my son and I were burning sage and praying for protection over the house. Then when I played the Shamanic Trance Chant CD from your website, my son started to instantly react by moving his body and arms…then he started to blow onto my face. Truly amazing! Many thanks again! Love and Peace.

Sharon

From Peace Mother to Sharon:

Swami Durgadas, please let Sharon know that her son has done this work in past lives. He is a Shaman... now it is only a matter of remembering, which he will do easily as she encourages him. By all ways reassuring him that what he is experiencing is all right and part of the process...by helping him understand whatever he has questions on; his unfoldment will take place perfectly. Victory unto the Light in All matters. May they both be triumphant in transforming all limited realities...forever dwelling in the Golden Mind, as Impeccable Warriors of Light...In Lak'ech!

AFTERWORD

I thank Divine Mother for this assignment and the opportunity She has given me to serve. I give great thanks to my Spirit Guides for waiting so patiently for this book to take form. I thank them for their Compassion and Trust they are happy with the completion of this Divine assignment.

I thank your Spiritual Protectors for guiding you to pick up this book, for it is an extremely auspicious sign for your Spiritual Path that you arrived at the point where you are ready for these Teachings. The more aware beings we have walking on this planet, the quicker we all reach our highest destiny.

You now have many techniques and tools to enhance your relationship with the other worlds. With this you have acquired greater awareness of the energetic laws that govern us here on Earth. Knowledge is Freedom and through this awakening to the many worlds living alongside us, you have gained your Freedom from torture, suffering and distress.

The key is to USE what you have learned. You do not have to use it all. But if you pick those things that you are able to do and experiment with the protection Teachings on a daily basis, you will gain Strength in the Spiritual Laws of protection.

I encourage you to take a couple of the ideas given here and make them your own by working with them. By doing so, you must emerge a happier person. For "cleanliness is next to Godliness" and this applies to your auric field and the energetic field of your home, as well as the body.

All-ways remember that **YOU** are the one with the POWER. You CAN dissolve any negative force! You just have to be willing to experiment until you find the right combination to turn a challenge into a positive outcome. To live is to learn, may you continue to pay astute attention and learn every-thing Life is offering you!

I look forward to walking the Shaman's Path with you once again through our forthcoming books which will complete our series. Some of these titles will include:

- The Shamanic Healing Art Journal
- The Golden Laws of the Impeccable Warrior of Light
- Divine Mother's Grace - Peace Mother Geeta Sacred Song's Autobiography
- Soul Retrieval for Success, Happiness and Health: The Fast Track to Enlightenment
- The Perfect Student, Perfect Teacher: Unravelling the Mystery of the Master Teacher.

If it is our good fortune, we will meet each other in person at one of the Peace Ceremonies. Until then, know that my blessings are with you, I have Faith in you to utilize this knowledge to become an Impeccable Warrior of Light and in so doing reach your highest destiny!

Push In Lak'ech!
This Mayan expression means
"I am you, you are me, we are One and the same!"

Peace Mother Geeta Sacred Song

Sacred Spiritual and Protection Tools

Audio CD's by Peace Mother and the Global Peace Musicians.

Peace Is Triumphant - Love Is The Answer
Be Victorious Maa - Dancing In The Light
Mystical Protective Shield & Space Clearing Mantra
Prosperity Mantras - Opening Doors to Infinite Blessings
Jai Jai Maa - Invoking the Blazing Light of Harmony
Om Namah Shivaya
Kali Durge Namo Nama
(Ancient Mantras for Spiritual Protection and Victory)
Shamanic Trance Chant
(Helps you glide into deep meditation)
Shiva Shakti - Love Is The Answer
(Balancing heart and mind & harmonizing relationships)
Om Namo Bhagavate Vasudevaya
(Thy Will Be Done Beauty-Full Lord)
(Surrendering to Divine Will)

Video (DVD's, Video tapes)
Live wisdom teachings & ceremonial peace concerts
with Peace Mother Geeta Sacred Song

Yantras:
Durga, Goddess of protection
Kali, Goddess of protection
Lakshmi, Goddess of prosperity and abundance
Saraswati, Goddess of Wisdom and Scriptures

Amulets: (Medicine bags / Crystals / Stones / Jade)
Healing (Purple), Health (Orange), Grounding (Green)
Love (Pink / Red), Prosperity / Wisdom (Gold),
Connecting with Angels (Blue)
Divine Mother jade amulets, various sizes

Ritual Oils:
Kundalini and 3rd eye activation, Healing, Protection, Attraction,
Dissolving Evil, Connecting with Angels, Love and Harmony, Prosperity,
Grounding and Strength, Cleansing & Strengthening the Aura, Power of
Attraction, cutting negative cords, Increasing good luck.

Sacred Spiritual and Protection Tools

Purification Essences:
Sweet Grass (Spiritual cleansing, brings in love)
Mayan White Copal (Spiritual cleansing resin)
Amber Incense
…And more

Sacred Powders:
For Healing, Protection, Dissolving Karma, Connecting to Spirit, Love
and Harmony, Attraction, Increasing Prosperity, Kundalini balancing and
activation.

Medicine Bags:
1" / 3" – gold coloured leather

Aztec Ayayote Rattle (stick): dispels negative forces from your body,
mind, aura, living or workspace

Spiritual House Cleaning Kits:
3 day (3 treatments) smoke kit , quickest, easy, most power full
The White Tornado (9 treatments) smokeless kit, easy to use

Kundalini Items:
Kundalini Corrector powder (helps reverse the damage done by
childhood sexual abuse)
Kundalini Activator (opens 3rd eye, activates spiritual center in body and
mind)

Protection Items:
Durga Silver coin
Silver and Copper protection capsules

Prayer Beads:
Crystal (clear, blue, purple, pink, turquoise, white and other colours)
Sandalwood
Rosewood female energy – intuition, softness)
Rudraksha (male energy – strength, focus)
Wooden Rosary with cross
Wooden Rosary with cross & Divine Mother images
Glass Rosary (small beads)
Protection Necklace for children

Sacred Spiritual and Protection Tools

Prayer Flags:
Divine Mother Tara (Protectress)
Cosmic Winged Horse (carries prayers to heavens)

Pictures and Posters:
Peace Mother
Nine Durgas, Kali, Kuan Yin, Tara, Ixchel, Virgine de Guadalupe, Mother Mary
Saraswati (Goddess of Wisdom & Creativity)
Lakshmi (Goddess of Prosperity)
Shiva & Shakti, Radha & Krishna, Lakshmi & Narayana (balances Sacred Masculine & Feminine energies)
Ganesh (Dissolver of obstacles)

Pashmina Meditation Shawls
Solid Colors, Two Tone Colors, Silk blend, 100% Pashmina

Miscellaneous:
Smudge bowls
Bandanas (For protecting 3rd eye and crown chakra)
Divine Mother Altar Cloth
Pretreated charcoal tablets for burning essences.

Visit our website for updated products list and contact information.
To order on-line, e-mail or phone contact:

A Center For Peace & Healing
Sacred Peace Center
1800 N. Bristol Street, Ste #C224,
Santa, Ana, CA 92706, USA
Phone: 1-866-987-3223
www.sacredpeace.org
websales@sacredpeace.org
info@sacredpeace.org

The following programs and workshops are available through the Sacred Peace Center to awaken the Bliss, Inner Peace, Ecstasy and Healing Power within the Human Spirit. These programs are supremely invaluable to Business, Education, Spiritual Community, Medical, Environmental and Health Groups.

Impeccable Warrior of Light and Love Spiritual Protection Intensive
Shamanic Training Intensive
Prosperity & Abundance Ceremony
The Path of the Goddess Initiation
The Shaman's Path
Drumming Workshops
Drum, Dance, Chant for Peace
Dissolving Karma Ceremony
"Drum the Dream" Circle
Shamanic Healing Circle
Shamanic Weddings
Jaguar Medicine Ceremony
Attracting & Maintaining Loving Harmonious Relationships
Medicine Wheel Wisdom: Opening the Portal to Peace
Land Blessings
Peace Walks

Subscribe online to our complimentary newsletter and receive information on Peace Mother's pilgrimages and workshops taking place in your area!

Sacred Peace Center

Address:	1800 N. Bristol St, Ste #C224, Santa Ana, CA 92706, USA
Phone:	1-866-987-3223
Websites:	www.sacredpeace.org
Email:	info@sacredpeace.org

INDEX

245